THE PRINCES
AND PRINCIPALITY
OF WALES

HIS ROYAL HIGHNESS, PRINCE CHARLES, PRINCE OF WALES

THE PRINCES
AND
PRINCIPALITY OF
WALES

FRANCIS JONES

WALES HERALD EXTRAORDINARY

CARDIFF

UNIVERSITY OF WALES PRESS

1969

Bx60000 84 11111

PRINTED IN GREAT BRITAIN

God Bless the Prince of Wales

AMONG our ancient mountains
And from our lovely vales
Oh let the prayer re-echo
God Bless the Prince of Wales. — *Chorus.*

With heart and voice awaken
Those minstrel strains of yore
Till Britain's name and glory
Resound from shore to shore.

Should hostile bands or danger
E'er threaten our fair Isle
May God's strong arm protect us
May Heaven still on us smile.

Above the Throne of England
May fortune's star long shine
And round its sacred bulwarks
The olive branches twine.

Duw Fendithio Dywysog Cymru

AR D'wysog gwlad y bryniau
O boed i'r nefoedd wen
Roi iddo gyda choron
Ei bendith ar ei ben. — *Cytgan.*

Pan syrthio'r aur wialen
Pan elo un i'r Nef
Y Nef a ddalio i fyny
Ei law frenhinol ef.

Ei faner ef fo uchaf
Ar goedwig fyw y môr
A'i liniau ef fo isaf
Wrth orseddfainc yr Iôr.

Dyrchafer gorsedd Prydain
Yng nghariad Duw a dyn
Yn agos at orseddfainc
Y Brenin Mawr ei Hun.

TO

HIS ROYAL HIGHNESS

PRINCE CHARLES, PRINCE OF WALES

THIS BOOK IS

BY GRACIOUS PERMISSION

MOST HUMBLY, DUTIFULLY, AND RESPECTFULLY

DEDICATED

I'W

UCHELDER BRENHINOL

Y TYWYSOG SIARL

TYWYSOG CYMRU

CYFLWYNIR

Y GYFROL HON

TRWY GANIATAD GRASOL

MEWN GOSTYNGEIDDRWYDD, DYLETSWYDD,

A PHARCH

PREFACE

BY SIR ANTHONY WAGNER, K.C.V.O.

GARTER PRINCIPAL KING OF ARMS

THE spell cast by Wales on the English imagination has not always been backed by knowledge. Of Welsh political history in particular the ordinary Englishman is grossly ignorant. His usual impression seems to be that the English conquered all Wales under Edward I, who gave the Welsh his baby son as their titular prince while abolishing their separate government, which was thenceforth united with that of England.

The reader of this book who starts with such beliefs will soon learn better. He will discover that important parts of Wales were subdued by the Normans soon after their Conquest of England. Conversely he will learn that legally and administratively the Principality remained a separate country until Henry VIII united it with England by two remarkable and far-reaching Acts of Parliament in 1536 and 1542. The developments here set forth form a fascinating and little-known chapter of administrative history.

If our reader further believes, as he well may, that the first 'English' Prince of Wales to claim descent from the old Welsh Princes was Arthur Tudor, he will learn with surprise that the distinction of descent from Llywelyn the Great belonged also to the future Richard II and all his successors save Henry IV, and that the Welsh ancestry of Edward IV was a source of pride and pleasure to his subjects in the Principality.

It is wholly proper that the author of this book should be a herald, as well as a Welsh-speaking Welshman; no less a herald, indeed, than Wales Herald Extraordinary. In former times the attachment of the Welsh to pedigrees was proverbial. It sprang from a social system based on kinship and became engrained so as to outlast that system. Many Welshmen have been heralds in England. In the 1460s the King Maker Earl of Warwick employed one David Griffith as Warwick Herald and Major Jones in this book mentions seven Welshmen who held heraldic office in the College of Arms between 1536 and the present day. No less interesting are the *deputations*, which he also mentions, by which the Kings of Arms appointed Welshmen living in Wales to act locally as their deputies.

To this tradition Major Francis Jones is the lineal heir, a fact recognized in his appointment by Her Majesty the Queen to the office of Wales Herald Extraordinary. The title links him to the Prince of Wales and in this book, like a bard of old, he celebrates the Prince's ancestors and forerunners. For me it is a great personal pleasure to welcome to the heraldic establishment Wales Herald Extraordinary with his book of the Princes of Wales in his hand.

AUTHOR'S NOTE

THIS book is intended as an introduction to the study of a subject that deserves a more extensive and scientific treatment than it has received in the past. A number of books have been written on the Princes of Wales, but these are mainly of a biographical nature, nearly all laudatory, and divorced from the historical context, while none is free from inaccuracies and the repetition of picturesque fancies. Much valuable information has been published in the form of essays in learned journals, but these are not always readily available and their specialist nature fails to provide a view of the subject as a whole. In this work I have gathered together the scattered materials, both from printed and manuscript sources, and have tried to treat the subject as an institution within the constitutional framework of England and Wales.

I am deeply grateful to Her Majesty The Queen for gracious permission to dedicate this book to His Royal Highness The Prince of Wales, and for allowing me to reproduce the photograph of The Prince and his Coat of Arms.

I am indebted to several friends for their constant encouragement and help. To Professor I. Ll. Foster, F.S.A., Professor of Celtic in the University of Oxford, and Mr. T. D. Tremlett, F.S.A., I am grateful for drawing my attention to sources that I might have otherwise overlooked; to Sir Anthony Wagner, K.C.V.O., Garter Principal King of Arms, Mr. E. D. Jones, C.B.E., Librarian of the National Library of Wales, and Mr. H. N. Jerman, C.B.E., of the Welsh Office, Cardiff, for reading the work in typescript and giving me the benefit of their specialized knowledge. I am deeply grateful to these gentlemen and I welcome this opportunity of publicly acknowledging my indebtedness to them.

FRANCIS JONES

CONTENTS

LIST OF ILLUSTRATIONS

MAPS

GENEALOGICAL CHARTS

BIBLIOGRAPHY

This bibliography consists of the main works consulted in the compilation of this book. Other works, mainly journals of various learned societies, are cited in detail in the notes and references to the text, as also are manuscript materials preserved in the Public Record Office, British Museum, and the National Library of Wales.

AIRY, OSMUND. *Charles II*. London, 1901.

ANON. *The Order and Sollemnitie of the Creation of the High and Mightie Prince Henry &c.* London, 1610.

ANON. *The Prince of Wales: A Poem*. London, 1702.

ANON. *The History of the Royal Family* . . . . London, 1713.

ANON. *A Succinct and Impartial History of all the Regencies, Protectorships, Minorities and Princes of England or Great-Britain and Wales, that have been since the Conquest, with a Proper Dedication to a Great Duke*. London, 1751.

Antiquarian Repertory. Vol. ii (1779): vol. iv (1784): vol. i, new edn. (1807).

ARTHUR, SIR GEORGE. *Seven Heirs Apparent*. London, 1937.

BACON, FRANCIS. 'Memorial of Henry, Prince of Wales', *Collected Works*. 1857–74. (14 vols.) Vol. vi, pp. 327–9.

BARRON, OSWALD (ed.). *Northamptonshire Families* (Victoria History of the Counties of England). London, 1906.

BELTZ, G. F. *Memorials of the Order of the Garter*. . . . London, 1841.

BIGHAM, THE HON. CLIVE (Viscount Mersey). *The Kings of England 1066–1901*. London, 1929.

BIRCH, THOMAS. *The Life of Henry Prince of Wales*. London, 1760.

Black Prince, Register of the, preserved in the Public Record Office. 4 parts, 1346–63. London, 1930–3.

BOWEN, I. *Statutes of Wales*. London, 1908.

BREESE, EDWARD. *Kalendars of Gwynedd*. London, 1873.

BRIDGE, F. MAYNARD. *Princes of Wales*. London, 1922.

BRIDGEMAN, G. T. O. 'Ancient Lords of Mechain', *Arch. Cam.* 1863: 'Princes of Upper Powys and The Welsh Lords of Kerry and Arwystli', *Mont. Coll.* i, 1868: *History of the Princes of South Wales*. Wigan, 1876.

Bruts, Text of the, from the Red Book of Hergest, ed. Sir John Rhys and J. Gwenogvryn Evans. Oxford, 1890.

Brut y Tywysogion, or The Chronicle of the Princes, ed. John Williams ab Ithel. (R.S.). London, 1860.

Brut y Tywysogyon. Peniarth MS. 20, (gol.) Thomas Jones. Gwasg Prifysgol Cymru, 1941.

BUDGE, JOHN. *Order and Solemnitie of the Creation of Prince Henrie, as it was celebrated in the Parliament-house on Monday, the fourth of June last past*. Printed at Britain's Bourse, for John Budge, 1610.

CHANCELLOR, E. BERESFORD. *The Life of Charles I. 1600–25*. London, 1886.

Chester's Triumph in Honor of her Prince as it was performed upon St. George's-day 1610 in the foresaid cittie. London, 1610.

CHRISTIE, MABEL E. *Henry VI*. London, 1922.

CHURCHYARD, THOMAS. *The Worthiness of Wales*. London, 1776. (Repr. of 1587 edn.)

Civitatis Amor. The Cities Love. An entertainment by water, at Chelsey and Whitehall. At the ioyfull receiuing of that Illustrious Hope of Great Britaine, the High and Mighty Charles To bee created Prince of Wales, Duke of Cornewall, Earle of Chester, &c. . . . . London, 1616.

CLARK, HUGH. *An Introduction to Heraldry*. London, 1866.

CLARKE, J. S. *The Life of James the Second, King of England &c. collected out of Memoirs writ of his own hand*. London, 1816. 2 vols.

CLIVE, R. H. *Documents connected with the History of Ludlow and the Lords Marchers*. London, 1841.

COBBETT, WILLIAM. *Parliamentary History of England*. Vol. v. London, 1809.

COLLINS, ARTHUR. *Life of Edward Prince of Wales* (The Black Prince). London, 1740.

COOK, E. THORNTON. *Kings in the Making, The Princes of Wales*. New York, 1931.

CORNWALLIS, SIR CHARLES. *An Account of the Baptism, Life, Death and Funeral of the most incomparable Prince Henry Frederick, Prince of Wales*. Written 1626, printed 1641, reprinted 1751.

Court and Times of James the First. 2 vols. London, 1848.

COWLES, VIRGINIA. *Edward VII and his Circle*. London, 1956.

COXE, H. O. (ed.) *Black Prince*. Ballad on the Life and Deeds of Edward Prince of Wales, son of Edward III, by Chandos Herald. Roxburghe Club. 1842.

DAVENPORT, CYRIL. *The English Regalia*. London, 1897.

DAVIES, J. CONWAY (ed.), *The Welsh Assize Roll* (1277–84). Cardiff, 1940.

DAVIES, J. S. (ed.). *An English Chronicle of the Reigns of Richard II, Henry IV, Henry V, and Henry VI*. (Written before 1471.) Camden Soc. London, 1856.

DAVIES, R. (ed.). *York Records*. Extracts from the Municipal Records of the City of York. London, 1843.

Dictionary of National Biography.

Dictionary of Welsh Biography. English edn. London, 1959.

DINELEY, THOMAS. *The Account of the official Progress of His Grace Henry The First Duke of Beaufort through Wales in 1684*. London, 1888.

DODD, A. H. *Studies in Stuart Wales*. University of Wales Press, 1952.

DODRIDGE, SIR JOHN. *An Historical Account of the Ancient and Modern State of the Principality of Wales, Dutchy of Cornwal, and Earldom of Chester*. London, 2nd edn., 1714.

DORAN, JOHN. *The Book of the Prince of Wales, Heirs to the Crown of England*. London, 1860.

DYER, T. F. THISELTON. *Royalty in All Ages*. London, 1903.

EDWARDS, AVERYL. *Frederick Louis, Prince of Wales, 1707–1751*. London, 1947.

EDWARDS, (SIR) J. G. *Calendar of Ancient Correspondence concerning Wales*. University of Wales Press, 1935; *Littere Wallie* (ed.), University of Wales Press, 1940.

EDWARDS, SIR OWEN M. *Wales*. London, 1924.

Encyclopaedia Britannica.

Encyclopaedia, Chambers's.

EVANS, HOWELL T. *Wales and the Wars of the Roses*. Cambridge U.P., 1915.

FINCH, BARBARA CLAY. *Lives of the Princesses of Wales*. London, 1883. 3 vols.

FISHER, J. *The Cefn Coch MSS*. Liverpool, 1899.

FLEMMING, JESSIE H. *England Under the Lancastrians*. London, 1921.

FLENLEY, RALPH (ed.). *A Calendar of the Registers of the Council in the Marches of Wales, 1569–1591*. London, 1916.

FLETCHER, I. KYRLE. *The British Court*. London, 1953.

FLOOD, F. SOLLY. *The Story of Prince Henry of Monmouth and Chief-Justice Gascoigne*. . . . (Reprinted from the Transactions of the Royal Historical Society. Vol. iii. Part I. Dec. 1885.) London, 1886.

FOX, J. C. (ed.). *The Official Diary of Lieutenant-General Adam Williamson, Deputy-Lieutenant of the Tower of London, 1722–1747*. Camden Soc. 3rd Ser. Vol. xxii. 1912·

'Free and Impartial Reflexions on the Character, Life and Death of Frederick, Prince of Wales' in *Miscellanies of the Philobiblon Society*, vol. vii, p. 10.

FRETTON, W. G. *Associations of the Princes of Wales with Coventry*. Coventry, 1872.

GAIRDNER, J. *Memorials of Henry VII; Life and Reign of Richard III*, 1898; *Historical Collections of a Citizen of London in the Fifteenth Century* (ed.). Camden Soc., 1876.

GILBERT, C. S. *An Historical Survey of the County of Cornwall*. . . . Plymouth and London, 1817–20. 2 vols.

GODFREY, WALTER H. *The College of Arms* . . ., London Survey Committee. 1963.

GORE, JOHN. *King George V. A Personal Memoir*. London, 1941.

GOUGH, RICHARD. *Sepulchral Monuments in Great Britain*. London, 1780–96.

GRAHAM, EVELYN. *Edward P*. London, 1929.

Grants, &c. from the Crown during the Reign of Edward the Fifth. Camden Soc. London, 1854.

GREEN, M. A. E. *Lives of the Princesses of England*. London, 1849–55. 6 vols.

GREENWOOD, ALICE DRAYTON. *Lives of the Hanoverian Queens of England*. 2 vols. London, 1909–11.

HACKETT, FRANCIS. *Henry the Eighth*. London, 1929.

HAILE, MARTIN. *James Francis Edward. The Old Chevalier*. London, 1907; *Queen Mary of Modena. Her Life and Letters*. London.

HALL. *Hall's Chronicle containing the History of England during the Reign of Henry the Fourth and the succeeding monarchs to the end of the Reign of Henry the Eighth*. London, edn. 1809.

HALLIWELL, J. O. (ed.). *The Autobiography and Correspondence of Sir Simonds D'Ewes, Bart., during the reigns of James I and Charles I*. London, 1845. 2 vols.; *Letters of the Kings of England*. London, 1846. 2 vols.

HALSTED, CAROLINE A. *Richard III*. London, 1844. 2 vols.

HARDING, G. P. *A Description of a Series of Illustrations to G. P. Harding's Manuscript History of the Princes of Wales from the time of Edward of Caernarvon to the Present Sovereign of England, containing a list of all The Portraits, Armorial Bearings, Royal Badges, Monuments, Seals, Illuminated Letters, Views and other Decorations.* London, 1828.

HARDY, W. J. *The Handwriting of the Kings and Queens of England.* London, 1893.

HARRIS, WILLIAM. *Historical and Critical Account of the Life of Charles II.* 1766. 2 vols.

HAY, D. (ed.). *The Anglica Historia of Polydore Vergil, 1485–1537.* Camden Soc. London, 1850.

HENNESSY, JAMES POPE-. *Queen Mary 1867–1953.* London, 1959.

Heralds Commemorative Exhibition 1484–1934. Held at The College of Arms. Enlarged and Illustrated Catalogue. London, 1936.

(LORD) HERBERT OF CHIRBURY. *Life of Henry VIII.* edn. 1706.

HEWITT, H. J. *The Black Prince's Expedition of 1355–1357.* Manchester U.P., 1958.

HEYLIN, PETER, *A Help to English History.* . . . London, 1675.

HIBBERT, CHRISTOPHER. *The Court at Windsor. A Domestic History.* London, 1964.

HIGHAM, F. M. G. *King James the Second.* London, 1934.

HOLMES, SIR RICHARD. *Edward VII. His Life and Times.* London, 1910. 2 vols.

HOLOHAN-WHEELER, V. *The History of the King's Messengers.* London, 1935.

HOPE, W. H. ST. JOHN. *Heraldry for Craftsmen and Designers.* London, 1913.

HOWARD, SIR ROBERT. *Reflections upon the Reigns of Edward II and Richard II.* 1690.

HOWELL, JOHN. *Blodau Dyfed.* Carmarthen, 1824.

HUISH, ROBERT. *Memoirs of George the Fourth.* London, 1830 (1831). 2 vols.; *Memoirs of Her Late Royal Highness Charlotte Augusta, Princess of Wales, &c.* . . . London, 1818.

IOLO GOCH. *Gweithiau Iolo Goch.* Charles Ashton, ed. Oswestry, 1896; *Cywyddau Iolo Goch ac Eraill*, ed. H. Lewis, Thos. Roberts, Ifor Williams, Cardiff, 1937.

JAMES, G. P. R. *History of the Life of the Black Prince.* 1822. (also edn. 1839).

JENKINS, R. T., and RAMAGE, HELEN M. *The History of the Honourable Society of Cymmrodorion.* London, 1951.

JESSE, J. H. *Memoirs of the Court of England during the Reign of the Stuarts*, 4 vols. London, 1846; *Memoirs of the Court of England from 1688 to the death of George II.* 3 vols. London, 1846; *Memoirs of King Richard III.* London, 1862; *Memoirs of the Life and Reign of George III.* 3 vols. London, 1867.

JOHNSTONE, HILDA. *Edward of Carnarvon, 1284–1307.* (Victoria University of Manchester, Historical Series No. 83). Manchester U.P., 1946.

JONES, E. D. (gol.). *Gwaith Lewis Glyn Cothi.* y gyfrol gyntaf. Gwasg Prifysgol Cymru a Llyfrgell Genedlaethol Cymru, 1953.

JONES, JOHN. *The History of Wales.* London, 1824.

JONES, J. LLOYD-. *Geirfa Barddoniaeth Gynnar Gymraeg.* Cardiff, University of Wales Press, 1946.

JONES, OWEN. *Ceinion Llenyddiaeth Gymreig.* London, 1876.

JONES, RHYS. *Gorchestion Beirdd Cymru.* . . . Shrewsbury, 1773.

JONES, SIR T. ARTEMUS. *The Union of England and Wales.* London, 1937.

JONES, T. GWYNNE (ed.). *Tudur Aled, Gwaith.* Cardiff, University of Wales Press, 1926. 2 vols.

JONES, WILLIAM. *Crowns and Coronations, A History of Regalia.* London, 1883.

JONES, WILLIAM GARMON. 'Welsh Nationalism and Henry Tudor', *Trans. Cymmr,* 1917–18.

KENDALL, PAUL MURRAY. *Richard the Third.* London, 1955. (2nd impr., 1956.)

KINGSFORD, C. L. *Henry V.* London, 1901., new edn., 1923; *English Historical Literature in the Fifteenth Century.* Oxford, 1913. Appx. XV.

KNIGHT, F. H. *The Historie of Edward the second Surnamed Carnarvan.* London, 1629.

LANG, A., and SHIELD, A. *The King over the Water.* London, 1907.

LAW, ERNEST. *The History of Hampton Court Palace.* London, 1890. 3 vols.

LEE, SIR SIDNEY. *Life of Edward VII.* London, 1925. 2 vols.

LEGG, L. G. WICKHAM. *English Coronation Records.* London, 1901.

LEGGE, A. O. *The Unpopular King. The Life and Times of Richard III.* London, 1885. 2 vols.

LEWIS, E. A. *The Mediaeval Boroughs of Snowdonia.* London, 1912.

LINDSAY, W. A. *The Royal Household.* London, 1898.

LLOYD, SIR J. E. *A History of Wales.* 3rd edn. 1939. 2 vols.

LLOYD, SIR J. E. (ed.). *A History of Carmarthenshire.* Vol. i. Cardiff, 1935.

London's Love, to the Royal Prince Henrie, meeting him on the River Thames, at his returne from Richmonde, with a worthie fleete of her citizens, on Monday, the last day of May, 1610, with a brief report of the water-fight and fire-works. London, 1610.

LONGMAN, WILLIAM. *The History of the Life and Times of Edward the Third.* London, 1869. 2 vols.

LUCAS, R. J. *George II and his Ministers.* London, 1910.

LUDERS, ALEXANDER. *An Essay on the Character of Henry the Fifth when Prince of Wales.* London, 1813.

MACAULEY, J. (ed.). *Speeches and Addresses of the Prince of Wales, 1863–1888.* London, 1889.

MAUROIS, ANDRE. *King Edward VII and his Times.* Trans. Hamish Miles. London, 4th edn., 1936.

McCARTHY, JUSTIN. *A History of the Four Georges and of William IV.* 2 vols. London, 1902, etc.

MELVILLE, L. *Farmer George.* London, 1907. 2 vols.

MOORE, NORMAN. *Illness and Death of Henry Prince of Wales in 1612, an historical case of Typhoid Fever.* London, 1882.

MORRICE, J. C. *Wales in the Seventeenth Century, its Literature, &c.* Bangor, 1918.

MORRICE, J. C. (ed.). *Gruffydd ab Ieuan ab Llywelyn Vychan, Detholiad o'i waith.* Bangor, 1910; *Gwaith Barddonol Howel Swrdwal a'i fab Ieuan.* Bangor, 1908.

MORRIS, J. E. *The Welsh Wars of Edward I.* Oxford U.P., 1901.

NICHOLS, JOHN. *The Progresses . . . of King James the First*. (4 vols.), vol. ii. London, 1828.

NICHOLLS, J. *A Collection of all the Wills of the Kings and Queens of England, &c.* 1780.

NICOLAS, SIR N. H. (ed.). *Acts and Proceedings of the Privy Council*. Record Commission, 1834; *The Historic Peerage of England*. London, 1857; *The Siege of Carlaverock*. London, 1828.

NICOLSON, SIR HAROLD. *King George the Fifth*. London, 1952.

Ordinances and Regulations for the Government of the Royal Household. Printed by the Society of Antiquaries. London, 1790.

ORMEROD, GEORGE. *History of . . . . Chester*. (ed. Thos. Helsby). Vol. i. London, 1882.

OWEN, EDWARD. *A List of those who did Homage and Fealty to the First English Prince of Wales, A.D. 1301*. Cardiff, 1901, privately printed.

PALGRAVE, F. *Antient Kalendars and Inventories of the Treasury of H.M. Exchequer*. London, 1836. 3 vols.

PALMER, F. B. *Peerage Law in England*. London, 1907.

PARKER, JAMES. *Glossary of Heraldry*. London, edn. 1847.

PARRY, EDWARD. *Royal Visits and Progresses to Wales . . . .* London, 1851. 2nd edn.

PATTISON, D. R. DUNN-. *The Black Prince*. London, 1910.

Peerage, The Complete . . ., ed. by the Hon. Vicary Gibbs, H. A. Doubleday, Duncan Warrand, Lord Howard de Walden, G. H. White. London, 1910–40. 13 vols.

PENNANT, THOMAS. *A Tour in Wales*. London, 1784. 2 vols.

PERKINS, JOCELYN C. T. *The Most Honourable Order of the Bath*. London, 1913.

PERRIN, W. G. *British Flags*. Cambridge U.P., 1922.

POLLARD, A. F. *Henry VIII*. Edinburgh, 1902.

POWEL, DAVID. *The Historie of Cambria . . . By H. Lloyd, gentleman . . . corrected, augmented and continued . . . by David Powel, Doctor in Divinitie*. London, 1584.

POWELL, T. G. E. *The Celts*. London, 1958.

POWICKE, F. M. *King Henry III and the Lord Edward*. Oxford U.P., 1947. 2 vols.

POWICKE, F. M., and others. *Handbook of British Chronology*. Royal Historical Society, Guides and Handbooks, No. 2. London, 1939.

QUINN. *The Prince's Epitaph* (Henry, Prince of Wales). London, 1613.

RAMSAY, SIR JAMES H. *Genesis of Lancaster* or The Three Reigns of Edward II, Edward III, and Richard III. 1307–1399. Oxford, Clarendon Press, 1913. 2 vols.; *Lancaster and York*. A century of English History (A.D. 1399–1485). Oxford, Clarendon Press, 1892. 2 vols.

Record of Caernarvon (Registrum vulgariter nuncupatum 'The Record of Caernarvon') ed. Henry Ellis. Record Commission. London, 1838.

REES, MYFANWY (ed.). *Ministers' Accounts for West Wales, 1277 to 1306*. Part I. Cymmrodorion Record Series. London, 1936.

REES, PROFESSOR WILLIAM. *South Wales and the March 1284–1415*, Oxford, 1924. Maps of South Wales and the Border in the XIVth century, *Ordnance Survey*, Southampton, 133. Accounts of the Ministers for the lands of the Crown in West Wales for the financial year 1352–3, *BBCS*, x, 1939–41. *The Union of England and Wales*, University of Wales Press, 1948. *An Historical Atlas of Wales*, Cardiff, 1951.

Report brought from the Lords on the Dignity of a Peer of the Realm. London, 1829. State Papers. Vol. v.

Reports of Commissioners on Crown Lands. State Papers. 1st Report (1787–92): 2nd Report (1787): 12th Report (1792): 16th Report (1793).

RHYS, JOHN, and BRYNMOR-JONES, DAVID. *The Welsh People*. London, 5th impression, 1909.

Richard II, Life and Reign of. By a Person of Quality. 1681.

RILEY, H. T. (ed.). *Chronica Monasterii S Albani. Willelmi Rishanger*. (R.S.). London, 1865.

ROBERTS, T., and WILLIAMS, I. (ed.). *The Poetical Works of Dafydd Nanmor*. Cardiff.

ROTHERY, G. C. *Armorial Insignia of the Princes of Wales*. London, n.d. (after 1911).

RYMER, T. *Foedera, Conventiones, Litterae, &c*. London, 1816–69. 4th edn.

SANDERSON, EDGAR. *King Edward VII*. London, 1910. 5 vols.

SANDERSON, WILLIAM. *A Compleat History of the Lives and Reigns of Mary Queen of Scotland and of her son and successor James the Sixth, King of Scotland, and (after Queen Elizabeth) King of Great Britain, France, and Ireland the First (of ever Blessed Memory)*. . . . London, 1656.

SANDFORD, FRANCIS. *A Genealogical History of the Kings and Queens of England and Monarchs of Great Britain, continued by Samuel Stebbing*. London, 1707.

SANDFORD, J. L. *Estimates of the English Kings, from William 'the Conqueror' to George III*. London, 1872.

SCOFIELD, CORA L. *The Life and Reign of Edward the Fourth*. London, 1923. 2 vols.

SELDEN, JOHN. *Titles of Honor*. London, 1631. 2nd edn.

SETON, W. W. 'The Early Years of Henry Frederick, Prince of Wales, and Charles, Duke of Albany', *Scottish Historical Review*, 13, pp. 366–79.

SHAW, W. A. *The Knights of England*. London, 1905. 2 vols.

SIDNEY, THOMAS. *Heirs Apparent*. London, 1957.

SITWELL, H. D. W. *The Crown Jewels in the Tower of London*. London, 1953.

SKEEL, CAROLINE A. J. *The Council of the Marches in Wales*. London, 1904.

SMITH, LUCY TOULMIN (ed.). *The Itinerary in Wales of John Leland in or about 1536–9*. London, 1906.

SMITH, P. W. MONTAGUE-. *His Royal Highness The Prince of Wales*. Pitkin Pictorials Ltd. Series. London, 1958.

SNEYD, C. A. (ed.). *Italian Relations of England*. Camden Soc. London, 1847.

SPEED, JOHN. *The Historie of Great Britaine* . . . . London, 1623. 2nd edn.

STEEL, ANTHONY. *Richard II*. Cambridge U.P., 1941.

STEER, FRANCIS W. (ed.). *Orders for the Household of Charles, Prince of Wales*. 1959.

STOW, JOHN. *The Annales of England*. London, 1592; *Annales or A General Chronicle of England*; begun by John Stow, continued . . . by Edmund Howes. London, 1631.

STRICKLAND, AGNES. *Lives of the Queens of England*. London, 1885 edn. 8 vols.

STUART, DOROTHY MARGARET. *Portrait of the Prince Regent*. London, 1953.

STUBBS, W. *Chronicles of the Reigns of Edward I and Edward II* (R.S.); *The Constitutional History of England*. 3rd edn. Oxford. Vol. i (1880), vol. ii (1883).

Studies in Medieval History presented to Frederick Maurice Powicke. Oxford U.P., 1948.

TAYLER, ALISTER, and HENRIETTA. *The Old Chevalier*. London, 1934.

TEMPERLEY, GLADYS. *Henry VII*. London, 1917.

THOMAS, A. H., and THORNLEY, J. D. (ed.). *Great Chronicle of London*. London, 1938.

THOMAS, W. J. *A Book of the Court*. London, 1838.

THOMPSON, E. M. (ed.). *Chronicon Ade de Usk. A.D. 1377–1421*. London, 2nd edn., 1904.

THORNLEY, ISOBEL D. *England Under the Yorkists, 1460–1485*. London, 1920.

Three Fifteenth Century Chronicles. Camden Soc.

TOUT, T. F. *The Place of the Reign of Edward II in English History*. Manchester U.P., 1914; *Chapters in the Administrative History of Mediaeval England*. Manchester U.P., 1920–33. 6 vols.

TREVELYAN, G. M. *England Under the Stuarts*. London, 1941 edn.

TURNER, C. *A Griefe on the death of Henry Prince of Wales*. London, 1613.

TURNER, F. C. *James II*. London, 1948.

Vetusta Monumenta. Society of Antiquaries Publication. Vol. iii, 1796, vol. v, 1835.

Victoria County Histories: counties of Berkshire, Gloucester, Oxford, Surrey, Worcester, and York.

VULLIAMY, C. E. *Royal George. A Study of King George III*. London, 1937.

WAGNER (SIR) ANTHONY. *Heralds and Heraldry in the Middle Ages*. 2nd edn., 1956; *English Genealogy*, 1960: both published by Oxford U.P.

WALL, J. C. *The Tombs of the Kings of England*. London, 1891.

WALLON, H. *Richard II*. Paris, 1864. 2 vols. (Fr.).

WARRINGTON, REVD. WILLIAM. *A History of Wales*. London, 1786.

WATERS, W. H. *The Edwardian Settlement of North Wales in its Administrative and Legal Aspects (1284–1343)*. Cardiff, University of Wales Press, 1935.

WEBSTER, JOHN. *A Monumental Column* (lament for Henry, Prince of Wales). London, 1613.

WHATES, H. R. *The Life and Times of King Edward VII*. London, 5 vols.

WILLEMENT, THOMAS. *Regal Heraldry: The Armorial Insignia of the Kings and Queens of England*. London, 1821; *Heraldic Notices of Canterbury Cathedral*. London, 1827.

WILLIAMS, DAVID. *A History of Modern Wales*. London, 1950.

WILLIAMS, F. *Domestic Memoirs of The Royal Family and of The Courts of England*. London, 1860. 3 vols.

WILLIAMS, IFOR (ed.). *Gwyneddon 3*. 1931; *Gwaith Guto'r Glyn,* Cardiff, 1939. University of Wales Press: *Canu Aneurin,* Cardiff, 1938.

WILLIAMS, W. LL. *The Making of Modern Wales*. London, 1919.

WILLIAMS, W. R. *The Parliamentary History of the Principality of Wales 1541–1895*. Brecknock, 1895.

WILSON, BECKLES. *George III as Man, Monarch and Statesman*. London, 1907.

WINDSOR, H.R.H. THE DUKE OF. *A King's Story*. London, 1951.

WINWOOD, SIR RALPH. *Memorials of Affairs of State*. London, 1725. 3 vols.

WRIOTHESLEY, CHARLES. *A Chronicle of England During the Reigns of the Tudors from A.D. 1485 to 1558*. By Charles Wriothesley, Windsor Herald, edited by W. D. Hamilton. 2 vols. Camden Soc., N.S. xi (1875), xx (1877).

WYNNE, WILLIAM. *The History of Wales . . . formerly published in English by Dr. Powel.* London, 1697.

YOUNG, SIR GEORGE, BT. *Poor Fred—The People's Prince*. Oxford U.P., 1937.

I

THE MONARCHICAL TRADITION IN
WELSH HISTORY

THE earliest literature, chronicles, legends, and traditions of the Welsh make it clear that they could not conceive of a period in their history when there had been no kings and princes. This is reflected even in their religion, for nearly all their saints derive from ruling families, and in their folk-tales such as the Mabinogion which possess an air of royalty and an atmosphere of courts. Following the Roman conquest these early kings disappear into the island mists, and after four centuries of alien Respublica and Imperator it might have been expected that they had departed for ever. However, throughout the centuries of Roman dominion, the Celtic kings slumbered but to wake, and no sooner had the legions sailed from the British shore than the kings re-emerged, and the kingship became once more the central fact of national existence. Although, subsequently, the Welsh sometimes overthrew, exiled, and even slew kings, it was always done in order to replace them with other kings; they never rebelled against the institution of kingship. The history of the nation is one of crowns and coronets.

There is no indication at what stage kings first appeared among the Celts. They are complete and ready-made when they first greet us in the pages of Classical writers. Archaeological evidence reveals that kings and chieftains had existed in prehistoric times, while the pomp and circumstance, the ritual and ceremonial that attended their sepulture in the great mounds and stone chambers indicate the eminent position they must have occupied in the days of their life.[1]

Military leadership formed a prominent, perhaps essential, element in Celtic kingship, and the element *cat* ('cad', battle) so often found in the names of the early kings indicates what was once their primary duty.

---

[1] See T. G. E. Powell, *The Celts*: Henri Hubert's two volumes, *The Rise of the Celts* and *The Greatness and Decline of the Celts*, trans. M. R. Dobie, London, 1934; J. M. de Navarro, 'The Coming of the Celts' in *Cambridge Ancient History*, iii. 41–73, Cambridge, 1938.

The most complete picture we possess of Celtic kings dates from the time of their decline. When the Romans hammered at their portals, the Celtic land was one of multiple kings constantly at war with each other, with no central government to co-ordinate the whole, and in this fact lay their weakness.

The Romans exploited to the full those conditions produced by the internecine struggles of the Celts. Fugitive kings were encouraged to plot behind Roman shields, and employed to foment further weakening strife among their kinsmen; dethroned kings were restored and paid for their restoration by becoming clients; the legions marched to support one Celtic king against another, and the victor converted into an ally, hailed as 'Friend' by an astute Senate. The final score was never in doubt, and despite desperate campaigns continental kings surrendered their crowns, and their dynasties vanished. And they vanished for ever. After the fall of Rome, many centuries later, no Celtic dynasty re-established itself in Europe.

(a) The Roman Conquest

When the Romans entered Britain they found a similar state of affairs —a land divided into numerous tribal kingdoms, under their own royal families, often at war with one another. Strabo says of the Britons 'their form of government is monarchical' and Diodorus that they were ruled 'by many kings and potentates'.

Numismatic, epigraphic, and literary sources have enabled us to learn the names of as many as forty-nine of the kings who ruled in Britain before its final reduction by Roman arms.[1]

The Roman operations of 55 and 54 B.C. were little more than raids, transient successes. In order to put an end to the help received by the mainland states from Britain, Caesar decided on invasion.

On an August day in 55 B.C. Caesar's convoy, carrying two legions and auxiliaries, arrived off the Kentish coast, somewhere between Deal and Walmer. The Britons massed to meet them, and the invaders appear to have been initially overawed by the task that confronted them; but,

---

[1] John Evans, *The Coins of the Ancient Britons*, London, 1864, and Suppl., 1890: Christopher Hawkes and G. C. Denning, 'The Belgae of Gaul and Britain' in *Archaeological Journal*, lxxxvii (1930), pp. 157–79; Derek Allen, 'The Beglic Dynasties in Britain and Their Coins' in *Archaeologia*, xc (1944), pp. 1–46; R. M. Mack, *The Coinage of Ancient Britons*, London, 1953.

led by the intrepid eagle-bearer of the Tenth Legion, the disciplined troops fought their way across the beaches and defeated their adversaries. The Romans remained in Kent for a short time, and, having repulsed a British raid, re-embarked and returned to Gaul. In the spring of the following year, Caesar again crossed, and this time the landing was unopposed. An army under Cassivellaunus, the most powerful of the British kings, was driven inland. Realizing the uselessness of fighting a set battle, the king disbanded his main force, retaining only some 4,000 war-chariots with which he harried the invading army. The Romans continued their march northwards to the area of St. Albans where they captured Cassivellaunus' capital and inflicted heavy casualties on the defenders. Terms having been made, a tribute imposed, and hostages delivered, Caesar returned to Gaul. However, the Roman success had been local involving only a part of south-eastern Britain.

For the next one hundred years, during which the Romans made no further inroads, the two leading British dynasties were those of Commius of the Atrebates and Cassivellaunus of the Catuvallauni, whose fortunes can be traced to a certain extent from their coinage. The Catuvallaunian dynasty achieved a hegemony over most of the neighbouring states, and became largely responsible for the distinctive development of the culture of south-eastern Britain. Cassivellaunus was succeeded by Tasciovanus, and he, in turn, by his son, the eminent Cunobelinus—'the radiant Cymbeline' of Shakespeare's play. His long and successful reign was beset towards its close by family troubles. About A.D. 40 he banished one of his sons, Amminius, who thereupon made his way to Caligula to enlist help to regain his lands. Cunobelinus died shortly before the Roman invasion, leaving his kingdom between two sons.

When the Romans, under Aulus Plautius, invaded Britain in A.D. 43, they came to a land that Caesar, had he been able to return, would have recognized as virtually unchanged—a land of many kings, many loyalties, many rivalries, and no unity. The Belgic kingdoms of the south-east and the Ordovices and Silures of Wales provided the main opposition to the invaders. Within a short time the Iceni and Brigantes capitulated, and a few other tribes submitted after little or no fighting. Cogidumnus of the Regni, who surrendered early, was allowed to retain local authority under the high-sounding title of *Rex et Legatus Augusti in Britannia*, and revelled in his newly found servitude by adopting the name Tiberius

Claudius Cogidumnus. Before the close of the year 43, Claudius received the submission of eleven more kings at Colchester.

The sons of Cunobelinus—Togodumnus and Caratacus—were of different mettle. The former fell, shortly after 43, leaving his brother to lead the resistance. Defeated in battle after battle, Caratacus revealed an unyielding resolution and refused to allow himself to become depressed by defeat or to consider saving his skin by submission. He made his way to the warlike Silures, with whose help he raised another army, persuaded the Ordovices to throw in their lot with him, and led the combined host to meet the Romans once more. Somewhere in Shropshire a decisive battle fought in the year 51 shattered Caratacus' army, and his wife, daughter, and brothers were taken prisoners. The king himself managed to escape, and made his way to the territory of the Brigantes to persuade Queen Cartimandua to help him to raise yet another force. Where the Romans had failed, a woman of Celtic race succeeded. Cartimandua promptly made Caratacus a prisoner and handed him over to the Romans. Sent to Rome to adorn a triumph, his bearing impressed the emperor as his valour had impressed the generals, and he ended his days in honourable captivity.

Cartimandua received her reward, and on later occasions, when the Brigantes rose in revolt, the Romans reinstated her. The victors were not as considerate when dealing with the Iceni. When Prasutagus, the Icenian king, submitted, he was allowed to retain his kingdom under Roman sovereignty, but after his death about the year 61, the widowed Queen Boudica and her daughters were subjected to indignities and humiliation at Roman hands. Infuriated at the treatment accorded their royal house, the Iceni rose and wreaked a terrible vengeance on the oppressors, who were hard put to maintain their position in the island from A.D. 61 to 64. The rising was eventually suppressed, and rather than fall into enemy hands the Queen and the princesses took poison. Like Caratacus, she too lives in the affections of the British, and her bronze figure, erect and imperious, stands above the waters of the Thames, whence many thousands of her countrymen sailed in later centuries to rule those 'regions that Caesar never knew'.

After this we hear no more of British kings. By A.D. 83 the Romans had occupied the land as far north as the Forth and the Clyde, and Agricola could inform his army that 'the flower of Britain had fallen long since'.

For nearly four centuries Britain formed part of the Roman empire. During those centuries no record of any British notable or leader has survived in contemporary evidences. Not all the royal and chiefly families were destroyed—we know that some accepted the status of clients, and Tacitus describes the Romanization of 'the sons and chiefs' and mentions that 'rival chiefs' were still contending among themselves for local power so late as A.D. 93. Yet no name or memory of a British notable occurs in Roman literature. Chiefs and peasants, saints and sinners, rebels and patriots are all blanketed in anonymity, as if they had never existed.

(b) Re-emergence of the Kings

The Romans departed during the years 410–28, leaving the Britons to fend for themselves. Grave perils beset them. From the west came marauding Irish to gain plunder and slaves, though many remained as permanent settlers, particularly in the north-west and south-west of Wales. From the Caledonian hills wild Pictish hordes pressed south-wards, and sometimes joined the Irish in piratical descents on the coast. From the east, across 'the flint-grey flood', came persistent Teutonic adventurers, as skilful with oar and sail as with blade and battle-axe. These perils were by no means new, for the last hundred years of Roman occupation had been a time of constant menace. Of the task now thrown on the Britons, Sir John Lloyd has observed that there is nothing to show that it was not manfully entered upon and vigorously carried out.[1] The notion, mainly inspired by Gildas's jeremiad composed in the mid sixth century, that they meekly submitted, that they had forgotten those manly virtues by which nations are preserved, has been disproved by the evidence now available. In the hour of peril the Britons entered upon the Heroic Age of their history, and the names of the kings and chiefs who led the people form the subjects of early poetry and chronicles, and continued to echo in the traditions and legends of the Welsh throughout the succeeding centuries.

Within a brief space after the withdrawal we find precisely the same pattern of political life as Caesar and Tacitus had observed on their arrival in our land. Once more it is a land of many kings and kingdoms.[2]

---

[1] *History of Wales*, 1939 edn., vol. i.
[2] The establishment of the numerous Welsh kingdoms and their subsequent development is discussed by Dr. Rees in his *Historical Atlas of Wales*, an indispensable guide in this field.

Who were these kings who now appeared on the scene? Where did they come from? How did they establish their power? Where were their kingdoms? We know that rich British landowners lived during the Roman period, that chieftains continued to exist among the tribal peoples in the highland zone. The genealogies of the resurgent kings show they derived from Celtic stocks, while a few were of mixed Roman-Celtic blood. Although we cannot accept these genealogies in their higher latitudes, nevertheless the half-dozen or so generations prior to A.D. 400 may be accepted as genuine, for the form of nomenclature and surviving traditions are in accord with known conditions obtaining during the period immediately preceding the departure of the Romans. It is noteworthy that the genealogies of the resurgent kings do not trace to those who had existed during the period 55 B.C.–A.D. 70. Of course we do not know the names of all the kings who had lived during those earlier years, and it is not impossible that the names of some of them may be preserved in the genealogies of the post-Roman kings, but there can be no doubt that the latter derived from British noble stocks.

Three facts stand out prominently in the period following the Roman departure. The first is the maintenance of the early territorial and tribal divisions, and particularly the identity of the lowland and highland zones: the inhabitants of the former turned their faces to the east to contend with Teutonic raiders, those of the latter faced west and north to meet the menace of the Pict and Irish: each zone fought its own battle for survival. The second is that the reborn kingdoms were established in the tribal areas known to have existed even in pre-Roman days, so that the territorial traditions to a great measure remained intact so far as the highland zone was concerned. The third point that strikes us is the speed and apparent ease with which the kingdoms were established after four kingless centuries.

The fate of Britain was decided in the lowland zone. The precise date of the arrival of Englishmen as permanent settlers is not known.[1] Merciless raids had been made during the preceding decades, but the Britons had been able to prevent the establishment of any considerable bridge-head. Somewhere around 450, a British king, Vortigern, is said to have applied to the Saxons for aid against some of his own countrymen who were pressing on his frontiers. The Saxons came to help—and stayed

[1] Sir Frank Stenton, *Anglo-Saxon England*, places the date between 446 and 454.

to conquer. Vortigern fled to the fastnesses of Wales and his descendants retained their position as minor kings in the wild district of Builth in northern Breconshire. The English invaders built up a bridgehead which they sought not only to maintain but to extend. Although large numbers of their countrymen continued to pour into the island, the task of the invaders proved by no means easy, and if the Britons were unable to expel them, they were able to impose great delays on them. Redoubtable warriors led vigorous counter-thrusts, like Ambrosius Aurelius (Emrys Wledig), a man of Roman ancestry, under whose leadership the Britons were able to check the English drive. Leaders like Arthur, who lived in the first half of the sixth century, defeated the English so decisively at Mons Badonicus in the Bath area that their advance halted for a further generation. The picture that emerges during the next hundred years is one of attack and counter-attack, raids, burnings, spirited actions at river-fords, fights to the last man and the last arrow, in a land where 'the hall blazed in the moonlight, the spear clanged, and shield answered to the shaft'.

The patient, stubborn Englishman paused awhile, then picked up his spear and plodded on. *The Anglo-Saxon Chronicle* tells how in 577 Cuthwine and Ceawlin fought with the Britons and slew three of their kings, Conmail, Condidan, and Farinmail, and took from them the cities of Gloucester, Cirencester, and Bath. This opened the valley of the lower Severn and isolated the Britons of Wales from their compatriots of Devon and Cornwall. In mid England the British armies were defeated and soon the control of the Severn valley was wholly lost. Further north, the conflict proved even more severe. There the English had to contend with the kings of the Brythonic houses of Coel and Dyfnwal, rulers of the areas that now form northern England and southern Scotland. English and Welsh chronicles attest to the severity of the protracted struggle. Against Theodoric, son of Ida of Northumberland, who ruled from 585 to 592, came the four kings, Urien son of Cynfael, Rhydderch Hael, Gwallog son of Lleennog, and Morgan son of Coleddog. Others who led the northern warbands included Llywarch Hen, Clydno Eidin, the brothers Gwrgi and Peredur, and Gwenddolau son of Ceidio. Urien king of Rheged, the area around Carlisle, and his son Owain figure prominently in these struggles.

Ultimately the northern kings were driven into Scotland where the tide of invasion receded, so that the British kingdom of Strathclyde remained in being for several centuries longer. In the year 615 Ethelfrith of Northumbria won a resounding victory near Chester over an army led by Selyf son of Cynan Garwyn, and grandson of Brochwel Ysgithrog, king of Powys. Shortly afterwards, the Welsh of Wales, as we must now call them, were severed from their kinsfolk in the north, and from this time onwards Welsh history may be discussed in isolation.

During these fierce struggles the Britons had failed to combine under one leader. Those of the north and the west do not appear to have realized the significance of the warfare in which their southern kinsfolk were engaged. But the conquest was not one of extermination. Doubtless great numbers of Britons were slain in course of the fighting, and many must have fled, but there is no evidence of any large-scale migrations from England into Wales during this period. Considerable numbers are known to have been absorbed into the Anglo-Saxon population.

(c) The Early Welsh Kingdoms

What was happening within Wales while these relentless encounters filled the English plains? There is no evidence that the mountaineers combined with their lowland kin to bar the invader, and it would appear that they took no positive action until the Anglo-Saxon tide was lapping the foothills beyond the Severn and the Dee. The saga quality of the lowland struggles is absent from Welsh history during the two momentous centuries A.D. 400–600.

It is important to understand that Wales did not consist of a population of refugees, ragged remnants from England, of hunted broken peoples; on the contrary, the Welsh kingdoms had been established before the English threat materialized.

The north-western group of states, consisting basically of what are now the counties of Anglesey, Caernarvon, Merionethshire, and parts of Denbighshire, developed into the unified kingdom of Gwynedd, which due to its geographical position and two vigorous dynasties, those of Cunedda and Rhodri Mawr, became the most important of Welsh states.

To the south-east of the rugged barrier of Snowdonia lay the land of the Brythonic Ordovices, which developed into the kingdom of

Powys, an area including what are now the counties of Flint, Montgomery, and Radnor, whose eastern boundary, over 80 miles long, marched with Mercia. Its topographical position rendered this kingdom liable to receive the initial onset of any attack from the eastern lowlands.

In south-east Wales, the old territory of the Silures, lay Glywysing, which splintered into a number of separate kingdoms—Morgannwg (Glamorganshire), Gwynllwg, Gwent, and Erging (Monmouthshire and parts of Herefordshire). These failed to unite to form a strong power, and never attained the position enjoyed by Gwynedd and Powys. They came under the rule of dynasties whose origins differed widely—the royal houses of Brychan, the line of Caradoc Freichfras, of Cadell Ddyrnllwg, of Teithfallt, and Erb. Further north were the kingdoms of Brycheiniog (Breconshire), Buellt (Builth), and Gwerthrynion.

The south-west, the old territory of the Demetae, comprised the kingdoms of Ceredigion (Cardiganshire), Dyfed (Pembrokeshire and West Carmarthenshire), and Ystrad Tywi (remainder of Carmarthenshire), which later united to form the powerful kingdom of Deheubarth. The earliest royal house of Dyfed was Irish in origin, and its descendants continued to rule until the ninth century.

The boundaries of these kingdoms ebbed and flowed with the fortunes of their dynasties. The kings warred against each other as much as against the English, so that no confederation of states and no centralization of authority resulted. The custom of dividing the realm between all the sons of the king led to formation of 'splinter' kingdoms, and a proliferation of interests. During the 600 years between the coming of the English and the coming of the Normans, Wales constituted a patchwork of kingdoms, over thirty of them are known, of which some were about the size of a modern parish, the largest being little more than three or four modern counties in extent.

The dynasties had been firmly established during the period 400–600, so that when the English reached the western borders they were faced by mountain-kings who ruled over well-organized states. In the *De Excidio*, composed about the year 547, the cleric Gildas provides a brief but vivid view of Welsh royalty, of five kings whom he trounced for tyrannical practices and their failure to conduct their lives along lines acceptable to the author. Despite his preoccupation with their transgressions, the picture that emerges from Gildas's description is that of masterful rulers, leaders of armies, seated firmly on the inherited or acquired thrones they were determined to defend; they held sway over well-ordered territories, dispensed firm justice, patronized native learning, and although clergy ministered within their realms the kings were often worldly and steeped in sins against which the Church fulminated.

The most powerful of these, Maelgwn of Gwynedd, 'the dragon of the island', of massive physique, taller than all his brother-kings, had conquered many neighbouring states, and had attained a pre-eminence by triumphs in war and deeds of violence. Yet he was generous and in his household gleemen praised him in songs that were sweeter in his ears than the hymns of the servants of God.

Gildas was particularly hostile towards Cynlas, 'the grey butcher', son of Owain Ddantgwyn, a Gwyneddan king whose state lay on the borders of Powys. Like Maelgwn, Cynlas waged war on his neighbours and made light of the marriage tie, but more grievous was his reputation as a contemner of God and an oppressor of the clergy. His sins, however, were hardly visited on his descendants, for they were still ruling in the early ninth century.

Then there was Vortiporius (Gwrthefyr), 'tyrant' of Dyfed, the 'bad son of a good father', grown grey in the devil's service and showing no signs of repentance as he drew towards the end of his days. His tombstone, incised with the words *Memoria Voteporigis Protectoris*, is the oldest known memorial to any British king. Under the same scornful lash came Aurelius Caninus, described as the last of his line, ruling on the southeastern border of Wales, and Constantine king of the Devonian peninsula, 'the tyrannical whelp of the unclean lioness of Dumnonia'.

But the sins of the monarchs and the prejudices of the churchman cannot obscure the power and authority of the former, and the survival of their memory in early poetry, chronicle, and legend indicates the position they had held and the impact they had made on their countrymen. The period 600 to 1066 was one of great difficulty for the Welsh, constantly defending themselves against English attacks, at the same time indulging in inter-dynastic warfare, the Celtic 'sport of kings'. From Cunedda alone descended eight lines who ruled in north and west Wales. The senior line produced notable figures such as Cadfan (fl. 620), whose tombstone still survives in Anglesey, and Cadwallon, who married a sister of Penda of Mercia. Before Cadwallon fell in the Tyne gap in 634

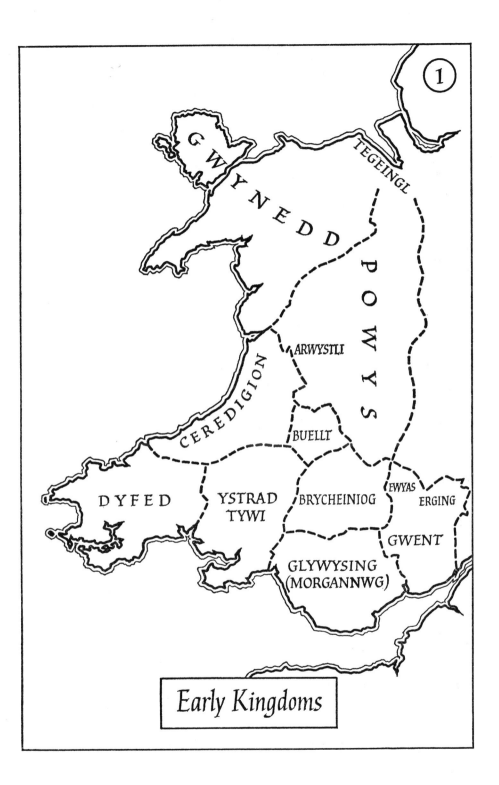

Early Kingdoms

he had defeated and occupied the formidable kingdom of Northumbria. Then came Cadwaladr Fendigaid (the Blessed, died 664), who enjoyed a reign of peace and quiet denied to his predecessors. Although little is known of him, Cadwaladr made a deep impression on the minds of

CHART I

Dynasty of Cunedda

(Line of Gwynedd)

Cunedda
|
Cadwallon
|
Maelgwn Gwynedd d. 547
|
Rhun fl. 550
|
Beli d. 599
|
Iago d. 613
|
Cadfan fl. 620
|
Cadwallon d. 634
|
Cadwaladr Fendigaid d. 664
|
Idwal Iwrch
|
Rhodri Molwynog d. 754.
|
Cynan Dindaethwy
|
Ethil (heiress) ═╤═ Gwriad
|
Merfyn Frych d. 844
|
Rhodri Mawr d. 878
|
See Chart II

succeeding generations who came to regard him as the hero who one day would return to recover the British realm.

During the four and a half centuries before the arrival of the Normans, the kingdoms continued to maintain themselves and their traditional disunity. Occasionally a king extended his influence by conquest or marriage, or a combination of both, but these instances represented dynastic or personal ambitions and were often temporary or ephemeral in character. In Gwynedd, for example, the line of Cunedda ended in an heiress who married Gwriad of the Isle of Man, whose ancestry traced to the Brythonic 'Men of the North'. The son of this union, Merfyn Frych, first ruler of Gwynedd of the new dynasty, improved his position by marrying Nest the presumptive heiress of the Powysian state. When Merfyn died in 844, his son, the redoubtable Rhodri the Great, succeeded to Gwynedd, and ten years later on the death of his unmarried uncle, Cyngen of Powys, that kingdom fell like a ripe plum into the hands of the delighted nephew, who thus became ruler of nearly half of Wales.

His good fortune did not end here. Meurig, king of Greater Ceredigion, which included Cardiganshire and most of Carmarthenshire, left one son, Gwgan, and a daughter, Angharad. Rhodri, with an inherited instinct for potential heiresses, married Angharad, and when her childless brother died in 872, the grief which the event might have occasioned the brother-in-law was assuaged by the acquisition of yet another kingdom. Thus by 872 the house of Gwynedd had acquired enormous territories without a single battle or skirmish. *Tu felix Venedotia, nube*. Rhodri was the greatest 'Habsburg' of them all. He had succeeded to Gwynedd in 844, Powys in 854, Greater Ceredigion in 872, and although often called king of 'All Wales' by later writers, this is not so, for outside his rule lay the southern kingdoms of Builth, Brycheiniog, Gwerthrynion, Gwent, Morgannwg, and Dyfed. His latter years were occupied by continual warfare against Danes and English, and the measure of his achievements may be gauged from the circumstance that after he had fallen in battle against the latter in 877, he became known to his countrymen as Rhodri the Great.

According to custom, Rhodri's realm was divided among his sons. Anarawd, the eldest, inherited Gwynedd, and Cadell took the territories in south-west Wales. Ironically, these sons of Rhodri the Great, heirs of rich and stable kingdoms, became responsible for giving the kings of England a semblance of legal claim to the overlordship of Wales.

Hardly had the people ceased to mourn the passing of the redoubtable Rhodri, than his sons turned their thoughts to invasion and plunder. The fair lands of the south tempted their ambitions. Before long the war-horns assembled the spearmen from the glens of Snowdonia, and

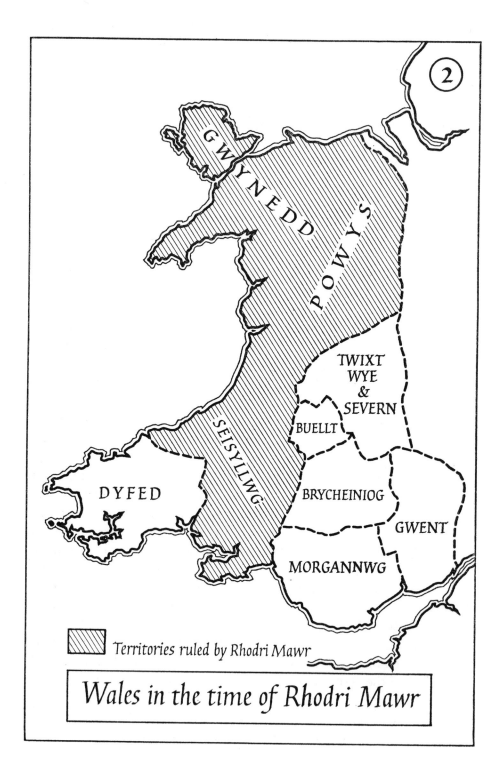

Territories ruled by Rhodri Mawr

Wales in the time of Rhodri Mawr

the sons of Rhodri were on the march. The minor kings could never hope to halt such a formidable host, and to save themselves, Hyfaidd of Dyfed, Elise of Brycheiniog, Hywel of Glywysing, Brochfael and Ffernfael of Gwent came to King Alfred during the years 878–81 to acknowledge him as their overlord in return for his protection. In the meantime the aggressors were themselves assailed by Mercia, but managed to hold their own after severe fighting, and in 881 decisively defeated Æthelred at the hard-fought battle of Conway. However, Anarawd knew that the Mercians would renew the struggle, and he, too, concluded that recognition of Alfred's overlordship represented the best way to secure immunity against further encroachments on his borders. Thus the majority, if not all, of the native princes became vassals of the great English king, and it is to this circumstance that his successors traced their title to homage from Welsh rulers. Under this arrangement they were to hold their territories with full sovereignty, retaining their laws and customs, and acknowledging Alfred as their lord. But this course was the lesser of two evils, and as the threats of invasion receded, acknowledgement of English overlordship became less and less attractive to the rulers of the western lands.

One of the most eminent kings of the House of Rhodri was Hywel Dda (the Good), who ruled the kingdoms of Ceredigion, Ystrad Tywi, and Dyfed, combined under the name of Deheubarth. His fame rests mainly on his codification of the Welsh laws, some of which persisted in various parts of Wales throughout the Middle Ages, and even in post-medieval times as customary and tenurial obligations. This achievement has overshadowed the acts of aggression and violence that proclaimed him a worthy descendant of Maelgwn Gwynedd. When in 942 Idwal of Gwynedd fell in battle against the English, and before his sons could seize the reins, Hywel annexed their state. About the same time he turned his arms against Powys and soon brought that kingdom under his sway. The aggression seems to have been condoned by the English king at whose court Hywel was a frequent visitor. His marriage to Elen, heiress of King Llywarch, a descendant of that Voteporigis so detested by Gildas, brought to her husband the fair kingdom of Dyfed. Although he, too, was sometimes called king of 'All Wales', certain kingdoms remained outside his rule, such as Morgannwg, Brycheiniog, and Gwent, whose rulers must have passed a life of nervous tension.

Wales nearly attained political unity under Hywel the Good, but after his death the state formed by his exertions and governed by just and firm laws fell apart. The men of Gwynedd rallied to the descendants of Anarawd and recovered their state. But Hywel's southern kingdom of Deheubarth still constituted a considerable power, and his grandson, Maredudd, who ruled from 986 to 999, renewed his efforts to re-establish the family hegemony. He succeeded in regaining Gwynedd and forced the state of Brycheiniog to acknowledge his rule. His nephew, Rhydderch ap Iestyn, installed himself as king in Gwent, and before his death in 1031 had secured the rule of the whole of South Wales. The next eighty years were marked by turmoil and confusion throughout Wales, legitimate rulers displaced by aspiring nobles, and constant warfare between dethroned kings, pretenders, and usurpers became a feature of those turbulent times.

During this anarchy, an ambitious noble, Llywelyn ap Seisyllt, came to the fore. By his marriage with Angharad, great-granddaughter of Hywel Dda, he had been brought within the orbit of royalist politics and his arrival was soon proclaimed by the vigour of his actions. He led an army into Gwynedd, which he subdued in 1018, then secured the kingdom of Deheubarth, so that he became the most powerful ruler in Wales. He died in 1023 leaving a son, Gruffydd ap Llywelyn. Angharad, the widow, was married shortly afterwards to Cynfyn ap Gwerystan, a Powysian noble, by whom she had two sons, Rhiwallon and Bleddyn. The three sons of Angharad proved themselves men of outstanding ability and performance. Gruffydd ap Llywelyn ruled Powys, seized Gwynedd in 1039, conquered Deheubarth two years later, and then overran Morgannwg and Gwent, thus bringing the whole of Wales under his rule. He even looked beyond the Dyke and entered into a treaty with Sweyn of Mercia, but the accession of Edward the Confessor in 1042 weakened Gruffydd's position, for Sweyn was banished, and the border lands granted to Norman favourites. When Ælfgar became Earl of Mercia in 1057, Gruffydd entered into a treaty with him, and cemented it by marrying his beautiful daughter Ealdgyth. However, the death of his father-in-law in 1062 deprived Gruffydd of the powerful support he had enjoyed during the preceding five years. The Welsh king's enemies moved against him, and the most determined of them, Harold the earl, obtained the Confessor's permission to carry out operations against Wales.

Gruffydd, oblivious of the danger, was taking his ease at the palace of Rhuddlan when Harold made a surprise attack at Christmastide of 1062. After a dramatic escape Gruffydd reached the safety of the hills. Harold then entered upon a deliberate campaign. The under-kings in South Wales submitted, and he thrust into Gwynedd with a corps of light infantry specially equipped and trained for mountain warfare. Driven from one refuge to another, Gruffydd found the rugged terrain that had so long served as Gwynedd's shield no barrier to the swarming English infantry. His supporters melted away, and he was assassinated in 1063. Gruffydd's half-brothers, Rhiwallon and Bleddyn, submitted, and were granted the kingdoms of Gwynedd and Powys after swearing to be faithful to King Edward, and to pay such tribute as had been paid long before to former English kings. Harold then married Ealdgyth, widow of the slain Welsh king, but in three years' time he lay stark on the slopes of Senlac, and Ealdgyth was again a widow.

It might be asked why the English did not conquer and occupy Wales, a task that could hardly have been beyond their capacity, particularly after the unification of England. Indeed, on several occasions English arms had thrust violently into the very heart of Wales and brushed aside the warlike pastoral kings that sought to bar their way, burnt homes and churches, and departed laden with plunder. Under Cenwulf the Mercian they had harassed North Wales so far as the stronghold of Snowdon in 816, and two years later their triumphant warbands had gazed at the Irish peaks from the headland of St. Davids. The armies of Harold had humbled the most powerful of their monarchs. But these were punitive expeditions, there had been no occupation, no annexation, no destruction of the dynasties, no displacement of the Welsh folk.

The fact is that the English kings had no desire to destroy or annex Wales. Their own land, too, had been torn by internal wars, and, in addition, menaced by external foes who not only conquered great areas of the English realm but had actually established a dynasty which ruled over Englishman and Dane alike. Even when united and powerful, England's policy towards the Welsh was 'live and let live'. Her rulers asked for nothing more than homage.[1] Alfred, his son Edward the Elder, and Edgar, were content if the Welsh kings attended their Witan and attested some of their charters. We have seen how the Welsh kings

[1] J. E. Lloyd, op. cit.

C

submitted to Alfred, and the English *Chronicle* records that Hywel and Clydog and Idwal, indeed 'all the Welsh race', sought his son Edward as their lord. They had also sought the protection of Offa. When Edgar sailed on the waters of the Dee, of the eight under-kings who pulled at the oars, three came from Wales.

The coming of the Normans changed all this. The Conqueror parcelled the English lands among his followers, but there were many who could not be rewarded or who regarded their rewards as inadequate. In the west lay a land where further prizes might be gained, and to annex and parcel it among their supporters became the object of the Norman kings.

(d) The Decline and Fall of the Kingdoms[1]

Wales had achieved political unity on the very eve of the Norman invasion of England, but this had been shattered by the intervention of Harold and the death of Gruffydd ap Llywelyn, and the country reverted to its traditional patchwork of independent kingdoms. Gruffydd had died when most needed, at a crucial moment in Welsh history, and had he lived, the unity he had created, enforced though it may have been, might have withstood the onslaughts that were being prepared by Norman adventurers. Even with the new peril looming on the eastern frontier the Welsh failed to form a united front, and from 1060 to 1100 the country was in the grip of unholy turmoil, wars against usurpers, revolts of recalcitrant nobles, quarrels between dynasties. Such conditions were most favourable to an invader, and it seemed as if the Welsh would never withstand the designs of the masterful race that had so signally defeated England in one battle and subjugated the whole of that country in the decade that followed. Although the Normans commenced operations against Wales in 1070, over two hundred years were to roll by before the native kingdoms were finally overwhelmed.

There were several reasons why the Welsh were able to check the invaders. Among the most important was the emergence of formidable warrior-kings like Gruffydd ap Cynan and Rhys ap Tewdwr, and the ability of Welsh armies to concentrate and to move rapidly in a country admirably suited for defensive warfare, in terrain where the decisive Norman arm, the mailed cavalry, could not be suitably employed. The

---

[1] This phase in Welsh history is admirably treated by Sir J. E. Lloyd in his *History*, and particularly by Dr. Rees in his *Historical Atlas*.

rapidity of manœuvre of Welsh infantry and light horse, which enabled them to deliver surprise attacks, remained characteristic of the operations that took place in the succeeding centuries. Another feature was the resilience of the Welsh and their quick recovery after even the most cruel reverses, so that the Anglo-Normans became involved not only in conquest but in reconquest.

Eight kingdoms and sub-kingdoms existed during the latter half of the eleventh century—*Gwynedd, Powys, Arwystli, Twixt Wye and Severn, Gwent, Morgannwg, Brycheiniog*, and *Deheubarth*. In the north, *Gwynedd* and *Powys* were ruled jointly by the brothers Bleddyn and Rhiwallon, sons of Cynfyn, to the exclusion of the representative of the former Gwyneddan dynasty, an exile in Ireland. The brothers were alive to the new menace, and during the years 1067–70, supported by Edwin of Mercia and Morcar of Northumbria, inflicted serious damage on the Normans, particularly in Shropshire. However, they had to contend also with their brother kings, and it was against these that the tandem-kings of Powys, Rhiwallon and Bleddyn, fell in 1070 and 1075. The ambitious and enterprising Trahaearn, king of *Arwystli*, pounced on Gwynedd, and extended his conquests southwards to Deheubarth, but the sons of Bleddyn managed to retain the territory of Powys. Gwynedd was eventually regained for the line of Rhodri by one who takes his place among the most distinguished of Welsh kings, namely Gruffydd ap Cynan, son of a fugitive Gwyneddan prince who had married Ragnhildr daughter of King Olaf of Dublin, son of Sitric Silkenbeard, descendant of Harold Fairhair. Determined, persistent, energetic, Gruffydd, after several abortive attempts, succeeded in 1081 in establishing himself in Gwynedd. After many vicissitudes, and a brief spell as prisoner of the Normans, he was forced to flee to Ireland where his youth had been spent. Misfortune merely served to strengthen his resolve, and in the following year he reappeared in North Wales, rallied his countrymen and led them from victory to victory so that by 1124 the whole of Gwynedd was firm in his grasp. When he died in 1137, aged and blind, the kingdom was secure and the succession assured. 'Eighty-two years was Gruffydd and then he died; and he was buried at Bangor in a vault at the left side of the great altar in the church. We pray that his soul may rest in the same manner, that is, in God, together with the souls of the other good kings, for ever and ever, Amen.' So wrote the author of his *Life*.

To the south of Powys, in what is now Radnorshire, lay *Twixt Wye and Severn*, ruled by the dynasty of Elystan Glodrudd, which, in the next century, bifurcated to form the two small states of Elfael and Maelienydd,

CHART II

The Dynasty of Gwynedd

(Main line only)

Rhodri Mawr
King of Gwynedd, Powys, and Ceredigion
d. 878

Gwynedd   Deheubarth ⟶

Anarawd d. 916   Cadell d. *c.* 909

Idwal Foel d. 942   See Chart III

Meurig d. 986

Idwal d. 996

Iago d. 1039

Cynan (exile in Ireland)

Gruffydd ap Cynan d. 1137

Owain Gwynedd d. 1170

Iorwerth Drwyndwn

Llywelyn the Great d. 1240

Gruffydd ap Llywelyn d. 1244 Reginald de Breose (1) ═ Gwladys ═ (2) Ralph
                 d. 1251 Mortimer

Llywelyn the Last d. 1282

Gwenllian d. 1337
a nun at Sempringham

and although overrun by the Normans, these minor dynasties managed to retain part of their lands and some of their privileges. Then came *Gwent*, ruled by descendants of Hywel Dda, and despite serious inroads by border barons, the dynasty showed a remarkable capacity for survival, and it was not until 1248, when the last of the line died, that Gwent became wholly absorbed into the Marcher lands. The kingdom of *Morgannwg* under Iestyn ap Gwrgant fell to the Normans about 1093, but parts remained in the hands of Iestyn's descendants until the middle of the fourteenth century. To the north of Morgannwg lay the small kingdom of *Brycheiniog*, but in the last decade of the eleventh century

CHART III

The Dynasty of Deheubarth

Rhodri Mawr d. 878

|

Cadell of Deheubarth d. *c.* 909

|

Hywel Dda d. 950

|

Owain d. 988

|

Einion d. 984

|

Cadell

|

Tewdwr Mawr

|

Rhys ap Tewdwr d. 1093

|

Gruffydd ap Rhys d. 1137

|

The Lord Rhys d. 1197

|

Gruffydd d. 1201	Rhys Gryg d. 1234	Rhys d. 1255
Owain d. 1236	Rhys Mechyll d. 1244	Rhys Fychan d. 1283
Maredudd d. 1265	Rhys Fychan d. 1271	Maelgwn d. 1294
Owain d. 1275	Rhys Wyndod d. after 1283	
Llywelyn of Iscoed d. 1309		

became a Norman lordship. In the south-west lay the important kingdom of *Deheubarth*, whose rulers had been driven into exile in Ireland in 1078 by the redoubtable Trahaearn of Arwystli. In 1081, the young heir, Rhys ap Tewdwr, with the help of Gruffydd ap Cynan, re-entered on his uneasy heritage. Rhys, like his northern cousin, proved himself a ruler of outstanding qualities, but in 1093 he fell in battle against the Normans who had occupied Brycheiniog. Nevertheless, his descendants

CHART IV

The House of Powys

Tegonwy ap Teon

Caenawg   Iorwerth Hirflawdd
                                           See Chart V
Coryf

Ceidau

Gwynnawg Farfsych

Gwynnau

Ednyfed

Lles Law Deawg

Caradawg

Bleddyn

Gwrhydr

Gwaethfoed

Gwerystan *viv. c.* 1000

Cynfyn

Bleddyn ap Cynfyn d. 1073

Maredudd d. 1132

Gryffudd d. 1128   Madog d. 1160

Owain Cyfeiliog d. 1197   Gruffydd Maelor d. 1191   Owain Fychan d. 1187

Gwenwynwyn d. 1216   Madog d. 1236   Llywelyn

Gruffydd de la Pole d. 1286 Gruffydd Maelor d. 1269   Llywelyn Fychan *viv.* 1241

Owain d. 1293   Madog d. 1277

continued to rule over portions of Deheubarth for the succeeding 200 years.

Some of the kingdoms covered considerable areas, others consisted of a few cantrefs, or even only one. Their borders rarely remained con-

CHART V

The House of Twixt Wye and Severn

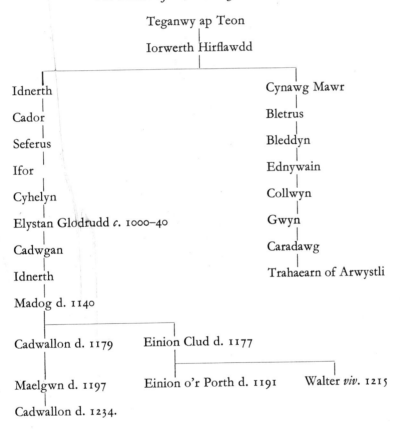

Teganwy ap Teon

Iorwerth Hirflawdd

Idnerth

Cador

Seferus

Ifor

Cyhelyn

Elystan Glodrudd *c.* 1000–40

Cadwgan

Idnerth

Madog d. 1140

Cynawg Mawr

Bletrus

Bleddyn

Ednywain

Collwyn

Gwyn

Caradawg

Trahaearn of Arwystli

Cadwallon d. 1179   Einion Clud d. 1177

Maelgwn d. 1197   Einion o'r Porth d. 1191   Walter *viv.* 1215

Cadwallon d. 1234.

stant, expanding and contracting with the fortunes of war, while the practice of dividing the land between the sons of the king as if it were a private estate, resulted in the creation of sub-kingdoms and proved an effective barrier to national unity. In addition there were areas ruled by petty kings under the overlordship of their more powerful neighbours and kinsmen.

The idea that Welsh kings were merely predatory chieftains, bushy-beards who lurked in dim caverns or forest glades, must be dismissed. They were dominant figures who lived well-ordered lives within a structure of law and custom, and although circumstances obliged them to spend much of their lives in the field, their rule was often enlightened and public-spirited. They patronized the arts, built churches, founded abbeys. Some were poets of distinction. The succession was assured and protected by an enlightened practice which caused the heir apparent (the *edling*) to be selected from among the sons of the king, not necessarily the eldest, but the most capable. Sometimes the choice fell on a nephew or a cousin, but always a member of the ruling house. The royal children were reared by foster-parents, noble families who acquired an intense affection for their charges, and who sometimes used their trust to further their own political and social ambitions.

The royal families lived in large wooden halls, the *llys*, or *neuadd*, whose construction formed part of the duties of their subjects. A king might possess several of these, distributed in various parts of his kingdom, which he and his court occupied during royal progresses. The chief palace of the kings of Gwynedd was at Aberffraw in Anglesey, those of the rulers of Powys and Deheubarth at Mathraval and Dynevor respectively. They were buried within the churches near their chief hall, or in the monasteries they had founded or endowed, and in the cathedral churches within their realms. Few died peaceful deaths, and numbers were buried on battlefields where they fell, on bracken-covered slopes, in mountain passes, in unmarked graves which 'the rain bedews and the thicket covers'.

One of the most important possessions, indeed the distinctive mark of a Welsh king, was the *teulu*, namely the warband, the household troops, consisting of noble and free-born youths commanded by a member of the royal family. Highly trained, skilled in the use of arms, the teulu lived in the king's hall, ready at a moment's notice to deal with disorders or to wage regular warfare against external foes. Phrases in the chronicles, 'the teulu attacked', 'the teulu were slain to a man', 'the teulu fell but the king escaped', and so on, proclaim the heroic standards of these high-spirited troops.

Disunity carries the seeds of death. Yet the amazing thing is that the redoubtable race that had laid England low in so short a time were to fail to overrun this land torn by disunity and rivalries. The Norman conquest brought unity to England, converting it into a highly centralized state in a brief space of time: in Wales the Normans merely added to the disunity they found there. This was due partly to the fact that while the conquest of England was undertaken by William as his immediate purpose, the conquest of Wales never became firm royal policy, and it was left to individual barons to establish themselves beyond Offa's dyke the best they could. Thus the subjection of Wales became a piecemeal process, and the acquisition of the regalities and privileges of displaced Welsh rulers by the marcher lords resulted in the establishment of what were virtually independent 'kingdoms' whose holders possessed far wider powers than their counterparts in England.

Norman penetrations commenced about 1070.[1] Three great earldoms were created, Chester (1070) and Shrewsbury (1071) as bases against Gwynedd and Powys respectively, and Hereford (1067) against the southern states. The process of conquest was pushed on with greater energy during the time of William Rufus, when the footholds gained in the previous reign became springboards for more ambitious objectives. As a result the Normans acquired many cantrefs along the border, and by 1093 had entered Gwent and Morgannwg, overrun Builth and Brecon, thrust into Cardigan and Pembroke, and in the north established strongholds as far as the banks of the Conway. However, as a result of the notable Welsh recovery in 1094, led by the kings of Deheubarth, Powys, and Gwynedd, a great deal of the land was recovered from the Normans after heavy fighting.

From 1100 onwards campaigns were conducted by acquisitive lords, by Clare, Braose, Mortimer, Corbet, FitzAlan, by the royal armies, while at the same time the Welsh princes continued to wage war on each other on the slightest provocation. Sometimes the princes combined with a Norman lord against another Welsh state, sometimes submitted to the King and became his allies against some too-powerful and aspiring marcher lord. Occasionally they formed alliances among themselves and carried out operations against marcher lords or Crown lands. Neither side showed much feeling of 'nationality', and intermarriage between the Norman lords and the princely houses took place at a very early stage.

[1] See (Sir) J. G. Edwards, *The Normans and the Welsh March* (British Academy: Raleigh lecture on history), Oxford, 1957.

The wife of Bernard Neufmarche who conquered Brecon in 1093 was granddaughter of that Gruffydd ap Llywelyn who had conquered all Wales before his death in 1063, and in later days the baronial houses of Bohun, Braose, Barri, Clifford, Mortimer, Martin, Windsor, Talbot, and Turberville all had Welsh blood in their veins. On occasions the Crown cultivated the friendship of princes who were encouraged to attack their more independent compatriots. The fugitive uncle, the dispossessed son, the disgruntled brother, the vindictive cousin—the English Court knew them all, and the English king employed them, often to the discomfiture of their kinsfolk in Wales. But these combinations were ephemeral, and both sides found sufficient excuses to repudiate agreements, so that the changes of side in Welsh medieval politics become especially bewildering. The princely chameleons of Powys were particularly notorious in this respect, such conduct being thrust upon them by the hostility of the rulers of Gwynedd and Deheubarth as well as by menace of the Normans along the eastern border. It was a confused, difficult time alike for king, prince, and baron.

The greater part of South Wales fell to the Anglo-Normans during the reign of Henry I, so that only the north-western part of Carmarthenshire remained in native hands. After the death of Henry in 1135, the Welsh recovered considerable territories, and re-established the kingdom of Deheubarth under the prince Gruffydd ap Rhys and his son the Lord Rhys; the ruler of Gwynedd, Gruffydd ap Cynan, and his son Owain Gwynedd drove the Normans back almost to the Cheshire border, while Madog ap Maredudd and his brother Owain Cyfeiliog extended the boundaries of Powys. The conquest of Wales had received an effective check, and three important Welsh kingdoms were completely re-established. Contention between the factions of Stephen and the Empress kept England occupied so that the Welsh gained a valuable breathing-space at a very critical time in their history.

The accession of Henry II in 1154 marked the end of anarchy in the English kingdom, and opened a new stage in Welsh affairs. The King, whose policy was to reassert the royal position, lost no time in putting his plans into effect. Although the Welsh kingdoms were ruled by energetic princes, their rivalries persisted, preventing any effective and sustained co-operation. Gwynedd was ruled by Owain Gwynedd (succeeded in 1137), a notable commander who extended his conquests eastwards against the forces of the Earl of Chester and the princes of Powys. The only major defeat he ever suffered occurred in 1157 when Henry II invaded North Wales and recovered the small tracts of Tegeingl and Yale, and obliged Owain to recognize him as overlord. When Henry invaded South Wales in 1164 to subdue the Lord Rhys, the princes everywhere rose under the leadership of Owain Gwynedd, and as a result the King's expedition failed. By 1167 Owain had recaptured the castles of Basingwerk, Rhuddlan, Prestatyn, and the land of Tegeingl, which he held without let till his death in 1170. After this the leadership of the Welsh kingdoms passed to the southern monarch, the Lord Rhys.

In the south, Henry recovered Carmarthen, and re-established the lords marcher. The Lord Rhys reacted vigorously, and in 1155 regained most of Deheubarth. Although four royal expeditions during the years 1158–63 forced him to submit on each occasion, he rose in arms immediately the King had retired. Finally, Henry acknowledged his right to Deheubarth, granted him the title of Lord of Ystrad Towy, and the office of Justiciar of South Wales, and named him his intermediary in affairs relating to the independent sub-kings of South Wales. Recognized as paramount among the southern princes, when Rhys attended the King's conferences at Gloucester (1175) and Oxford (1177) his retinue included the princes of Elfael, Maelienydd, Gwerthrynion, Afan, Senghenydd, Caerleon, and Gwent Iscoed.

When Henry died in 1189, Rhys regarded his compact with the Crown as dissolved. Assembling his armies, he attacked the Norman lords, and soon brought them (with the exception of the small area round Pembroke) under his rule, then turned eastwards and forced William de Braose to accept his terms. The Lord Rhys died at the height of his power, in 1187, and was buried in St. David's Cathedral.

After the death of Owain Gwynedd and the Lord Rhys their kingdoms became torn by rivalries between their sons and kinsmen. However, in 1203 Llywelyn ap Gruffydd, grandson of Owain, held the reins of Gwynedd firmly in his hands, and set about extending the influence of his kingdom. By a combination of diplomacy and warfare this distinguished prince obtained an acknowledgement of his overlordship from all the independent princes, and from 1215 onwards was paramount in Wales, having also curbed the designs of the marcher lords. In 1230 he assumed the title of Prince of Aberffraw and Lord of Snowdon. A

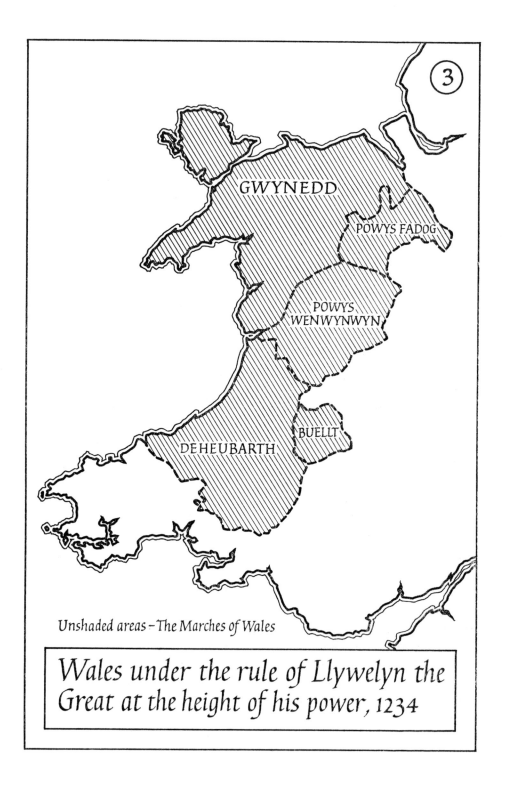

GWYNEDD

POWYS FADOG

POWYS
WENWYNWYN

DEHEUBARTH

BUELLT

Unshaded areas – The Marches of Wales

Wales under the rule of Llywelyn the
Great at the height of his power, 1234

resourceful commander, an astute statesman, decisive in field and council, Llywelyn proved himself a worthy member of a line of outstanding rulers, and from this time on it was to Gwynedd that Welshmen turned for guidance and inspiration. He died in 1240 at the age of 67, and was buried in the Abbey of Aberconway.

The matrimonial ventures of Llywelyn the Great and his children are remarkable for their alliances with Anglo-Norman houses. Llywelyn had set the pattern, for his second wife was Joan the daughter of King John. Of his children, Gruffydd married as his second wife Ragnhild daughter of a king in Man; David, Isabella de Braose; Gwenllian, William de Lacy; Helen, firstly John the Scot, and secondly Robert de Quincy; Gwladys, firstly Reginald de Braose, secondly Ralph de Mortimer; Margaret, firstly John de Braose, secondly Walter Clifford; while Angharad was the only daughter who married a Welshman, Maelgwn Fychan, a prince of the southern dynasty.

David, Llywelyn's only son by Joan, succeeded to Gwynedd, but failed to retain his father's power. Powys and Deheubarth shook off the northern hegemony, and the efforts of David's half-brother, Gruffydd, to acquire a share of the sovereignty further weakened Gwynedd's position. David's short troubled reign ended with his death in 1246, when his two young nephews, Owain and Llywelyn sons of Gruffydd, became rulers. In 1247 a royal invasion forced the two princes to accept the humiliating terms of the Treaty of Woodstock, under which they were to retain only that part of the kingdom lying to the west of the river Conway as a gift of the King, to whom they had to render homage. Powys and Deheubarth, who had already broken with Gwynedd, also submitted, so that the King had reduced the Welsh states to a status something akin to marcher lordships.

For the next seven years Gwynedd remained in this subordinate position, exacerbated further by endless dissensions between the brothers. Then in 1255 one of those sudden upsurges so often found in the history of the dynasties transformed the whole scene, and the house of Gwynedd, which had produced so many inspiring leaders when its fortunes seemed at their lowest, reasserted itself in spectacular manner. In 1255 Llywelyn ap Gruffydd finally established himself as the sole and complete master of Gwynedd. Turning eastwards he regained that part of Gwynedd taken into the King's hands under the Treaty of Woodstock, and before the end of 1256 he extended his conquests to the boundaries of the palatinate of Chester. He then overran Cardigan, which he handed to Maredudd ap Owain, grandson of the Lord Rhys. Moving with great speed his army conquered the lordship of Builth, and advanced into Carmarthen whose native prince submitted. Having restored the southern kingdom to its former dynasts, Llywelyn harried and despoiled the Norman lordships in the south-west. By 1262 he had driven the lords marcher from Brecon, Elfael, and Maelienydd, so that by the following year he had not only regained the whole of his own kingdom but restored the independence of all the other Welsh kingdoms whose rulers now acknowledged him as overlord.

During these operations, Llywelyn had been greatly helped by the incapacity of Henry III to oppose him, for that monarch was beset by troubles with his own baronage under de Montfort, and his treasury was in no state to allow him to indulge in a Welsh war. In 1267 the Treaty of Montgomery brought peace to the land. The King acknowledged Llywelyn's title as Prince of Wales, his right to the overlordship of the other Welsh rulers, confirmed his conquests of the marcher lordships of Builth, Brecon, Gwerthrynion, and Elfael, and, finally, admitted his claim to Maelienydd.

Llywelyn would have been well advised to have consolidated his now considerable position; instead, he continued active operations against neighbouring marcher lords. But England was recovering from her internal troubles, and when Edward I ascended the throne in 1272 he wasted no time in taking steps to restore the royal position. When, after many applications, Llywelyn refused to render homage, the King invaded the country with three armies. Llywelyn submitted, and the Treaty of Aberconway in 1277 marked the end of the influence of the Welsh prince. He lost all his previous conquests and his rule was confined to the territories west of the Conway, while the princes of Powys and Deheubarth had to acknowledge Edward as their liege lord. Llywelyn was allowed to retain the title of Prince, but had to acknowledge the King's supremacy. Thus at one stroke Llywelyn had been reduced to a relatively minor lord, Gwynedd to a truncated relic of its former greatness, and the territories of the princes elsewhere in Wales became little more than large fiefs. When on 3 October 1278 Llywelyn married Eleanor daughter of Simon de Montfort, at Worcester Cathedral in the presence of the

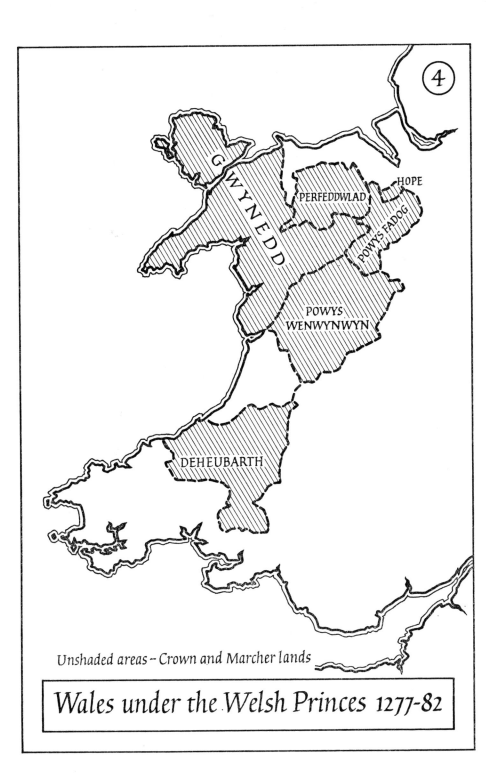

④

GWYNEDD

PERFEDDWLAD

HOPE

POWYS FADOG

POWYS WENWYNWYN

DEHEUBARTH

Unshaded areas – Crown and Marcher lands

Wales under the Welsh Princes 1277-82

King and Queen, it seemed as if he had accepted a final settlement and would abandon dynastic ambitions in favour of his new position as a tenant in chief. But it was not to be.

In March 1282 the dogs of war were unleashed with a vengeance. Llywelyn took the field, and some of the princes of Powys and Deheubarth rallied to his cause. He scored several local successes, and hopes that he would repeat his earlier conquests ran high. But Edward had determined to solve the Welsh question once and for all. A formidable force assembled—Englishmen, Gascons, Picards, and Welsh 'friendlies' like Gruffydd ap Gwenwynwyn and his sons from southern Powys. The earls of Surrey and Lincoln were there, the Justiciar Tibetot, de Valence, Mortimer, the counts of Armagnac and Bigorre, Alexander and Guy de Bergerac, the Captal de Buch, the Viscount de Tarcazin, and Amadeus of Savoy. The King moved methodically, his strategy consisting of converging attacks on Gwynedd. Before any decisive battle could be fought, Llywelyn fell in a chance skirmish while reconnoitring positions by the river Irfon near Builth, on 11 December 1282. His head was struck off and sent to the King, who caused it to be crowned with ivy and placed on the highest pinnacle of the Tower. The body of the slain prince, through the representations of his cousin the Countess of Salisbury, was buried in the Abbey of Cwm Hir, a Cistercian house that owed its foundation and many benefactions to the Welsh royal families. The most precious treasures of the Welsh, the golden crown of Arthur and the 'Croesynad' (a piece of the true Cross) gilded and adorned with gold and precious stones, were sent to the King, who conveyed them in great solemnity to Westminster Abbey, attended by the Archbishop of Canterbury and other prelates and a vast concourse of people. He placed the 'Croesynad' and other Welsh regalia on the high altar, as his son Alphonso had done earlier with the ring of Llywelyn.

Llywelyn's brother David—'chiefest fire-brand in this fatall combustion' according to Speed—continued to hold out but failed to halt the royal armies as they stormed into the heart of Snowdonia. After April 1283 the rising collapsed, and in June of that year David fell into the hands of his enemies. As he had held lands directly of the King, he was tried at Shrewsbury in October 1283 for breaking his fealty, found guilty, and sentenced to be drawn, hanged, beheaded, disembowelled, and quartered.

CHART VI. *Some Descendants of Llywelyn the Great*

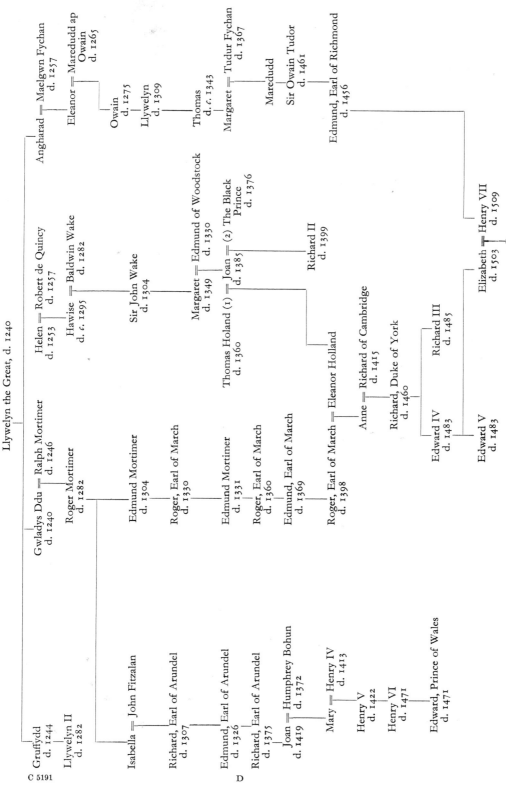

Llywelyn the Great, d. 1240

Here was the *Götterdämmerung* of the House of Gwynedd. Yet, and it is a dramatic fact, before a further hundred years had rolled by, a Plantagenet king in whose veins ran the blood of Llywelyn the Great was to ascend the throne of England, and before the Middle Ages came

CHART VII

The Welsh Ancestry of Richard II

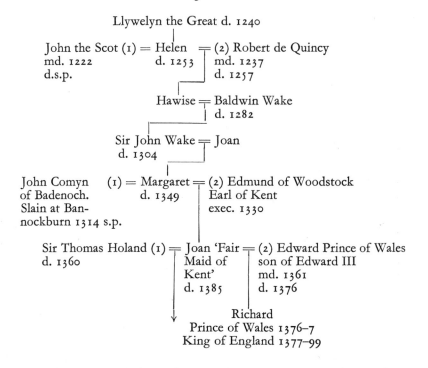

Llywelyn the Great d. 1240

John the Scot (1) = Helen   = (2) Robert de Quincy
md. 1222   d. 1253 | md. 1237
d.s.p. | d. 1257

Hawise = Baldwin Wake
           | d. 1282

Sir John Wake = Joan
d. 1304

John Comyn   (1) = Margaret = (2) Edmund of Woodstock
of Badenoch.   d. 1349 | Earl of Kent
Slain at Ban- | exec. 1330
nockburn 1314 s.p.

Sir Thomas Holand (1) = Joan 'Fair = (2) Edward Prince of Wales
d. 1360 | Maid of | son of Edward III
                                     | Kent' | md. 1361
                                     | d. 1385 | d. 1376

Richard
Prince of Wales 1376–7
King of England 1377–99

to their close there were to be six more Plantagenet kings, descendants of the same Llywelyn. Such are the tricks that genealogy plays on imperial politics.

(e) *The Fate of the Dynasties*

The outlook of the Welsh princes had been, all along, personal and dynastic. They fought for their own kingdoms rather than for the land of Wales as a whole; they were never able to bury their rivalries, so that unity never became possible, or, to them, even desirable.

Edward remained for some time in Wales after the destruction of the last native kingdom. The lands of the Principality were confiscated and taken into the King's own hands. He began to build a ring of strong castles in the conquered areas, at Caernarvon and Conway in 1283, Harlech in 1285, Beaumaris in 1295, strengthened and garrisoned the old Welsh castles of Bere, Dolwyddelan, and Criccieth, and established boroughs at those places, with the exception of Harlech.

On 3 March 1284 the Statute of Rhuddlan was proclaimed,[1] and for the succeeding three and a half centuries Wales was ruled according to its clauses. The King's view of the conquest is outlined in the preamble —'The land of Wales, with its inhabitants had been subjected to us previously in feudal right. And now God, by His grace, all obstacles whatever coming to an end, has converted it totally and in its entirety with our own dominion, and has annexed it to the crown of the said kingdom as part of the same body.' The provisions applied to the conquered lands vested in the Crown, and defined the boundaries of the Principality, which now consisted of counties modelled on English lines, namely, Anglesey, Caernarvon, Merioneth, Cardigan, and (northern) Carmarthen, administered by royal officers. The rest of the country remained in possession of the lords marcher, while a few lordships, distinct from the Principality, were held by the Crown. The Welsh were allowed to retain many of their ancient customs especially those relating to land tenure, and several native local officials incorporated into the new administration.

Apart from the barbarous treatment of Prince David, the victorious monarch behaved with moderation. His aim, to remove the political power of the princes and the nobles, resulted in a peculiarly interesting phenomenon, namely the survival of the royal and noble stocks and their eventual transformation into a powerful ruling class, many descendants of whom retain their pre-eminence in Welsh life to this day.

The last two princes of *Gwynedd* had been killed, one in action, the other by the processes of law. Gwenllian, daughter and heiress of Llywelyn, was carried to the English court where she was reared until old enough to take the veil, and died a nun at Sempringham in June 1337. Piers Langtoft speaks of her as personally known to him, and mentions also 'her cousin Gladous daughter of David' who died a

---

[1] Printed *in toto*, with an English translation, in *Statutes of the Realm*, i. 55–68.

professed nun at Sixtille in 1336. David's two sons, Owen and Llywelyn, were sent in September 1283 for safe custody to Bristol Castle, and as we hear no more of them it seems fair to infer that they ended their lives in captivity. One English source states that as many as seven of David's daughters were made captives. The King's policy, to destroy the immediate succession, was not entirely divorced from feelings of humanity, for in a letter to the Prior and Prioress of Alvingham, dated at Ludlow 11 November 1283, he stated that his object was 'not to punish the children of Llywelyn and David' for their fathers' revolt, but 'we, from regard to charity, have thought fit in wholesome sort to make provision for them. Wherefore, we beseech you, brethren, that you admit to your order and the habit of your house, any one or more of the said children of Llywelyn and David his brother, whom we shall name to you . . .'. Nevertheless, the heirs of the main line of Gwynedd pined away in the castles and nunneries of England, so that possible leaders of future revolt were removed from the scene. One notable exception was made. Llywelyn's younger brother, Rhodri, went to England in 1272 and made his peace with the King, who knighted him and granted him a yearly pension of £40 and valuable lands in Chester and Surrey. As Sir Roderick ap Griffin knight, he accompanied the Queen Mother on her visit abroad in 1275. His son Thomas ap Sir Rhodri inherited his lands and lived at the manor of Tatsfield in Surrey, and acquired the manors of Bidfield in Gloucestershire and Dinas in Mechain Iscoed. The son of this Thomas was the famous Owen of the Red Hand who went to France where he fought against the English and planned to invade Wales to restore his dynasty. Owen's murder in 1378 removed the nearest legitimate descendant of the Gwyneddan house. After this, the representation of Gwynedd became vested by the irony of genealogy in the house of Mortimer, descendants of Gwladys Ddu daughter of Llywelyn the Great, who gave Yorkist kings to England. The King had given support to one cadet line of Gwynedd, descendants of Cynan ap Owain Gwynedd, in order to embarrass Llywelyn, and this line retained its possessions in Merioneth.

The princes of *Southern Powys*, who had suffered much at Llywelyn's hands, and, through generations of intermarriage, were more Anglo-Norman than Welsh, had thrown in their lot with the King. No nunneries or castles received the scions and daughters of this house. The

King rewarded these princes, creating them tenants in chief of Powys and Mawddwy, territories which became transformed from principalities to feudal lordships, their holders into feudal barons.

Although the princes of *Northern Powys* had supported Llywelyn, and suffered the woes of the vanquished, they managed to survive destruction. Gruffydd Fychan, whose lands became forfeit in 1282, secured the support of the Earl of Surrey, who by the way had received most of the forfeited territories, with the result that in 1284 the King granted the land of Glyndyfrdwy to Gruffydd to hold as tenant at will, but by 1321 his descendants held it in chief, a very notable performance. The family continued to flourish until its representative, Owen Glyndwr, revolted in 1400. Owen, descendant of Audleys, Corbets, and Le Strange as well as of Welsh royal houses, married an Englishwoman, and all his four daughters married Englishmen—Scudamore, Grey of Ruthin, Croft, and Monnington, so that the representatives of this kingdom are found today in English shires, and some of them sit in the House of Lords. In Wales, one of the most distinguished cadet lines of the dynasty, that of Brogyntyn, is now represented by Lord Harlech.

The senior line of *Deheubarth* escaped the slings and arrows of outrageous conquest, for in 1282 its representative, Llywelyn ap Owain, was a mere boy, and did not rise against the King. He retained his lands, Iscoed, Anhuniog, Caerwedros, one-half of Gwynionydd, and Trefgarn, and when he died in 1309 his inquisition recorded that he held them of the King in chief. Neither were his descendants disturbed, and when the line ended in coheiresses they brought the lands to the family of Owen Glyndwr (who later forfeited his share) and to William de la Pole, lord of Mawddwy from whom descend the present Earls of Bradford, and to Tudor ap Gronw of Anglesey from whom came the House of Tudor. The junior lines of Deheubarth were less fortunate. That of Rhys the Hoarse, having survived the tempest of 1282, plunged into irretrievable disaster shortly afterwards. His grandson, Rhys ap Maredudd, whose wife, mother, and grandmother came from Anglo-Norman baronial families, withheld support from the Welsh cause in 1282. As a reward he received the Cardiganshire commotes of Mabwnion and Gwynionydd (except for the parts held by his kinsman Llywelyn ap Owain of Iscoed), and Mallaen and Caeo in Carmarthenshire previously held by his kinsmen Gruffydd and Cynan, who had joined Llywelyn. His position was sealed by the accolade of knighthood. However, Sir Rhys had afterthoughts, and in 1287 rose against the King, but was defeated, captured, and led to execution at York in 1291, while his two sons disappeared behind the walls of Norwich Castle. Sir Rhys's sister, Gwenllian, married a minor Welsh noble in Carmarthenshire, and Edward, the first imperial Prince of Wales, granted an annual pension of £20 to her.

Another cadet of Deheubarth, Rhys Fychan, had supported Llywelyn, and together with his sons Rhys and Gruffydd, and his kinsman Rhys Wyndod, was captured in 1282–3 and thrown into English dungeons. Rhys Fychan went first to the Tower, whence he was transferred to Windsor where he remained in honourable captivity. When he died in September 1302 the King ordered his remains to be 'well and courteously interred' within the church of Windsor, according to his rank, and at the King's expense. And so, somewhere in Windsor, home of English royalty, lies, in some unmarked grave, the dust of the Welsh prince, honoured in death by his conqueror, the greatest of the Plantagenets.

I have considered it necessary to emphasize the twilight hours of the native princes since the tradition of the 'ruthless king' has been all too frequently, and indeed unfairly, presented by both Welsh and English writers. The truth helps to explain how it was that many of the Welsh royal families, far from being exterminated, continued in occupation of the lands which their ancestors had held for so long.

The fortunes of some of the minor princes who had been 'mediatized' before 1282 follow a similar pattern. The dynasty of the mountain kingdom of Arwystli, which had suffered as much from its powerful neighbours of Gwynedd and Powys as from Anglo-Norman ravages, somehow managed to maintain fitful sovereignty down to 1200. About that year Gwenwynwyn of Powys occupied Arwystli, but it was later annexed by Gwynedd, who allowed the former Arwystlian royal house to exist within its boundaries as landowners, whose subsequent history illustrates the way in which the floating wreckage of the foundered dynasties was used by the King to harass the very princes who had encompassed their downfall. The King's tool in this business was Sir Adam de Montgomery, son of Phillip de Montgomery son of Alexander de Montgomery who had married Amice daughter of Hywel ab Ieuaf the last king of Arwystli (died 1185). In 1277 Sir Adam instituted an action in the courts calculated to embarrass Llywelyn of Gwynedd, who laid claim to overlordship in this territory.[1]

A branch of the Arwystli dynasty had ruled *Cydewain*, a territory some fifteen miles long and about ten miles broad in north Montgomeryshire. After the death of its last prince, Owain ap Meredudd, in 1261, Llywelyn of Gwynedd seized Cydewain. Owain had no sons, and his heiress, Angharad, married firstly Owen ap Meredudd, a prince of South Wales, and secondly Sir Walter de Pedwardine, a Shropshire magnate and a Justice in the Marches. She proved a spirited lady and from 1277 onward carried out lively warfare in the courts claiming Cydewain and certain royal privileges against Roger de Mortimer to whom the King had granted the land, while other cadets of the dynasty, legitimate and illegitimate, presented similar claims. All failed, and Mortimer remained in the saddle.

The royal family of *Gwent*, descended from Hywel Dda, had been among the first to meet the Norman onset, yet managed to retain a grip on parts of the kingdom, particularly in the Caerleon area. The main line ended with Morgan ap Sir Howel, who died in 1248, a powerful land-owner, from whose heiress the family of Lord Tredegar descends. The main line of Morgannwg survived as feudal lords of Afan, and when the male representation failed about 1360, the lands and honours of the family were carried by the heiress Jane of Afan to her English husband, Sir William Blount.

The history of the dynasty that ruled *Twixt Wye and Severn* (modern Radnorshire) is one of gradual disintegration. Descended from Elystan Glodrudd, the dynasty bifurcated to rule the two sub-kingdoms of Elfael and Maelienydd. Although both lost their sovereignty towards the middle of the thirteenth century, their descendants continued to hold lands and privileges, and a record of 1271 describes Madog and Gruffydd and Iorwerth, sons of Owain, as 'domini de Elvael'. As in the cases of the other dynasties, the descendants of the house continued as land-owners after they had been deprived of sovereignty.

Although in some ways the date 1282 seems to mark the final curtain in the drama of the Welsh princes, the reality is less sombre. The end of the princes was not doom, disaster, and destruction; it was mediatiza-tion; a cutting down to size. That some heads fell was inevitable, the wonder is that many more did not fall.

[1] For a detailed account see J. Conway Davies, *Assize Roll*.

The poignant lament on the death of the last Llywelyn, the prince who had died at his post, written by Llywelyn son of the Red Judge, shows how deep the feeling for the fallen prince was amongst his countrymen. Traditional 'prophecies', always the balm of bruised nationalism, were heard on hearth and in field, 'prophecies' that a descendant of Cadwaladr the Blessed would one day sit on the throne in London, that alien oppression would pass away. The brutal execution of David had shocked but not cowed them, and that event together with the wishful thinking expressed in the 'prophecies' played a part in maintaining the morale of the conquered nation. This feeling is shown in the way the people flocked to the banners of their ancient dynasties so soon after their disastrous defeat.

In 1294 a widespread rising showed the King that his conquest had not been so final as he had hoped. The men of North Wales were led by Madog ap Llywelyn of Merioneth, a descendant of a cadet of Gwynedd who had benefited from Edward's toleration; Madog, son of a dispossessed noble, led the Glamorgan men, and Maelgwn Fychan of the line of Deheubarth led the men of West Wales, and in mid Wales the revolt was general. This obliged the King to postpone his expedition to Gascony, and turn westwards once more. Madog was captured and thrown into the Tower, and Maelgwn Fychan slain in South Wales in the spring of 1295. The rising was crushed.

As a result of these outbreaks many more Welsh chieftains entered English prisons, but the King treated the people with surprising leniency, and with all his castles back in his hands and the administration established by the Statute of Rhuddlan operating once more, he felt that the danger was over.

The insurgents had directed their main attacks against royal officials and the lords marcher. It is significant that the men of Glamorgan who had risen under Morgan submitted on condition that they were to hold their lands of the King himself and not of the Earl of Gloucester. When, later in 1316, Llywelyn Bren, a minor hill-chieftain in Glamorgan, rose in arms, his insurrection was directed against an unjust lord marcher, not the Crown.

The Welsh attitude has been summed up by Dr. E. A. Lewis in these words:

The Welsh people of this period were much bent on having a prince of their own. Even the creation of Edward of Carnarvon to be the first English Prince of Wales was popularly received throughout the Principality. Whenever the rule of *created* princes of this type, or the administration of their representatives, erred on the side of tyranny and extortion, the Welsh peasantry either attempted to make princes of their own, or extended ready welcome to any local chieftain having lineal claims to the position.[1]

In the third decade of the next century the Welshmen of North Wales petitioned King Edward III to be allowed their customs and usages as 'in the time of the ancient princes of Wales'.[2] The bard Iolo Goch summarized this fidelity in the lines—

> Oftentimes have I wished
> To have a lord of ability—glorious portent,
> From among us ourselves.

Indeed from 1282 down to the accession of the Tudors the Welsh were distracted by a dual loyalty, clearly shown in the poetry of the bards. The odes composed to native magnates emphasize their descent from royal and noble ancestors and there is little doubt that the magnates themselves were proud of such lineage. The ordinary people continued to look to them for protection and patronage. On the other hand, the Welsh were also loyal to the English kings and the imperial Princes of Wales. They never faltered in their support of Edward II and Richard II, their bards never wearied of singing the praises of Edward III. During the war of Glyndwr, Welshmen fought on both sides, and afterwards some acquired English denizenship to escape the penalties imposed on the race by Henry IV. These confused loyalties did not disappear until the advent of Henry VII. The accession of the Tudors resulted in a symbiosis, so that from 1485 onwards all Welsh loyalties have been given wholly to the King in London.

(f) The Imperial Princes

From 1283 to 1301 the Principality was merely a name; it had no prince. From the time of Cunedda to the fall of Llywelyn, nearly nine hundred years, Gwynedd and Deheubarth had never been without their own kings and princes. Now, for the first time, they were administered by officials whose blood was certainly not kingly and often not noble.

---

[1] *The Medieval Boroughs of Snowdonia*, p. 222.

[2] *Ancient Petitions*, nos. 7289, 10058; *Cal. Pat. Rolls, 1330–4*, p. 61, and cf. *Cal. Close Rolls, 1337–9*, pp. 91–92.

For some eighteen years the Welsh of these historic regions were without a royal personage as their immediate lord, but this came to an end in 1301, when the King created his eldest son to be their Prince. He was Edward, born in Caernarvon in 1284, a native of Wales, who could well have been called Edward of Gwynedd. The King had taken away, and now the King had given.

Contemporary evidence shows that the creation of Edward was well received, and among those who gave homage and fealty to him in 1301 were members of well-known chiefly houses.[1] What attracted the Welsh to this Prince and to his successors, and indeed to the Crown, was the fact that now they could appeal directly to the most august quarter for redress of grievances. Generally speaking they received sympathetic treatment, and there are examples of Welshmen migrating from marcher lordships to the Principality where more settled conditions prevailed. Despite Edward's many weaknesses the Welsh remained loyal to him both as prince and as King, and were plotting to secure his release when he met his end in Berkeley Castle. They showed the same loyalty to the Black Prince, and numerous bodies of the Welsh troops fought in France, at Crécy, Poitiers, and elsewhere. A poem written by Iolo Goch reviews their exploits in Scotland and France, in which the King is praised as 'the eagle of Windsor' and 'the grey Leopard'.[2] When the young Roger Mortimer, Earl of March, was recognized as heir to the Throne in 1385, Iolo Goch eulogized him, emphasizing his descent from Gwladys Ddu and from the 'lord of Aberffraw', claiming that the red colour in his coat of arms is 'the blood of the red dragon', declaring that Welshmen looked forward to 'the crowning of a kinsman of Gwynedd'.

The policy of the English kings from the time of the first Edward to that of Henry VII was directed towards pacification. Certain punitive ordinances contained in the Statute of Rhuddlan gradually lapsed. Welshmen were appointed as officials both for peace and war in the Crown lands and in the Principality. Edward II even brought them within the framework of the English legislature, and in 1322 and again in 1326–7 forty-eight Welshmen from the Principality were summoned to Parliament. *The Register of the Black Prince* provides us with names of Welsh military leaders chosen to muster and lead levies to ports for embarkation to France, or to English centres where they joined the royal army

---

[1] *Vide infra*, p. 63.   [2] Ashton, pp. 112–20.

on its march northwards against the Scots. Numerous Welsh troops served in the wars of Edward III, and the names of the chieftains who led them are preserved in *The French Roll of 19 Edward III* and other records of the realm.[1] Their old laws were respected and records of Assize and other courts contain numerous references to Welsh lawyers, described as 'Pleaders of the Law of Howel Dda'; Welshmen were permitted to give evidence in their native tongue as proved by the presence in the law courts of men described as *latimer* in the records.

Only in borough towns were the English wholly predominant and even those, as time went on, succumbed to the influx of Welsh settlers. But the main national strength of Wales lay in the rural areas, and here the ancient nobility and the pedigreed farmers were in control and continued to give to Welsh life a feudal and aristocratic air that characterized it until the religious, political, and industrial changes of the nineteenth century.

(g) *The Wars of the Roses*

During the fifteenth century the Welsh people became intimately involved in baronial politics. Despite the penal laws following upon Glyndwr's war, Welshmen were asserting themselves and acquiring an influence in local government. They took a prominent part in military campaigns and the names of David Gam, Roger Vaughan, Mathew Goch, Sir Richard Gethin, Sir Griffith Vaughan, Sir William ap Thomas, the widespread house of Herbert, Sir Rhys ap Thomas, and the descendants of Ednyfed Fychan in North Wales indicate the virility of the race. In the south, Gruffydd ap Nicholas was entrusted to hold Sessions for Humphrey, Duke of Gloucester, and in the north the great house of Penrhyn was to supply Chamberlains for the Prince, while on the Borders members of the Mostyn family were acquiring similar influence.

In 1455 Wales found itself involved in the Wars of the Roses. The land was almost equally divided between the contending parties. Lancaster drew its support almost entirely from West Wales, the Principality, the lands held by the Duchy of Lancaster, the county of Flint, the earldom of Pembroke (held by Jasper Tudor), and the Stafford lordship of

---

[1] See also General the Hon. G. Wrottesley, 'Crécy and Calais', in *Historical Collections of Staffs*, vol. xviii (1897); and H. J. Hewitt, *The Black Prince's Expedition of 1355–1357*, Manchester U.P., 1958.

Brecknock. The Yorkists held most of eastern Wales, where the Mortimer interest was strong, the Earl of Warwick's lordship of Glamorgan, the Nevills in Gwent, and in the south-east those stout Yorkists the Herberts. Edward IV, 'mighty bull of the Mortimers' as the Yorkist bard, Guto'r Glyn, described him, was popular, and by sending his son the young Prince of Wales with a special Council to Ludlow showed the royal interest in Welsh affairs.

The course of those years of confusion and tragedy is so well known that we need not dwell on it here. The bards were busy with metrical support for their favoured lords, and here again dual loyalty raised its head. From a 'national' point of view both contestants possessed attributes that commended them to the affections of the Welsh. When Henry Tudor became the hope of the Lancastrians,[1] bards of that party saw in him the Welshman destined to fulfil the old prophecy, and the poems describe his descent from Welsh noble houses with flamboyant enthusiasm. On the other hand, the Yorkist bards had an equally strong card to play. As heirs of the Mortimers, the Yorkists could claim descent from Llywelyn the Great, and so from Cadwaladr the Blessed, and the bards who supported the white rose found that the name of Gwladys Ddu made as good politics as genealogy. Indeed, the bard Dafydd Llwyd ap Llywelyn ap Gruffydd claimed in one of his poems that as a 'Welshman' Edward IV was to be preferred to the Tudors!

Some of the Welsh Yorkists had been raised to eminence during these sorry struggles. In 1461 William Herbert had been appointed Justice of South Wales, and six years later Justice of North Wales as well. In 1462 he was made a Knight of the Garter and in 1469 created Earl of Pembroke, only to be executed after the Battle of Banbury where the flower of the Welsh marches fell. William Griffith of Penrhyn was Marshal of the King's Hall to Edward IV and served on a number of royal commissions in North Wales. Sir Rhys ap Thomas became the strongest figure in south-west Wales, and had he so wished could undoubtedly have seriously hindered Henry Tudor's march in 1485.

During the reign of Edward IV special attention was paid to the unruly conditions existing in Wales and the Marches. In 1473 the King appointed a Council to guide the affairs of the Prince, which developed into the Council of Wales and the Marches, and which from 1473 to 1689

[1] See W. Garmon Jones', 'Welsh Nationalism and Henry Tudor', *Trans. Cymmr*, 1917–18.

carried out administrative and judicial functions from its headquarters at Ludlow, centre of the old Mortimer power. Both Edward IV and Henry VII had intended that Ludlow should become the 'seat and court of the Prince of Wales', and that participation in the work of the Council should provide him with training and experience for his future kingship as well as bringing him into closer contact with the affairs of the Principality. This laudable project did not survive the death of Prince Arthur in 1501.

After 1483 a greater affection for Henry Tudor developed, and the bards who had supported the white rose transferred their support to the red. Had the character of Richard III been other than what it was, it is doubtful whether the defections of 1485 would have taken place. As it was, Sir Rhys ap Thomas, Lord Stanley, Justice of North Wales, and others espoused the cause of the challenger, and after August 1485 a triumphant Tudor rode into London to be crowned as King Henry VII. 'For 797 years before, there came one night to Cadwallader, last King of the Britons, some sort of an apparition with a heavenly appearance; this foretold how long afterwards it would come to pass that his descendants would recover the land. This prophecy they say came true in Henry, who traced his ancestry to Cadwallader'—so Polydore Vergil recorded in his *Historia*. The people saw in the crowning of Henry the culmination of those earlier 'prophecies'—a descendant of Cunedda, of Cadwalader, and Rhodri Mawr occupied the throne in London. It was a moment of jubilation, the fulfilment of their monarchical sentiments and aspirations. The bards were chanting in the hills once more. Lewis Glyn Cothi saw in Henry a king 'of the line of Dardanus', 'of Beli', of 'the line of Troy'.

> Among the victorious army
> Harry, the venturesome stag, was crowned,
> The privileges of the Feast of All Saints protect him,
> The line of Locrinus received its second coronation.

The new king had no doubts about the legality of his position, and is the only monarch to incorporate the dignity of the Principality into his royal style. One of the first letters he wrote after Bosworth started with these words—'Henry by the grace of God, King of England and France, Prince of Wales, and Lord of Ireland'.[1]

[1] J. O. Halliwell, *Letters of the Kings of England*, i. 169.

(h) The Act of Union 1536

The significance of Bosworth was not that its victor was a Lancastrian, but that he was a Welshman. It is true that the new king had a Welsh descent, that he had been born in Wales, that he rewarded his Welsh supporters, who were welcomed at his court. His marriage to Elizabeth of York had a double significance, for apart from uniting the claims of the rival houses, it ensured that the children would be descendants of Llywelyn the Great. To his eldest son the first Tudor monarch gave the name Arthur after the British hero who had lived for a thousand years in Welsh legend and song, created him Prince of Wales, and sent him to Ludlow to rule his principality and marches. The bards hailed the infant joyfully, and Dafydd Llwyd called on the saints to protect him—

> Let Mary and Saint Mwrog secure
> Our Prince and his cradle
> Let the hand of Beuno and Ilar
> Preserve him from all ill,
> And the hand of Derfel the great guide
> And the hand of Christ.

But despite all this the new king was not a Welsh nationalist. Apart from a few anxious weeks, he had never lived in Wales, and after his accession never visited it. It is true that the red dragon on the green and white background had flown over him at Bosworth, that he introduced the dragon as a supporter in the royal arms, that he commissioned a galaxy of bards to trace his agnatic ancestry to its distant source, even unto Brutus and the blood of Troy. His interest in his pedigree and heraldry flattered the Welsh, and it is by such trivia that the affections of subjects can be captured by a shrewd monarch.

It was left to Henry VIII to take a step with the most far-reaching practical implications. By a series of Acts in the years 1536–42, he united Wales to England, and removed legal differences between Englishmen and Welshmen. One of the most important landmarks in Welsh history, the Act contained nothing that smacked of conquest or repression, and may be considered as the culmination of the policy of the pacification of Wales initiated by Edward I. The semi-dependent lordships were abolished, and the whole country formed into shires on the English pattern. English law was introduced, and representation in Parliament was granted to the Welsh counties and boroughs. For the first time in its history Wales had become a unified political entity. The name Wales now comprised the whole country, and the term Principality, in time, grew to be synonymous with it, so that the Princes of the Principality became the Princes of all Welshmen. The history of Wales from this time onwards to our day contains little that differs from that of the predominant partner.

There is no doubt that the Act was popular, and the attitude towards it may be inferred from an address said to have been delivered to King Henry VIII by a Welshman on behalf of his fellow countrymen.[1] The speaker asks that the Welsh may be allowed to enjoy the same laws and privileges as those enjoyed by other subjects of the King; he recounts the gallant resistance to Romans, Saxons, and Danes; English kings who could not conquer Wales gave the land to the lord marchers who were allowed to retain *iura* regalia; the Welsh finally submitted to Edward I, and defended Edward of Caernarvon 'when not only the English forsook him, but ourselves might have recover'd our former liberty, had we desired it'; they remained loyal to Edward III and Richard II; and if they had resisted Henry IV, the attitude of foreigners towards him was surely excuse enough: Welshmen had shed their blood ungrudgingly for England on the fields of France, and they had declined to take advantage of the Civil Wars (of the Roses) to regain their independence: their devotion to Henry VII 'bearing his name and blood' from them, never failed: therefore, they now beg defence against their detractors who mock the ruggedness alike of their mountains and their speech; their mountains at least supply not only Wales, but England, with good beef and mutton, while Welshmen speak their language in the throat 'as believing that words which sound so deep, proceed from the heart'.

Two noteworthy matters arise out of the settlement of 1536. The first is that the boundaries of the counties conform closely to those of the ancient Welsh states, on which, as we have seen, the marcher lordships and the Principality had also been based. Had, for instance, the kings of the line of Elystan Glodrudd returned in 1536 they would have recognized their kingdom in the shire of Radnor; the kings of Ceredigion would have noticed that the shire of Cardigan corresponded exactly to their ancient territory. And this is true of the other territorial divisions.

[1] Lord Herbert of Chirbury, *Life of Henry VIII*, edn. 1706, p. 190.

Thus the continuity of the basic political divisions of Wales, which can be traced back to Roman times, remained largely undisturbed, and a new life was given to the regionalisms and particularisms that had distinguished (and bedevilled) Welsh history. The second is even more remarkable. The families that now monopolized local government, as members of Parliament, High Sheriffs, justices of the peace, coroners, etc., were largely descendants of royal and noble families which could be traced back to the eleventh century (some even further), and were domiciled in those very areas that their ancestors had once ruled. Thus, in the sixteenth century the native families re-entered upon their heritage, obtained fresh lease of life. In England, the Tudor period was the time of the rise of new families, of able and brilliant upstarts, new men, 'gentlemen of the first head', the two- or three-generation men, who had made fortunes in trade, professions, and in various forms of speculation. In Wales the opposite was the case. Genuine upstarts were few and far between; the new Welsh gentry was composed of old Welsh aristocracy, that indestructible class which had survived conquest, oppression, rebellion, penal laws, and economic depressions. The coats-of-arms that still decorate portals of Welsh country-houses were not granted by English heralds, but derived from the royal houses and from great chieftains like Hwfa of Anglesey, Ednyfed Fychan, Tudor Trevor, Cadifor ap Dinawal, Gwaethfoed, Cadifor Fawr, Collwyn ap Tangno, Moreiddig Warwyn, and a host more. As there had been a large number of royal and noble families in medieval Wales, it follows in the nature of things that their descendants must be numerous.

Such then were the families that were to lead Wales from the Tudor period onwards; they retained and nourished the monarchical outlook, and loyalty to the Crown has remained one of their most enduring characteristics.

(i) Post-Tudor development

The accession of the Tudors united all Welshmen in their loyalty to the Crown, and brought them into closer and more intimate association with the capital, the Court, and central government. The first history of Wales written in modern times, the work of Humphrey Llwyd, published in 1584, contained a special section devoted to 'the Princes of

Wales of English-Blood' who had by then become an integral part of Welsh history. They hailed the advent of James I as a monarch of their own blood, emphasized the Celtic origin of the Stuarts, and particularly the fact that the new monarch's great-grandmother was a daughter of Henry VII. Genealogists produced yards of illuminated parchment to demonstrate how much Cymric blood flowed in his veins, and two enthusiastic Welsh parsons published a book containing detailed pedigrees to show that here was a true representative of the royal line of Cadwaladr. Indeed, one bard went so far as to hail him as

> Brenin Siams . . .
> Cymro o hâd Cymro yw hwn

(King James . . . a Welshman by stock, a Welshman is he). These were the words of Richard Phillips,[1] and others like Roger Kyffin, Edwart Urien, and Huw Robert Lleyn sang in similar strain. The creation of Henry of Stirling as Prince of Wales in 1610 brought forth a poem of blithe acclaim from the quill of Edwart Urien, and some two years later a mournful elegy by John Philip marked the untimely death of the youthful prince.

John Lewis of Radnorshire dedicated a 'History of Great Britain' to the King, and addressed his preface to 'The High and Right Noble Prince Henry', whose family, the Stuarts, he says, descend 'linially from the ancient British kings and Princes' through 'Gwaltr Stewart' whose mother was Nest, daughter of 'Griff ap Llywelin Prince of Wales'. The truth of this assertion is perhaps less important than the spirit and attitude that inspired it.

Welshmen took a leading part in political life, and Welsh families like the Cecils and Herberts established themselves in the very heart of government, while men like Sir Rhys ap Thomas and his eldest son were associated with the households of the first two Tudor Princes of Wales. Many others became prominent as members of Parliament and as 'London-Welshmen'. It was a Welshman, Sir William Maurice of Clenennau and Brogyntyn, a personal friend of James I, who suggested to that monarch that he should assume the new title, 'King of Great Britain', while the Lord Keeper John Williams proved himself one of the wisest councillors of Charles I. In the households of the first two Stuart

---

[1] N. L. W., Llanstephan MS. 123, fols. 7 ff.

Princes of Wales appointments were held by men like Sir John Wynn of Gwydir, Richard Gwynne, Sir Edward Lewis of the Van, Sir John Vaughan (later Earl of Carbery), Ambrose Thelwall, Sir Thomas Trevor, and that descendant of the Princes of Powys, Sir Oliver Cromwell, uncle and godfather of the future Protector.

Perhaps at no period in history has the monarchical character of the Welsh been more evident than during the unhappy Civil War of the seventeenth century. The Welsh stood firmly for the King and remained so to the end. Even when England was in the hands of Parliament, the Celtic areas, Wales and Cornwall, continued to take their stand under royal banners, and it is significant that the only part of Wales to support Parliament was southern Pembrokeshire with its predominant English-speaking population. With the exception of two, the Welsh members of the Long Parliament were all Royalists, and of these two exceptions only one remained constant in his opposition to the King. One of the bards called on the King to

> Display againe thine ensigne,
> Wee'ld assure thee, Welsh are thine.

Among leading Royalists were the ancient houses of Owen of Clenennau, Mostyn, Bodfel, Bulkeley, Trevor, Salisbury, Vaughan of Crosswood, Vaughan of Golden Grove (Carbery), the Stepneys, Sir Richard Lloyd, Sir Marmaduke Lloyd, the Prices of Newtown, Monachty, and Brecon, and the Griffiths of Cefnamlwch. Bards like John Griffith, Huw Morris of Pontymibion, Rowland Vaughan of Caergai, and the Philips family of Ardudwy tuned their harps to the royal cause. When Harlech Castle fell in 1647 after a long siege, William Philip of Ardudwy composed a poem in praise of its defenders, and after the tragedy of 29 January 1649 his brother Griffith apostrophized the martyred monarch as 'Brenin Siarl, bur, union, sant' (the King Charles pure, upright, saint). Waspish verses were directed at leading Roundheads, and the Protector's descent from the Princes of Powys made his actions all the less excusable.

Perhaps the monarchical spirit of the Celt was best typified in the conduct of the Royalist David Jenkins, son of Jenkin ap Richard of Hensol. Captured in 1645 and impeached at the bar of the House of Commons, Jenkins refused to kneel, calling the place 'a den of thieves', and when threatened with hanging, retorted that he would hang with the Bible under one arm and Magna Charta under the other. A fine of £1,000, and imprisonment at Newgate until released in 1657 at the age of 75, failed to break the spirit of this resolute old man, 'a vigorous maintainer of the rights of the Crown, and a heart of oak' as Anthony à'Wood described him.

There were, of course, notable exceptions, such as Colonel John Jones of Maesygarnedd, Sir Hugh Owen, an anglicized baronet of south Pembrokeshire, Sir Thomas Myddelton, and Colonel Philip Jones of Fonmon, who supported Parliament in field and council. There were turncoats on both sides. But the generality of the people stood for the King, and vast numbers of Welsh mountaineers and countrymen who formed the bulk of the royal infantry laid down their lives amidst the hedgerows of the English shires.

The Restoration was hailed in Wales with joyous relief expressed by the bards in rhyme and song. The Stuarts were popular, for with all their virtues and weaknesses they represented certain traditional modes acceptable to so conservative a people as the Welsh. Of the four Stuart Princes of Wales, one died during promising boyhood, the second became King and lost his head, the third left the country as a fugitive but returned to enjoy his own again, while the fourth, a babe of five months, was borne into continental exile some two weeks before his father's flight in December 1688.

For twenty-six years after the expulsion of James II no prince was presented to the Welsh, among whom a strong body of Jacobite opinion existed. In South Wales, Sir Richard Philipps of Picton Castle, Edward Lewis of the Van, the Kemeys of Cefn Mabli, and other prominent squires supported the Jacobite Society of Sea Sergeants, and in North Wales the powerful Sir Watkin Williams Wynn and his fellow squires hankered after the House of Stuart, and their club, the Cycle of the White Rose, held its annual festival on the birthday of James Francis Edward the exile of St. Germain. These clubs provided the gentry with opportunities for private talks behind the fiction of social intercourse.

But Jacobite ardour cooled, and when a Hanoverian Prince of Wales was created in 1714, the people were disposed to acquiesce in the new settlement, and few Welshmen became involved in the 'Fifteen' and the later 'Forty-Five'. Edward Lewis of the Van was fined for sedition in 1715, but the remainder of the gentry were too cautious to risk their lives and substance in what was rapidly assuming the melancholy romanticism of a lost cause. Nevertheless, during the next fifty years Welsh gentlemen, farmers, and rural parsons continued to be indicted at local sessions for expressing Jacobite opinions in songs, sermons, and excited conversation. As late as 1751 a fervent Jacobite poem appeared in John Prys's *Almanack*, which contained the vigorous prayer: 'May the brave Charles, unrivalled in grace, be glorious and crowned with gold. O Stuart! guileless and kindly, our dear Prince, tame their (Hanoverian) unruly ways.'

But the bulk of the people had become reconciled to the Hanoverian succession, and the genealogists now proclaimed the descent of King George from the House of Tudor, the Plantagenets, from the imperial Princes of Wales, from the dynasties of Gwynedd and Rhodri Mawr. It has been said that any proposition may be proved by an appeal to statistics, and so far as national claims are concerned the same may be said of dynastic genealogy. All kings are cousins, the enthroned, the dethroned, the exiled, and all share the same august ancestry. The phantom of Gwladys Ddu haunted St. James's as well as St. Germain.

After the accession of George I, Wales received a Princess as well as a Prince. The people quickly noted that the birthday of Caroline of Anspach, Princess of Wales, fell on St. David's Day. Accordingly a number of London Welshmen, headed by the Earl of Lisburne, decided to form 'The Honourable and Loyal Society of Antient Britons', and to seek the patronage of the new Prince and Princess. On 5 April 1715 the stewards of the society were received in audience and the Prince consented to become President. On 23 September following, the society presented a loyal address to the Prince signed by all the leading London Welshmen and 200 gentlemen of the Principality, following which a knighthood was conferred on Thomas Jones, secretary and treasurer of the society, who had taken a prominent part in its formation. Every St. David's Day the society listened to a Welsh sermon in London, after which they dined in state, each Antient Briton wearing 'favours of good silver ribbon with the motto *Caroline and S David*', while the stewards bore green staves 'with the arms of the Principality on top'.

On the formation of the first Cymmrodorion Society in 1751, the Prince of Wales became its Patron. One of its rules read, '. . . when the current business is over, they shall drink *Health to the Prince of Wales and*

Prosperity to the Principality. When the Cymmrodorion Society was re-formed over a century later, in 1873, one of its rules directed that the anniversary of the society should be held on 9 November, being the birthday of the Prince of Wales (later Edward VII). Another London-Welsh Society, the Gwyneddigion, formed before 1785, expressed loyalty in its chief toasts, *King and Church* and *Prince and Principality*.

The feast of the patron saint of Wales had been specially observed in the courts of the Tudors and the Stuarts, a tradition continued under the Hanoverians. On this anniversary the King and Queen, the other members of the Royal Family, and the lords and ladies of the Court, all wore leeks in their hats and on their dresses. It was a day, also, when Welshmen expressed their loyalty to the Prince, when they petitioned him for special support for their pet projects. On St. David's Day, 1765, the governors of the Society of Antient Britons came to St. James's to solicit the Prince's patronage for an institution to support and educate poor and destitute natives of the Principality. The address, presented by Sir Watkin Williams Wynn, contained the following sentiment: 'Your royal parents remember no period of their lives too early for doing good—and when a few years shall call forth your virtues into action, your Royal Highness may perhaps reflect with satisfaction upon your faithful ancient Britons, thus laying themselves at your feet.' The object of their solicitation, then a chubby child of some three years of age, is said to have answered, 'Gentlemen, I thank you for this mark of your duty to the King, and I wish prosperity to the Charity', which, according to a journal of the day, he delivered 'with great propriety and suitableness of action'. Equally acceptable to those ancient Britons was the purse of £100 which he gave as a gift to their treasurer.[1] A copy of this address, ornamented with a drawing of the infant Prince receiving the deputation, hung for many years on the walls of the old Welsh Charity School in Gray's Inn Road.

The Prince (later George IV) remained a lifelong supporter of the Charity, to which he subscribed a hundred guineas annually, and received grateful homage every St. David's Day. On that festival in 1773, 'a great number of nobility and gentry, natives of Wales, went to St. James's to pay their duty to the Prince of Wales', and on the same feast in 1811 the nobility and gentry of Wales, accompanied by the children of the Welsh Charity School, went in procession to Carlton House to acclaim their

[1] Huish, *Memoirs of George IV*, p. 13.

Prince. On the saint's festival in 1813, we learn that the Marquess of Downshire, president of the Antient Britons, together with the other officers of the Society, assembled in their carriages at the Welsh School in Gray's Inn Road. They then formed a procession, all wearing a plume of feathers and silver leeks in their hats, followed by the boys and girls, also wearing silver leeks, marching behind a band of musicians, the whole being led by the City Marshal who had charge of the proceedings. Halts were made outside the residences of Samuel Homphrey, and at Downshire House, where cheers were given for Homphrey and the Marchioness of Downshire. They then entered the church to listen to prayers 'read in the Ancient British Language, with all the purity of native accent' by the Revd. Hugh Jones of Lewisham. From the church the procession wound its way through Pall Mall and St. James's Square, where the children curtsied and cheered outside the houses of Sir Charles Morgan, Sir Watkin Williams Wynn, and the Duke of Norfolk. Then came the great moment, when the procession drew up outside Carlton House, where the children 'in a reiterated loud acclaim testified their strong sense of gratitude to their august and Royal Patron by whose munificence the charity has flourished'. From Carlton House the procession went on to the Freemasons' Tavern, where it was joined by a large party of noblemen and gentlemen who dined, and drank the loyal toasts, while the children sang an Ode to Chastity 'in a peculiarly sweet manner'. After the Marquess of Downshire left the chair, his place was taken by Sir Watkin Lewes, and the Earl Percy was voted President-Elect, after which many more toasts were drunk, the remainder of the evening being spent 'with the utmost harmony and conviviality'.

The Welshmen of those days neglected no opportunity to mark their affection for their Prince. Goronwy Owen wrote a *cywydd* to the Prince of Wales in 1753. The birth of Prince George in 1762 was celebrated in poems by Ieuan Fardd and Rhys Jones, and the Cymmrodorion Society resolved that their president should present Ieuan's poem to the King himself. Another poem to the Prince of Wales, composed in 1767 by the Revd. William Lloyd, rector of Cowden in Kent, was put to music and sung to the Cymmrodorion by the blind harpist, John Parry.

The dual loyalties had disappeared, and loyalty to the Crown had developed into a durable, indivisible quality. Nevertheless, the inherent affection for the ancient heroes remained, but this had become a nostalgic sympathy possessing no political significance. Subjects of poems and compositions at Eisteddfodau had a royal air about them. At Corwen in 1789, a chair was offered for a poem on one of twelve subjects, which included, 'The recent recovery of King George III', 'Queen Charlotte', 'The Prince of Wales', 'Dr. Willis the King's Physician', and 'Owain Glyndwr'. In 1821 the medal of the Gwyneddigion Society went to the Revd. Walter Davies (Gwallter Mechain) for a poem on 'The Fall of Llywelyn the last Welsh Prince', and in the following year the Cymmrodorion Society offered medals for poems on 'The Birth of Edward (II) at Caernarvon', and 'The Accession of the Tudors'.

From 1820 to 1841 the Principality remained without a Prince, and in the latter year Prince Albert Edward was born, and when a few weeks old created Prince of Wales and Earl of Chester. Tremendous enthusiasm greeted the event. Verses in praise of the Queen, the Prince Consort, and the new Prince of Wales sparkled in the columns of Cambrian newspapers and were recited on hearths, in literary meetings, and Eisteddfodau. Ceiriog hailed the Prince as 'Arthur of the Round Table' and successor of Llywelyn the Last. The feelings of the nation eventually found expression in the enchanting music and words of the anthem, 'God Bless the Prince of Wales'.

Its origin is associated with a truly Welsh institution, the Eisteddfod, and, more appropriate still, to an Eisteddfod held within the walls of historic Caernarvon Castle.[1] The committee met on 11 October 1861 to discuss preparations for the Eisteddfod to be held in that castle in August 1862. The significance of the time and place was not lost on its members. As the Prince would come of age in that year, and as the castle was the birthplace of the first Prince of Wales, they decided to commemorate both events in a special way. Ceiriog was invited to compose a cantata, arrangements were made to set it to music, and for soloists and choirs to render it at the forthcoming festival. Ceiriog then composed the words for *Cantata Tywysog Cymru* and also arranged the dramatis personae, representing King Edward I, Queen Eleanor, Sir Griffith Llwyd, the Welsh foster-mother of the first Prince of Wales, princes of Gwynedd, Deheubarth, Powys, and other medieval rulers, chieftains, and nobles. A highlight of the performance was to be the carrying of a banner charged with the three feathers to the stage. The composer of the music,

[1] Described in detail in *Gweithiau Ceiriog*, vol. i (1872), Bk. iii; vol. iii, Bk. vi.

Owain Alaw, was appointed conductor. Sung with great spirit by the principals and massed choirs the cantata met with immediate success.

Present at the Eisteddfod was Henry Brinley Richards,[1] one of the foremost musicians of the day. On the morning following the rendering of the cantata, Richards congratulated Ceiriog, and as Wales did not possess a suitable anthem, he suggested that one should be composed and launched, particularly in view of the approaching marriage of the Prince (on 10 March 1863). Ceiriog agreed to write the words, and Richards to compose the music. Thereupon Ceiriog wrote two verses (he later added a third) under the title 'Ar Dywysog Gwlad y Bryniau',[2] the first four lines of the opening verse to form the chorus.

Ceiriog sent the verses to Brinley Richards, who shortly returned them together with the music. Ceiriog, Llew Llwyfo, and other eisteddfodwyr then sang the anthem in public concerts, and were enthusiastically received by the audiences. About two months after the Welsh verses had been first sung publicly, Richards suggested that an English version of the words should be printed. A number of efforts were studied, but eventually Richards and Ceiriog decided on the one submitted by George Linley. The title in the English form, 'The Prince of our Brave Land', was changed to 'God Bless the Prince of Wales', and the haunting melody that greeted the Prince of Wales on his marriage to Alexandra of Denmark in 1863 has deservedly become one of the most popular of British airs.

From 1841 to 1901, Wales was to enjoy the longest principate in her history. Visits to various parts of Wales brought the Prince into closer contact with the Welsh, and the visits of succeeding Princes served to strengthen further the ties between the royal house and the Principality, and to nourish the monarchical instincts of its people. The first visit of the present Prince to Welsh soil in 1958, so soon after his creation, touched their imagination, for, of all the Princes of Wales, he alone can claim descent from every ancient dynasty that once ruled west of Severn. As he stood in Anglesey he could hardly have failed to see across the Menai Straits the wooded mainland of Caernarvonshire, and the towering heights of Snowdonia, natural fortress of his ancestors, Gruffydd ap

---

[1] Born at Carmarthen in 1819, died 1885. A founder of the Royal College of Music, *vide* D.W.B.

[2] 'On the Prince of the Land of Hills.'

Cynan, Owain Gwynedd, and Llywelyn the Great. Those princes are long gone, their bones are dust, but on the slopes of Snowdonia live hill-farmers whose ancestors had followed the standards of those ancient warrior-kings. When a reporter from the *Guardian* approached one of them and asked him what he thought of the fact that Prince Charles had now been made Prince of Wales, the farmer, with a naturalness of one who has inherited a long tradition, replied 'Well now, myself, I think it will be a very good thing for the boy.'

2

EXTENT OF THE PRINCIPALITY

WHEN we use the term 'Principality' today, no one has any doubt as to its precise meaning. It means the whole of Wales. However, the territorial extent of the medieval Principality was something quite different, and that being the case it becomes necessary to define its ancient limits and to indicate why and when the name came to comprehend the whole of the Welsh land.

As we have seen, the term 'Wales' had no political meaning before the Act of Union of 1536. Prior to the coming of the Normans, 'Wales' consisted of a land of many states, and the inroads of the Anglo-Normans not only perpetuated but intensified its fragmentary character, so that it developed into a patchwork of Welsh kingdoms, Crown lands, and marcher lordships. The formation of a Principality under the English Crown in 1284 merely gave a cohesion to one of those fragments.

For our present purpose the Treaty of Conway[1] imposed by Edward I on the defeated Prince Llywelyn ap Gruffydd in 1277, forms a convenient starting-point for the discussion. By that treaty the Welsh lands were partitioned as follows:

(*a*) *Principality of Wales*, namely Caernarvonshire to the west of the river Conway, and the whole of Merionethshire, where Llywelyn retained full sovereignty, with the official style of Prince of Wales; Anglesey was also granted to him, for life only, to be held of the King by feudal service. These lands were often described in English records as *pura Wallia*.

(*b*) *Lands conquered by the King during the 1277 war*, namely the northern half of Denbighshire and the land of Flint, taken directly into the King's hands; the southern part of Denbighshire was granted to David ap Gruffydd to be held of the King; the northern half of Ceredigion and the lordship of Cardigan were taken into the King's hands, while the

[1] For text see *Rymer*, i. 545.

remainder of that county, together with the extensive Carmarthenshire lands of Cantref Mawr and part of Cantref Bychan, were granted to Rhys Fychan, a prince of Deheubarth, to hold as a tenant in chief.

The remainder of Wales which continued to be held by the lords marcher and the Crown was not affected by the treaty.

The death of Llywelyn ap Gruffydd in December of 1282 and the execution of David in the June following marked the complete victory of the King. All the properties of the fallen princes were confiscated, and by the Statute of Rhuddlan, proclaimed on 3 March 1284, Edward made a final settlement of the problem that had vexed him so long. This Statute, addressed to 'all his subjects of his land of Snowdon and of other his lands in Wales' did not concern the lordships of the march. By its provisions the lands were grouped as follows:

(a) *The Principality*, as defined in 1277, was formed into three counties on the English model—Anglesey, Caernarvon, and Merioneth, and the King's conquests in Deheubarth were formed similarly into the two counties of Cardigan and Carmarthen.[1] The last-named included the castle and borough of Carmarthen with the demesne lands of Llanllwch, Cantref Mawr, New Castle Emlyn, Emlyn Uch Cuch, and the castles and lordships of Dryslwyn and Dynevor. The new counties were to be administered by sheriffs, coroners, and other officials, the main centres of administration controlled by a justice, chancellor, and chamberlain, established at Caernarvon in the north and Carmarthen in the south.

(b) The lands of *Rhos and Rhufoniog*, erected into the new lordship of Denbigh, were granted to the Earl of Lincoln; *Dyffryn Clwyd*, erected into the lordship of Ruthin, was granted to Lord Grey: *northern Powys* (Powys Fadog), whose rulers had thrown in their lot with Llywelyn, was divided into two lordships, *Bromfield and Yale*, and given to the Earl of Surrey, and the lordship of *Chirk* to Roger Mortimer.

(c) The lands of *Tegeingl*, together with detached *Maelor Saesneg*, were connected with the county of Flint, which came under the King's Justice of Chester.

(d) The lordships of *Hope*, *Montgomery*, and *Builth* remained in the King's hands.

---

[1] These began their continuous existence as counties in 1241. See J. G. Edwards, 'Early History of the Counties of Carmarthen and Cardigan', *Eng. Hist. Review*, xxxi (1916), pp. 90–98.

It is important to note that the lands described in (*a*) above formed the basis of the Principality of Wales held by the English Princes of Wales from 1301 onwards. To this, from time to time, were added, at the King's pleasure, certain Crown lands, and marcher lordships which became confiscated or escheated to the Crown, but it must be noted that these did not become an integral part of the Principality.

From 1282 to 1301 there was no Prince of Wales, and the lands of the old Principality as defined by the new statute remained in the King's hands. During the years 1287 to 1291, further territories fell to the Crown, and since they were later added to the Principality it becomes necessary to define them. They appear in legal documents as 'the lands formerly of Res ap Mereduk'.

The genealogy of Rhys ap Maredudd, a scion of the dynasty of Deheubarth, reveals him to be as much a Norman as a Welshman. His grandfather, the Prince Rhys Gryg (died 1234), had married Joan, daughter of Richard de Clare, 4th Earl of Hertford. His father was Maredudd, lord of Dryslwyn, his mother a niece of Gilbert de Clare, the Earl Marshal. Rhys ap Maredudd married firstly a Welsh woman, and secondly, by Papal dispensation, on account of consanguinity, Auda de Hastings, daughter of Henry, Lord Hastings.

This branch of the old royal house had managed to retain parts of its ancestral territories. In an agreement made in 5 Edward I between the King and the lord Maredudd, the latter is recorded as holding the castles of Dynevor and Dryslwyn, and lands in Maenordeilo, Mallaen, Caio, and Mabelvyw, with all their rights and privileges.[1] During the war of 1282–3, Maredudd's son Rhys withheld support from Llywelyn, and Edward rewarded him with the Cardiganshire commotes of Mabwnion and Gwynionydd, the Carmarthenshire commotes of Mallaen and Caio, and in 1283 bestowed the honour of knighthood upon him. Thus the princeling became a lord marcher, holding in chief of the King. His new-found loyalty did not last, and in 1287 he revolted. After transient successes and exciting escapes he was captured four years later, and executed.

As a result, his lands escheated to the Crown. These consisted of the castle of *Dryslwyn*, the commotes of *Catheiniog, Caio, Mabelvyw, Mabedryd*, and a *half* of the commote of *Mallaen Iscoed*. Such, then, were 'the lands

---

[1] *Rymer*, ii. 81.

formerly of Res ap Mereduk', which became an integral part of the Principality held by the King's eldest son and heir apparent.

On 7 February 1301 King Edward created his son Prince of Wales and Earl of Chester, and granted to him the following lands,[1] which represent the extent of the Principality of the first English Prince of Wales:

(a) *All the King's lands of North Wales*, namely the counties of Caernarvon, Merioneth, Anglesey, and Hope and lands in the Four Cantreds.

(b) *All the King's lands of West and South Wales*, namely the counties of Carmarthen and Cardigan, the castles and manors of Haverford(west) and Builth, and all lands lately held by 'Res ap Mereduk'.

(c) *The county of Chester*, the *county of Flint*, and the manors of Maclesfield and Overton and the land of Maelor Saesneg.

These lands and their appurtenances, rights, and privileges were to be held by the Prince Edward and his heirs, Kings of England, rendering the same services to the King as the King had rendered to his father King Henry for the same lands.[2] The charter expressly excepted the *castle and town of Montgomery* which had been assigned as part of the dower of Queen Margaret on her marriage to the King in 1299. Mandates[3] to Philip ap Howel, keeper of the castle and town of Builth, William Chykun, keeper of the castle and town of Aberconway, John de Haveryng, keeper of Anglesey and the castle of Beaumaris, Thomas de Makelesfeld, keeper of the manors of Maclesfeld, Overton, and of Maelor Saesneg, Walter Haclut, keeper of the castle and town of Haverfordwest, and to the bishops, earls, knights, freemen, and all other tenants of North, West, and South Wales, Anglesey, and Hope, ordered them to be intendent to Edward the King's son. A similar mandate was directed to the magnates and tenants of the county of Chester.

[1] *Charter Rolls*, 29 Edw. I, m. 9. (36), 7 Feb. 1301.
[2] This refers to the grant of 14 Feb. 1254 when Henry III invested the lord Edward with all Crown possessions in Wales, as an appanage, in view of his intended marriage to a princess of Castile. That grant included Ireland, Gascony, the palatinate county of Chester, and all the Crown lands in Wales, which included the *Middle Country* in county Denbigh, the castles of *Diserth* and *Deganway*, the lordships of *Cardigan, Carmarthen, Montgomery*, and *Builth, the three castles of Upper Gwent* (Grosmont, Skenfrith, White Castle)—*Rymer*, i. 297, 309.
[3] *Charter Rolls*, 29 Edw. I, m. 9. (35).

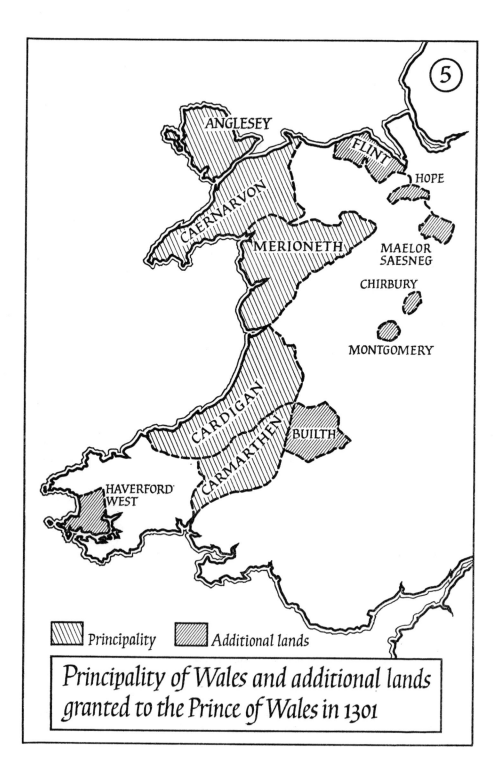

ANGLESEY

FLINT

HOPE

CAERNARVON

MERIONETH

MAELOR
SAESNEG

CHIRBURY

MONTGOMERY

CARDIGAN

BUILTH

CARMARTHEN

HAVERFORD
WEST

5

Principality   Additional lands

Principality of Wales and additional lands
granted to the Prince of Wales in 1301

A further charter, dated 10 May 1301, gave to the Prince the castle and town of *Montgomery* (excepted in the previous grant), and the hundred of *Chirbury*, to be held by the grantee and his heirs, Kings of England, as the King himself had held them, rendering for the lands within the Four Cantreds, the counties of Chester, Cardigan, and Carmarthen, and the other lands which the King lately gave to the Prince, such services as the King had rendered for the same lands to his father King Henry.[1]

The limitation governing the estate—to be held by the Prince and his heirs, Kings of England—ensured that the Principality should continue to be held by the Prince when he became King. This meant that he would be obliged to make a new creation and grant to his son and Heir Apparent if and when he decided to make him Prince of Wales. By the words of this limitation, the separation of the Principality from the heir to the Throne was for ever avoided.

A record of the homage and fealty of the tenants of his new Principality and earldom has survived in the form of an exemplification, which includes about 660 names.[2] The oaths were taken at various places between 13 April 1301 and 5 February 1307, the great majority belonging to the years 1301 and 1302. Most of the oaths were taken before the Prince's representatives, for he himself did not visit Wales for this purpose, at places within and without Wales—Chester, Thorple, Kenilworth, Carlisle, London, Odiham, Flint Castle, Ruthin, Rhuddlan, 'Langele', Conway, 'Conelkey', Tykehull in Yorkshire, Streche in Nottinghamshire, Perth in Scotland, Kennington (in London), and 'Wederhall'. The more important tenants appeared in person to render their fealty direct to the Prince. The lands held by the tenants are specified in some cases, but usually their names are listed under counties, commotes, cantrefs, and towns.

Some well-known names appear on the roll—Reginald de Grey for Ruthin, etc., Henry of Lancaster for Monmouth, Fulk fitz Warin,

---

[1] *Charter Rolls*, 29 Edw. I, m. 7. (28), 10 May 1301.

[2] Entered on *Patent Roll*, 18 Edw. III, Pt. I, mm. 24, 23, and printed *in extenso* in *Calendar*, pp. 227, 234, being an Exemplification made (5 Mar. 1344), of a Certificate by the Treasurer and Barons of the Exchequer, of the names of those who did homage and fealty to the Prince of Wales and Earl of Chester. It has been printed also, but less accurately, in *A Roll of those who did Homage and Fealty to the First English Prince of Wales*, A.D. 1301, by Edward Owen, Cardiff, 1901.

William Martyn of Cemaes, Roger de Mortimer, Griffith de la Pole of Powys, who did homage and fealty at London on 20 July 1302, the Count of Savoy, and by order of the King, Henry de Lacy, Earl of Lincoln, for the lands of Rhos and Rhufoniog; Sir Gruffydd Lloyd, knight, described elsewhere as 'the prince's knight';[1] Tudor ap Grono ap Ednyfed Fychan of Anglesey, Sir Richard Puleston of Englefield, Kenwrig Ddu the Forester of Ewloe, Ithel Fychan of Helygen, Sir Richard de Sutton for Malpas, John, Earl of Warrenne, for Bromfield, Yale, and Hope, Sir Edmund de Mortimer for Kerry and Cydewain, Anian, Bishop of Bangor, David, Abbot of Maenan, William Heraud of Haverfordwest, Ayron of Snowdon, Griffith ap Athewayn, and Llywelyn ap David, lords of Dinmael and Crogen respectively, the brother ap Havet of Merioneth, master of the Hospitallers of North Wales, and the brother Adam, Abbot of Bardsey. As there are very few names from South and West Wales, it is probable that the men of those parts rendered their oaths before the Justice, and that the record has been lost.

The form of the grants to succeeding Princes of Wales remained substantially unchanged. That made by King Edward III on 12 May 1343[2] to his son Edward, 'then Duke of Cornwall and Earl of Chester', specified the following territories—the lordships and lands of North, West, and South Wales, the lordship, castle, town, and county of Caernarvon; the lordships, castles, and towns of Conway, Criccieth, Beaumaris, and Harlech; the lordships and counties of Anglesey and Merioneth; the lordship, castle, town, and county of Carmarthen; the lordship, castle, and town of Llanbadarnfawr; the lordship and stewardship (*senescalcia*) of Cantref Mawr; the lordship, castle, town, and county of Cardigan; the lordships, castles, and towns of Emlyn, Builth, Haverfordwest, and Montgomery; and all the lordships, lands, and tenements of 'Res ap Mereduk'; all to be held with their appurtenances and rights, including the voidances of bishoprics, the advowson of Cathedral churches and other livings.

On the same day, mandates were sent to the Earl of Arundel and Gilbert Talbot, Justices of North and South Wales respectively, to

<hr />

[1] *Cal. Patent Rolls*, 35 Edw. I, m. 8, 7 June 1307.
[2] *Charter Roll*, 17 Edw. III, m. 19, printed in *The Report on the Dignity of a Peer*, v, p. 43; B.M. Royal MS. 18 A, lxxvii, p. 276.

deliver their offices to the Prince, together with the castles, towns, and counties of Caernarvon, Anglesey, Merioneth, Cardigan, and Carmarthen; and to the Chamberlains of North and South Wales, to deliver their offices with the seals, rolls, writs, and memoranda, and to the Constables of castles, Edward de St. John of Conway, William Trussel of Beaumaris, John Lestrange of Criccieth, and Walter de Mauny of Harlech, to deliver their castles to the Prince. The mandate to the Keeper of Dynevor ordered him to deliver that castle to the Prince 'only if it belongs to the principality and lands given him or if it belongs to the King, with all things in it, by indenture in the usual form', and a similarly worded mandate was sent to the Keeper of Dryslwyn Castle. On the following day a mandate *de intendendo* directed the bishops, earls, barons, knights, free men, and tenants of North, West, and South Wales to be intendent to the Prince.[1]

The charter did not define the lands of Chester, for the Prince had already been created earl of that palatinate on 17 March 1337. The roll of fealty, which also includes some interesting presentments, has survived.[2] An extremely detailed document, it contains far more names than does the roll of 1301, and includes those of the South Wales homagers not found in the earlier roll. At the end of June 1343, one of the King's clerks, William de Emeldon, was appointed to take into the King's hands the lands of the Principality, and then to deliver them to the Prince, and at the same time to survey the armour and victuals in the castles and manors.[3]

Accompanied by four commissioners, Emeldon carried out the task with exemplary dispatch. In just over three weeks, between 31 July and 23 August 1343, he called at fifteen places in the Principality, made his surveys, received the oaths of tenants, presented new seals to officials, and inquired as to moneys that the tenants were prepared to subscribe as a 'gift' to their new overlord. Occasional rifts appear in the lute. Several of the tenants side-stepped the question of the 'gift', asking for time to think the matter over, the absence of some important personages was noted, and in one place the Commissioners were confronted by direct defiance. But on the whole they travelled through a peaceful and

[1] *Cal. Charter Rolls*, v, pp. 14–15.

[2] P.R.O. *Miscellanea of the Exchequer*, 4/34, printed *in extenso* in *Original Documents* (Suppl. to *Arch. Cam.*), 1877, pp. cxlxviii–clxxv.

[3] *Cal. Patent Rolls*, 1343–45, p. 56.

well-ordered region, and the numbers of Welshmen holding extensive lands, some described as 'Welsh barons', indicate the extent to which racial animosities had been allayed. On the other hand, practically all the officials bore English names.[1]

On 31 July the Commissioners started their circuit at *St. Asaph*, where David ap Bleddyn, Bishop of St. Asaph, took the oath of fealty. At Conway on 1 August they took the oaths of Thomas de Upton, Constable and Mayor of the town, John Godynogh and Richard Wythe, bailiffs, Mathew de Englefield, Bishop of Bangor, and the burgesses of Conway, nearly all being Englishmen. On 3 August at *Beaumaris* they took the oaths of John de Warwick, Constable of the castle, Mayor of the town, and Sheriff of Anglesey, and the bailiffs, coroners, and burgesses, nearly all English; Dominus Robert de Hamburgh, former Chamberlain of North Wales, and others; while John de Hoson, Seneschal of Queen Isabell for the comote of Menai, which she held for life, swore to respect the Prince's interests. They had a busy time on 5 August at *Caernarvon* where a large crowd of burgesses and countrymen took the oath, among them John de Burton, Constable of the castle and Mayor of the town, the bailiffs, coroner, and burgesses, all bearing English names, Thomas de Upton, Sheriff of Caernarvonshire, the woodwards of Creuddyn, Isaf, and Uchaf, and 'Ughoor' [Uwch Gwyrfai]; the tenants of the country, all Welsh, were headed by Madoc Gloddaeth, a notable chieftain of that period. Asked what they were prepared to subscribe to the Prince in money, the magnates of both Caernarvonshire and Anglesey, together with the bishop and clergy of the diocese of Bangor, asked for leave to defer their answers until the following Michaelmas. At *Criccieth* on 7 August William de Hopton, Constable of the castle and Mayor, and minor officials and burgesses, all Englishmen, took the oath. At *Harlech* on 9 August, where the assemblage was predominantly Welsh, the oaths were subscribed by Bartholomew de Salle, Constable and Mayor, Thomas Fychan, Bailiff, and other burgesses: Howel ap Gronou, sheriff of the county of Merioneth, the abbot of Cymmer, and the 'barons of Edeyrnion' —Rees ap Madoc, Griffith ap David ap Elise, Madox ap Elise, Teg Madoc, Owain and Llywelyn sons of David ap Griffith—who took the

[1] For accounts of this circuit see R. W. Banks, 'On the Welsh Records in the Time of the Black Prince', in *Arch. Cam.*, vol. iv, Series 4 (1873), pp. 157–88; and more especially D. L. Evans, 'Some Notes on the History of the Principality of Wales in the Time of the Black Prince (1343–1376)', in *Trans. Cymmr* (1927), pp. 25–110.

oath of fealty as 'Welsh barons'. Emeldon made a note that the abbots of Valle Crucis, Strata Marcella, and Basingwerk, Griffith de Glyndyfrdwy (ancestor of Owain Glyndwr), and 'the barons of Abertanat' failed to appear.

On 12 August Emeldon and his fellows called at Llanbadarnfawr by Aberystwyth. Here an overwhelming number of Welshmen assembled. The oath was taken by John de Mawardyn, locum tenens of the knight Sir John de Montgomery as Constable of the castle, William Denys, Seneschal and Coroner of Cardiganshire, Robert Scudamore, Griffith ap Llywelyn, Bailiff itinerant of the Seneschalcy, the Abbot of Strata Florida, and by the commons which included notables like Robert Clement, David Bongam, Iorwerth Fychan ap Ieuan ap Gurgan, Howel ap Gwion, Ieuan Lloyd ap Evan ap Griffith, Griffith ap Ieuan Bwl, and many more.

Then through wooded Teivyside on to *Emlyn* where they were busy on 12 August taking the oaths of officials and tenants, nearly all Welshmen, notables like Llewelyn ap Gwilym,[1] the locum tenens of the Lord Gilbert Talbot, Constable, Receiver, and Bailiff of Emlyn, Llewelyn ap Cadwgan, Madoc Fychan, David ap Madoc Benbwl, Robert Martin, and others. At *Cardigan Iscoed* on 14 August the company was again principally Welsh. Here the oaths were subscribed by William Denys as Seneschal and Keeper of the Rolls of Cardiganshire, John Mathew prepositus of Cardigan town, and the men of the comote of Iscoed, which included William Warlow, Walter le Deyer, John Geraud, Griffith and Rhys Fychan sons of Rhys Emlyn, William ap Philip Hagar and others. Emeldon recorded that William Turberville held the office of Constable of Cardigan Castle under the King's grant with a yearly fee of ten shillings. Among the jurors at Cardigan were well-known men like Geoffrey Clement, John Knovil, Roger de Mortimer, Owain ap Llywelyn ap Owain, a member of the old royal house of south-west Wales, Meredydd ap Rhys, and Thomas ap Howel ap Owen. Among the suitors were 'the heirs of Gronow ap Tudyr', descendants of Ednyfed Fychan (died 1246) who had been granted lands in Cardiganshire by Llywelyn the Great.

On 15 August they were at *Haverfordwest* where practically all the homagers were English—William Harald, Seneschal, Constable, and Receiver of the castle, the prior of Haverford, and the commons of the 'town and county', men from families of local eminence bearing the

---

[1] Descendant of Cyhylin of Dyfed, and kinsman of the bard Dafydd ap Gwilym.

names Dowstowe, Wysman, Joce, Tankard, Roche, Robelyn, Hoton. Among them, William Gwrda represented an anglicized branch of an old Welsh noble house.

On 15 August they reached *Carmarthen*, administrative capital of south-west Wales. There they took the oath of the eminent Rhys ap Gruffydd, 'chevalier', locum tenens of the lord Gilbert Talbot, formerly Justice of South and West Wales and Seneschal of Cantref Mawr, John, the Abbot of Talley, the Abbot of Strata Florida, Pontius, the Prior of St. Clear's, and others, the great majority being English. The fealty of the following barons by tenure was accepted—Rhys ap Griffith ap Hywel, David ap Llywelyn ap Philip, Richard de Stakpol, Guy de Brian senior, and Richard de Penrhos. The absence of Lawrence de Hastings, Earl of Pembroke, William de Clynton, Earl of Huntingdon, and James Lord Audley drew comment from the alert Emeldon.

At Carmarthen the commissioners met their first check, and it came from a Churchman. Henry Gower, Bishop of St. David's, being invited to do fealty, answered that he had received the King's summons to attend a Council at Westminster on Wednesday after the Feast of the Nativity of the Virgin, and would then, in his own person, approach the Prince and willingly, 'do all that of right he was bound to do', and promised to inquire as to what aid his clergy would be disposed to give. This, as we shall see, was the opening gambit in a long struggle between bishop and prince. Proclamation was then made of the grant of a new seal to John de Pyrye as Chamberlain of South and West Wales, and that no one should obey other than the Prince's new seal. The lord Thomas de Castro Godrich delivered up the old seal of office, with a silver chain attached, which the Commissioners put into a bag sealed with their seal, to be returned to the King's Chancery in London.

On 19 August they called at the strongholds of *Dryslwyn* and *Dynevor*. As we have seen,[1] some uncertainty existed as to whether these castles formed part of the Principality, but inquiries into the matter had decided in the Prince's favour. At the former the oaths of the Constable, the lord Rhys ap Gruffydd, and of others were taken, and at the latter the oaths of the Constable, George de Chabenor, and his fellows, who, like the homagers of Dryslwyn, were practically all Englishmen.

When on 21 August, they came to *Builth*, where all the officers and

[1] p. 65, *supra*.

homagers were Welshmen, the commissioners met resistance. First, they noted that Owain ap Ieuan, locum tenens of Philip ap Rees, Constable and custos of the castle, did not obey the King's summons, but absented himself, having ordered David Goch, the castle porter, not to admit the commissioners. On the porter's refusal to open the gates, he was arrested and consigned to his own dungeon. Emeldon then seized the castle in the King's name and delivered it to the commissioners, who, in turn, committed it to the keeping of the lord Rhys ap Gruffydd. The new Constable and the commons, all Welsh, then took the oath. At Rhys's request, the unfortunate porter was released, but the former Constable and his deputy were attached, and sureties taken for an appearance to answer for their contempt.

Emeldon reached his journey's end on 23 August at *Montgomery*. Having taken the oaths of Roger de Annewyk, the Seneschal, Walter Bakon, the Constable and Forester, the Prior of Chirbury, and a number of others who bore English and Welsh names, Emeldon and the commissioners rolled their parchments, packed their trunks, and set out on the road to London.

As a widowed Princess of Wales received dower from the lands of her late husband, the succeeding princes sometimes received only part of the Welsh inheritance. Thus in 1376 Edward III, with the assent of the Council, assigned to Joan Princess of Wales, widow of the Black Prince, as her dower the county of Merioneth with Harlech castle, the commotes of Cymytmaen and Dinllaen in Caernarvonshire; a yearly rent of £13. 6s. 8d. from the abbot and convent of Bardesey; the town and castle of Cardigan, the commotes of Iscoed, Geneurglyn, Perfedd, Creuddyn, Hanynyok, Mefenydd, Mabwynion, Gwynionydd, Caerwedros (all in Cardiganshire), the commote of Mabudrud in Carmarthen, the town of Trefilan in Maenorsullen; reserving to the King the perquisites of the county courts of Caernarvon, and of the towns, hundreds, and commotes of Cymydmaen and Dinllaen, and the places and perquisites of petty sessions held at Cardigan and Llanbadarn, as well as the maiden fees of the counties of Carmarthen and Cardigan. On 13 October 1376 David Craddock and Hugh le Young, chamberlains respectively of North and South Wales, were directed to deliver these lands to the Princess.[1] The grant of the Principality made to Richard, the new Prince

---

[1] *Cal. Close Rolls*, 1374–7, pp. 405–6.

of Wales, on 20 November 1376 decreed that he was to receive *two-thirds* of the lands in Wales, the duchy of Cornwall, the county of Chester, and of lands elsewhere in England lately held by his father, and the whole of the county of Flint, with the reversion of the one-third then enjoyed in dower by Joan his mother.[1]

The next time that the lands of the Prince were defined in any detail was in 1399. On 15 October of that year, King Henry IV issued three charters.[2] By the first he created his son Henry Prince of Wales, Duke of Cornwall, and Earl of Chester; by the second confirmed him in the lands of the Principality, namely all the King's lands in North, West, and South Wales, the lordship, castle, town, and county of Caernarvon; the lordship, castle, and town of Conway; the four commotes of Isaph, Uchaf, Nanconway, and Creuddyn in the county of Caernarvon; the lordships, castles, and towns of Criccieth and Harlech; the county of Merioneth; the lordship, castle, and town of Llanbadarnfawr; the lordship and seneschalcy of Cantref Mawr; the lordship, castle, and town of the county of Cardigan; the lordships, castles, and towns of Builth and Montgomery; the lands formerly held by Res ap Mereduk; together with the vacancies of sees, advowsons of cathedrals, churches, etc., pensions, corrodies, the offices of chancellors, raglors, ringilds, woodwards, constables, bailiffs, foresters, coroners, etc., and the reversions of the lordships and castles of Haverford(west) with the prise of wines there, Newcastle in Emlyn, and the lordships of Nevin and Pwllheli which Thomas Percy Earl of Northumberland held for life by the gift of Richard II; and the reversion of the county and lordship of Anglesey and the castle of Beaumaris held by Henry Percy son of the said earl for life.[3]

The third charter, after reciting the creation and investiture of Prince Henry as Earl of Chester, confirmed him, 'according to custom', in the palatine counties of Chester and Flint, the castles of Chester, Beeston, Rhuddlan, Hope, and Flint, with all lands thereto belonging, the manors of Hope and Hopedale, the cantred of 'Inglefeld'; the advowson of St. Asaph Cathedral church, the vacancies, issues, etc., of the temporalities

[1] *Cal. Close Rolls,* 1374–7, p. 420.

[2] *Charter I*, Henry IV, Pt. I, m. 27 and m. 20 (26). The Latin texts are printed *in toto* in *Arch. Cam.*, 6th series, xi (1911), pp. 234–7.

[3] On 12 Oct. 1399 the King had granted the county and lordship of Anglesey and the castle of Beaumaris to the Earl of Northumberland; see text in *Original Documents* (Suppl. *Arch. Cam.*), 1877, pp. x–xi.

of the bishoprics of St. Asaph and Chester; and the reversion of the manor of Frodsham held by Redegunda, formerly wife of Degari Seys, knight, to whom Richard II had granted it for life.

The last time for the Principality to be defined in detail in such grants occurred in 1454 when King Henry VI created his son Edward Prince of Wales and Earl of Chester.[1] On 15 March of that year he granted him the King's lordships and lands in North, West, and South Wales; the lordship, castle, town, and county of Caernarvon; the lordship, castle, and town of Conway; the four commotes of 'Haph', 'Ughaph', Nanconway, and Creuddyn; the lordships, castles, and towns of Criccieth and Harlech; the county of Merioneth; the lordship, castle, town, and county of Carmarthen; the lordship, castle, and town of Llanbadarnfawr; the lordship, castle, town, and county of Cardigan; the lordship and castle of Haverford, with prise of wines there; the lordship and castle of Newcastle in Emlyn; the lordships of Nevin and Pwllheli; the lordship and county of Anglesey; castle of Beaumaris; the lordships, lands, and tenements formerly of Res ap Mereduk; an annual charge of £130. 6s. 8d. issuing from the lordship, castle, and town of Builth, which Richard Duke of York once held; and an annual charge issuing from the lordship, castle, and town of Montgomery.

Although the extent of the Principality had been clearly defined in the foregoing charters, nevertheless extensive tracts not specified in the grants did in fact own the jurisdiction of the Prince at various times.[2] These had formerly belonged to the Welsh princes but had not been incorporated in the counties as defined by the Statute of Rhuddlan or included in the subsequent grants to the Princes of Wales. When such lands fell vacant, a special escheator was appointed to guard the Prince's rights in these 'apurtenant' or 'foreign' estates, and it is clear that the Justices of North and South Wales possessed some undefined authority over some of them. Efforts by various Princes to extend their power over the marcher lordships and certain Crown lands were fiercely resisted and led to prolonged lawsuits.

Bones of contention were plentiful. One of the most important of these territories, the lordship of Denbigh, had been granted by the King

---

[1] *Rolls of Parliament*, v, pp. 290–5.

[2] The question as it affected North Wales has been discussed by W. H. Waters in *The Edwardian Settlement*, pp. 87–96.

to Henry Lacy on 16 October 1282, but in 1344 it was shown that the lordship had always been appurtenant to the Principality, held of the Prince by knight service, and did not pertain to the King in chief.[1] In the event, the lordships of Denbigh, Bromfield, and Yale remained under the jurisdiction of the Prince. Reginald de Grey, who had received the lordship of Dyffryn Clwyd from the King on 23 October 1282, nevertheless did homage and fealty to the Prince in 1301. Cynllaith and Glyndyfrdwy were other territories that provided problems for the medieval lawyers. Madoc ap Griffith, who died in 1304, held one-half of the commote of Cynllaith *outside* the county of Merioneth, and one-quarter of the commote of Glyndyfrdwy *inside* that county, and for this latter portion he owed suit to the county court of Merioneth. During the minority of Madoc's heir, Griffith, these lands were farmed by John Lestrange of Knockin, who accounted for them at the Exchequer of Caernarvon, and when the heir came of age in 1321 the Justice of North Wales was ordered by the King to deliver the patrimony to the heir. The la Pole lands in Powys Gwenwynwyn were also claimed for the Prince, but in 1316 they were adjudged to be held of the King in chief. The lord of Mawddwy, Griffith son of William de la Pole, refused to acknowledge the overlordship of the Prince although he had made certain payments to the Exchequer of Caernarvon. When the Black Prince attempted to extend his authority to Powys, John de Charleton resisted, and proved that he held in chief of the King; and his efforts to make the lords of Laugharne and Gower in South Wales to attorn to him proved equally unavailing. The clergy of the diocese of St. David's scored a remarkable triumph, for they were able to upset an actual grant made by the King to his son. In 1343 the grant to the Prince specifically included the Welsh bishoprics, but when the Bishop of St. David's died in 1347 the clergy opposed all the Prince's efforts to establish a supremacy over the See, and with a spirit that recalls the earlier struggles of the Archdeacon Giraldus, the churchmen carried on the fight for ten years, and finally triumphed when the King ordained that St. David's should appertain to the Crown for ever and ordered the Prince and his ministers not to interfere further in the matter.[2]

---

[1] *Cal. Close Rolls*, 1343–6, p. 306.
[2] *Cal. Close Rolls*, 1354–60, p. 382: *Cal. Charter Rolls*, 1327–41, p. 188, and 1341–1417, s.d. 31 Dec. 1383.

In the grant to Prince Richard in 1376, the advowson of the Cathedral church of St. David's was excepted, because it had 'of old pertained to the Crown'.[1] And so the hero of Crécy and Poitiers failed to rout the tonsured clerics of West Wales despite the fact that the charter of 1343 had made it abundantly clear that he was to have jurisdiction over them. The other Welsh bishops never succeeded in becoming independent, and their bishoprics could be, and were, transferred to the Prince.

The Prince exercised limited rights over certain other areas. In the case of Arwystli it was adjudged that the officers of the Principality could interfere in judicial cases only by virtue of a special commission; while Mechain Iscoed was to be held in chief of the King, and yet to come under the authority of the Justice of North Wales. The Black Prince succeeded in asserting his authority over Kerry and Cydewain, the castle of Dolforwyn, the castle, town, and lordship of Montgomery and the hundred of Chirbury, which were confirmed to him in 1360 after he had shown that they formed part and parcel of the Principality, and that the castle of Montgomery was 'the key to the Principality'.[2]

Although only the lands of the defined Principality came under total and direct government of the Prince, he exercised a certain authority over lands outside that Principality, as shown by the names of tenants ordered by Edward III in 1343 to be intendent to the Prince. This significant and revealing list[3] included the names of the Bishops of St. Asaph, St. David's, Bangor, and Llandaff; and the lords William Montague of Denbigh; John de Warenne of Bromfield and Yale; Richard Earl of Arundel, lord of Chirk, Oswestry, and Clun; Roger Grey of Ruthin and Dyffryn Clwyd; the lord of Abertanat; John de Cherleton of Powys Gwenwynwyn; Griffith ap William (de la Pole) of Mawddwy; Roger Mortimer of Maelienydd, Cydewain, Gwerthrynion, Kerry, and Wigmore; Thomas de Beauchamp, Earl of Warwick, lord of Elvael; Humphrey de Bohun, Earl of Hereford, lord of Brecknock, Hay, and Huntyngdon; the lord of Bwlch-y-dinas (near Talgarth) and Clifford; Laurence de Hastyngs, Earl of Pembroke, lord of Abergavenny and Oysterlowe; Elizabeth de Burgh, lady of Clare and Usk: Hugh d'Audley, Earl of Gloucester, lord of Newport; the lord of Crickhowel; Hugh le

---

[1] *Cal. Close Rolls*, 1374–7, p. 420, 20 Nov. 1376.
[2] *Cal. Close Rolls*, 1360–4, pp. 80–82, 22 Nov. 1360.
[3] *Cal. Charter Rolls*, v. 14–15: mandate *de intendendo* dated 13 May 1343.

Despencer of Glamorgan; John de Mowbray of Gower; Henry de Lancaster, Earl of Derby, Lord of Kidwelly, Carnwallon, and Iskennen; Thomas de Bradeston of Builth; Bartholomew de Burghersh of Ewyas; the lady of Ewyas Lacy; the lord of Dore and Harold Ewyas; Henry, Earl of Lancaster, lord of Grosmont, White Castle, and Monmouth; and William de Clynton, Earl of Huntingdon, lord of St. Clears and Cilgerran.

Thus, in 1343, the King had acknowledged the authority of the Prince over these lordships. However, the subsequent opposition of the lords to the Prince and his Council decided the King to re-establish his own authority, and, accordingly, by a statute in 1354 decreed that the lands of the lords marcher were to be, for ever, attendant to the Crown and not to the Principality.[1] When Edward III created his grandson Prince of Wales, the grant made on 20 November 1376 contained the following clause—*reserving to the King the fees of lords of the march of Wales who of old were tenants of the Crown, and the advowson of the cathedral church of St Davids which of old pertained to the Crown.*[2] Having learnt by experience, the King now ensured that the difficulties generated by his late son were not to be repeated by the grandson.

After this, little is heard of any efforts to extend the authority of the Prince outside those lands forming the basic Principality or Crown lands in Wales specifically granted to the Prince for the time being.

From the Statute of Rhuddlan to the Act of Union the position remained virtually unchanged. Wales continued a mosaic of lordships, each governed by its own particular laws and customs. During the Wars of the Roses the power of the lords marcher and the feudal baronage generally, waned, and later the strong hand of the first two Tudor monarchs, with their policy of centralization and strengthening the royal prerogative, weakened them still further. Nevertheless, the patchwork quilt remained, and in 1536 numerous lordships still existed in a land as disunited and fragmented as ever it had been under the native dynasties. There was no such political unit as Wales—merely a region, a territory of many lordships having the character of semi-independent states, in the majority of which the King's writ did not run.

In the year 1536 Henry VIII slammed the door in the face of the

---

[1] Statute 28 Edw. III, c. ii.
[2] *Cal. Close Rolls*, 1374–7, p. 240, see Owen, *Pems*, iii. 151.

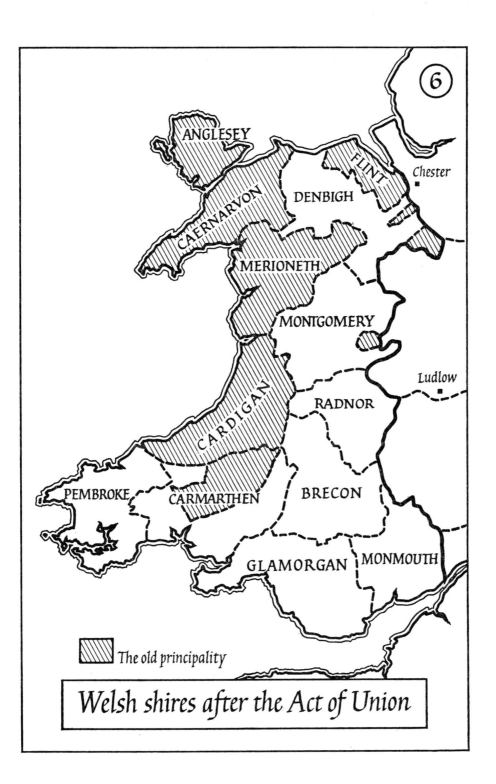

Welsh shires after the Act of Union

The old principality

marcher lords. By an Act[1] in that year he abolished the varied jurisdictions in Wales, and added, to the ones already existing, six new counties, Denbigh, Brecon, Radnor, Montgomery, Glamorgan, and Monmouth, all of which were made up of the medieval lordships. Other lordships were added to the existing counties of Carmarthen, Cardigan, Pembroke, and Merioneth, and on the border a number reputed to be wholly or partly in 'Wales' were transferred to the counties of Salop, Hereford, and Gloucester.[2] Thus the whole of Wales became organized on the English model, the shires and boroughs received parliamentary representation, and an improved judicial system was introduced. The Courts of Great Sessions, which had been held within the Principality since 1284, were now extended to include all the country except the county of Monmouth.

The provisions of the Act did not wholly destroy the lords marcher, who were permitted to retain many of their lesser privileges, but in effect they became little more than ordinary lords of the manor. Retaining seigniorial rights over their lands, they continued to receive customary dues, rents, reliefs, certain tolls, wreck, deodands, treasure trove, to hold courts leet and courts baron and receive perquisites and fines thereof. But they lost power of life and death, had no cognizance of Crown pleas, murder, robbery, theft, rape, arson. The map of medieval Wales had been rolled up.

From 1536 onwards the term 'Wales' had a political connotation, whereas before it had none. The country was united for the first time in its history, and the name Welshman now comprehended, not only one of Welsh ancestry or speech, but a man who lived in Wales, whatever his pedigree or language. No distinction in law existed between a Welshman and an Englishman resident in Wales, or between one Welshman and another Welshman.

How did the old Principality fare in this redistribution? What was the position of the Prince of Wales under the new dispensation? According to the Act of 1536 'the Domynyon, Principalitie and Countrey of Wales'

---

[1] The most convenient work on this subject is Dr. William Rees's *The Union of England and Wales*, where the Act of 1536 is printed *in extenso*, from Parliament Roll 27 Henry VIII (No. 60), P.R.O. C 65/145.

[2] The Act of 1536 defined the detailed composition of these counties and the disposal of the lordships, and some further minor rearrangements were made in 1541. See Rees, op. cit.; W. Ll. Williams, *Making of Modern Wales*; Rhys and Jones, *The Welsh People*, ch. viii, and app. C; C. A. J. Skeel, *Council of the Marches in Wales*, p. 41 et seq; *Y Cymmrodor*, vols. ix, xii, xiii, xiv; Bowen, *Statute of Wales*; Sir Artemus Jones, *The Union of England and Wales*.

was 'incorporated, annexed, united and subject' to England, and came under the direct lordship of the monarch as 'verye hedde kinge lorde and ruler'. There was no distinction made between the Principality of the Prince and the other lands in Wales. The Prince had been, in effect, a lord marcher, the most important one in Wales, and in the new redistribution was treated in the same way as any other lord marcher. He retained, as the others retained, certain powers within his Principality (i.e. within the lands defined in medieval grants as the Principality of Wales) and, as we shall see, the former Principality retained its identity so far as fiscal arrangements were concerned down to the nineteenth century. So late as 1793 the term Principality and 'the revenues of the Principality' comprehended only those lands which had formed part of it prior to 1536. Nevertheless, as the years went by, the term Principality became extended to include the whole of the new Wales, and the title Prince of Wales came to mean Prince of all Welshmen and of the thirteen counties. In courts of law the term was used to cover all Wales, and in the late seventeenth century the records of the Great Sessions used the formula 'the Principality of Wales' in that sense.

When the two sons of King James I were created Princes of Wales—Henry in 1610, Charles in 1616—no charter was passed granting them the lands and revenues of the Principality. The only post-Tudor grant of the lands and revenues was that made by George I to his son in 1715,[1] but this did not specify them in detail beyond naming the counties in which the lands were situated; and it is interesting to note that in addition to the twelve counties the county of Monmouth was also named.

Since some Welsh lands were attached to the Palatinate of Chester in medieval times, a brief reference to them may be permitted here. The first Prince of Wales to receive the earldom of Chester was the Black Prince, and the machinery of its government differed very little from that of the Principality. The Welsh members consisted of the county and town of Flint, which included the manors of Hope, Hopedale, and Euloe, the castle and lands of Rhuddlan, the towns and townships of Coleshill, Caersws, Bacherge, Vaenol, Mostyn. The chief officers for the Welsh lands were the sheriffs, escheators, and raglors of the county of Flint, the Constable of Rhuddlan Castle, and the escheator of Tegaingl (Englefield). Territorially these became part of Flintshire under the new dispensation.

---

[1] Public (General) Acts I, Geo. I, c. xxxvii.

3

GOVERNMENT OF THE PRINCIPALITY

WHEN Edward I reorganized the Principality in 1284, the careful arrangements made for its government remained in force until 1536, and some of them persisted in modified form for over two centuries after that date. Although organized on the model of English counties the government of the Principality, in fact, retained more of the characteristics of a great barony or palatinate, with the Prince as its lord, and when no such lord existed the monarch exercised the authority instituted by the Statute of Rhuddlan.[1] The 'chain of command' was as follows:

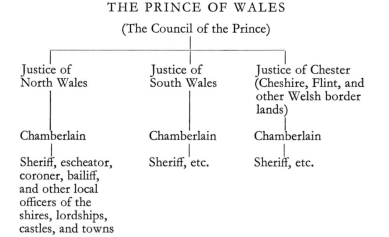

THE PRINCE OF WALES

(The Council of the Prince)

Justice of North Wales	Justice of South Wales	Justice of Chester (Cheshire, Flint, and other Welsh border lands)
Chamberlain	Chamberlain	Chamberlain
Sheriff, escheator, coroner, bailiff, and other local officers of the shires, lordships, castles, and towns	Sheriff, etc.	Sheriff, etc.

During medieval times the Prince received guidance from a Council appointed by the King. Little is known of the extent of the powers and exact functions of this Council, apart from the fact that it was to assist him in the administration of his territories in the Principality as well as those in England and in the Marches.

[1] See W. H. Waters, *The Edwardian Settlement of North Wales*.

Of the seven Plantagenet Princes of Wales, five had their own Councils and Households. The members of the Council varied between eight and fifteen. Edward of Caernarvon's Council consisted of fifteen members, that of the Black Prince about twelve, the Council and Household of Edward of Westminster (Lancaster) numbered ten and thirty-eight respectively. Edward of Westminster (York) on the other hand had a Council of eight members in 1471, increased to twenty-five in 1473, but since he presided over the Council of Wales and the Marches his position was somewhat exceptional. During their brief principates, neither Richard of Bordeaux nor Edward of Middleham had Council or Household, the former prince being in charge of his mother, to whom his yearly allowance of 1,000 marks was paid, the latter being maintained by the King. The two Tudor princes, Arthur and Henry, were the last to possess a Council of their own, since which no such body has been constituted.

This Council was the final court of appeal for the Principality in legal matters. It met, normally, in London and its orders to the officials in the Principality were issued either on the authority of the secretary of the Council or 'By the advice of the Council' as some documents are subscribed, or directly from the Prince. In the time of the Black Prince, for instance, many of the orders were signed 'By Command of the Prince himself'.[1]

The councillors consisted of prelates, peers, and other magnates, few of whom had any personal connexion with Wales. The most active of these Councils was that of the Black Prince, whose policy was to extend his influence, and since he constantly needed troops and money for his continental ventures, it became necessary to take particular note of all sources likely to provide these essentials. For a short time in the latter half of the fifteenth century the Prince's Council was absorbed into the Council of Wales and the Marches,[2] as I have noted earlier, but after the death of Arthur in 1501, no other Prince of Wales was associated with that body. At the close of the Middle Ages the Prince's Council as such ceased to exist, its place being taken by the senior administrative officers

[1] See *The Black Prince's Register*: see also *Journal of the Chester and North Wales Architectural, Archaeological, and Historical Society*, xl (1957), pp. 1 ff. and references there.

[2] A Council to regulate the affairs of the Principality and the Marches was appointed on 20 Feb. 1473 (Patent Roll, 12 Edw. IV, Pt. II, m. 21). See also *Y Cymmrodor*, xii, xiii, xiv: C. A. J. Skeel, op. cit.: and *Calendar of the Registers of the Council in the Marches of Wales, 1569–1691*, ed. Ralph Flenley.

of his Household, who, so far as is known, formulated no policies for the Principality.

As the Princes had no residence in Wales—they normally lived in the capital or its environs or within the King's court—and as few ever visited the country, the government was left to officials on the spot. The real power lay in the hands of the Justice of North Wales (sometimes termed Justice of Snowdon) and the Justice of South Wales (sometimes termed Justice of West Wales or of South and West Wales). Occasionally one man administered the whole of the Principality, being then entitled Justice of Wales, such as John Havering in 1300. In addition, a Justice of Chester directed the governance of that palatinate and the Welsh lands within its jurisdiction.

An important personage, the Justice was the 'vice-regent' of the Prince (or King), and acting head of the government, in fact a justiciar and ruler. He possessed an Exchequer and Chancery, located at Caernarvon in the case of North Wales, and Carmarthen in case of the South and West. These exchequers and chanceries remained distinct even when a single justice acted for the whole. Derived from powerful families, the Justices were either barons or lords marcher, such as Otto de Grandison, the first Justice of North Wales (appointed 1284), and John Havering, his deputy, John Grey de Ruthin (Justice of North Wales 1315–16), Roger Mortimer of Chirk (Justice of North Wales 1316–22), Roger Mortimer of Wigmore (Justice of North Wales 1327–30), William Martin of Cemaes (Justice of South Wales 1315–16), Maurice Berkeley (Justice of South Wales 1316–17), and Edmund FitzAlan, Earl of Arundel (Justice of Wales 1322–6). Before the end of the Middle Ages royal personages held the appointment, Richard Duke of York and Edward Prince of Wales being Justices of all Wales in 1469 and 1476 respectively. The Justices and their chief officers, the Chamberlains, were Anglo-Normans, and no Welsh name appears among them until the latter half of the fifteenth century. Since their interests as English lords often necessitated the presence of the Justices in their own fiefs, they appointed deputies to act for them in Wales, often Welshmen, like Sir Gruffydd ap Rhys and Sir Rhys ap Gruffydd ap Howel in the fourteenth century. The chief officers of the counties, the sheriffs, were also Anglo-Normans, but eminent Welshmen were sometimes included, so that out of the fifteen sheriffs of Anglesey during the years 1284–1343, five were

PLATE I

Eastgate sculp

CAERNARVON CASTLE, *in* NORTH WALES.

Publish'd according to Act of Parliament, by Alex.r Hogg, No.16. Paternoster-Row.

CAPITAL OF THE NORTHERN PRINCIPALITY

PLATE II

CAERMARTHEN CASTLE, *in* CAERMARTHENSHIRE.

Published according to Act of Parliament by Alex.^r Hogg, N.º 16 Paternoster Row.

CAPITAL OF THE SOUTHERN PRINCIPALITY

J.G.Wooding. sculp.

Welshmen. The coroners, who required a more intimate knowledge of local affairs, were nearly always Welshmen.

The Justice received his salary out of the issues of the lands under his jurisdiction. In 1359 the Justice of South Wales received £100, his deputy £20. The traditional fee was 200 marks per annum, and when they 'kept' the castles and towns of Caernarvon and Carmarthen each Justice received an additional £100. When one person acted for all the Principality he received a much higher salary, as, for instance, Roger Mortimer in 1308 who received 350 marks per annum, plus the £100 for the custody of Caernarvon Castle. The castles were governed by constables, usually Englishmen with military experience, and occasionally the Prince gave constableships to members of his retinue by way of reward for service, such as Simon de Burley, companion of the Black Prince and guardian of his son, appointed Constable of Carmarthen for life in 1377.

The highest court of law within their jurisdiction was that of Great Sessions, as laid down in the Statute of Rhuddlan, which the Justice held in his own person, or by deputy, sometimes assisted by other justices specially appointed for the occasion.

The chief fiscal officers, heads of the exchequer, were the Chamberlains, who were not recruited from the ruling families; they were always clerks in holy orders, and received a fee of £20 per annum. In South Wales they often came from the Priory of Austin Canons at Carmarthen, such as the Prior Robert in 1312–15, and the Prior John de Chandos in 1328–31. The Chamberlains, too, were usually of English or Norman extraction, but in the latter half of the fifteenth century Welshmen were appointed, members of the family of Griffith of Penrhyn in North Wales, and magnates like William, Lord Herbert, and Sir Rhys ap Thomas in the south. At a later stage the offices of Justice and Chamberlain were held by one man, such as the Duke of Buckingham in the reign of Richard III, and Sir Rhys ap Thomas and Lord Ferrers of Chartley in early Tudor times. Some were appointed for life, like Sir William Stanley who was made Justice of North Wales in 1485–6.

The sheriffs looked after the counties, were often constables of castles, and presided over county and commote courts. Local officials accounted to them, and they in turn to the Chamberlains. Below the sheriffs came a horde of minor officials, largely Welshmen, the rhaglaw (superintendent of the commote), beedles, reeves, bailiffs, constables, maer, latimer (interpreter), the pencais (sergeants of the peace), stewards, foresters, and so forth.

During the years a Prince held the Principality its records bore two dates, that of the King's reign and that of the principate. Thus the accounts of William de Rogate, Chamberlain of West Wales in 1304, were dated 'from Michaelmas in the thirty-first year of the reign of our Lord King Edward and the third year of the principate of Lord Edward Prince of Wales, son of the aforesaid king . . . '.[1]

As we have referred to the association between the Princes and the Council of Wales and the Marches, it becomes necessary to examine that association in more detail. Before the end of the Wars of the Roses, conditions in Wales and the Marches had reached a state of near-anarchy. Edward IV was the first monarch to take active steps to restore the rule of law, and accordingly in 1473 sent his infant son Edward, Prince of Wales, and the Queen, to keep court at Ludlow. A Council to regulate the affairs of these territories was appointed on 20 February 1473, and Bishop Alcock became its first president. The King also granted lands in the Marches to the infant Prince, and on 29 December following gave him power to appoint other Justices in the Principality and the Marches. We know little of the proceedings of the Council during this early period, which appears to have sat in various places. A stray reference shows that the Prince and the Council visited Shrewsbury in April 1478, where he made 'certayne ordonances for the weale and the tranquillitie of the same town'. No more is heard of a Prince in the Marches until Prince Arthur came to Ludlow in 1493, and during his lifetime the Council was known as 'Prince Arthur's Council'. Although Henry VII's intention was to make Ludlow a residence for the Prince of Wales, the next holder of the title, Henry, did not go there at all. Princess Mary Tudor held a court there, but after that no royal personage had any associations with Ludlow or with the Council of Wales and the Marches, which, under a Lord President, continued to operate, with the exception of the Commonwealth period, until its abolition in 1689.

After the Act of Union, which removed the diversity of jurisdictions in Wales, all that remained to the Prince was his title, together with the lands and issues which he owned as a private landowner, while his former subjects became his tenants, subject to the authority of the Crown

---

[1] *Ministers' Accounts for West Wales 1277 to 1306*, ed. Myfanwy Rees, Pt. I, *passim*.

and English law. He no longer ruled, required no Council to formulate policy, no officers to enforce decrees. All that was left for him was to appoint officials to hold courts and collect rents and dues. Many of the older appointments survived, it is true. There were constables of castles, but they were ruined castles. Appointments that had been invested with great power in medieval times became shadows without substance.

The learned Dodridge[1] has compiled a list of the officers who served the Prince within the Principality, together with their annual fees, 'collected out of divers ancient Accompts'. As will be seen in the following précis of the more important officials, the titles indicate the nature of their duties. Unless otherwise stated the salaries were 'per annum'. For North Wales the officers were: Justice, Chamberlain, Auditor, Comptroller of Pleas, Fines, Amerciaments, Redemptions and Ransoms, Attorney, Surveyor of castles, manors, lands, etc., Constable of Caernarvon Castle, Captain of Caernarvon town, Porter of the Gate of Caernarvon town, Constable of Conway Castle, Captain of Conway town, Keeper and Porter of the Gate of Conway, Constable of Harlech Castle, Constable of Beaumaris Castle, Captain of Beaumaris town, Porter or keeper of the Gate of Beaumaris, Chief Forester of Snowdon, Steward of the town of Newborough, Marshall and Keeper of the Justice House in Caernarvon town, Clerk of the Great Sessions, Woodward, Auditor, Receiver, and Surveyor of Merioneth.

The officers for the Principality in South Wales were the Justice, Chamberlain and Chancellor, Auditor, Attorney, Constable and Usher of Carmarthen Castle, Sheriff of the county, Steward of commotes, Clerk of the county courts and petty sessions, Crier of the said courts, Steward of the Welsh courts, Pencais of the commotes of Widigada and Elvet, Steward and Clerk of the said commote courts, Bailiff Itinerant for Carmarthen, and Bailiff Itinerant of Cantref Mawr; Constable of Cardigan Castle, Sheriff of Cardiganshire, Clerk of the county courts, towns, and petty sessions and of the counties of Cardigan, Carmarthen, Pembroke, and town of Haverfordwest, Crier of the said courts, Clerk of commotes in Cardigan, Steward and Clerk of the Rolls of the Welsh courts, Clerk of the Rolls in the commote of Isirwern, Bailiffs Itinerant of Cardigan and of Llanbadarn, Captain of the town of Aberystwyth, Escheator for the counties of Cardigan and Carmarthen, Clerk of Great Sessions of the two

[1] Dodridge, pp. 55 ff.

said counties, and Attorney for the counties of Carmarthen, Cardigan, Pembroke, Brecon, and Radnor.

In addition, a Court of the Exchequer of the Prince's Revenues existed at Caernarvon and Carmarthen, which involved further payment to officials for the performance of administrative duties. There was a whole host of minor posts, some of which were created from time to time to meet contingencies, but these gradually disappeared from the lists, like the Steward of Bardsey, the Keeper of Penmaenmawr, the Steward of Pembroke, the Governor of Milford Haven, and so on.

Most of the foregoing posts occur in medieval records and also at the end of Elizabeth's reign.[1]

Salaries were modest. In the northern Principality the highest was £50 to the Justice, a sum varying between £40 and £60 to the Constable of Caernarvon Castle, while at the lower end of the scale the Marshal of the Justice House received £1. 6s. 8d. Officers of the southern Principality were less well paid, varying between £40 paid to the Justice and 4s. to the Pencais of Widigada and Elfet.

The gradual elimination of local particularisms and seigniorial jurisdictions, the effect of the policy of uniformity, the changes and developments in national and county administrations, and adaptation to suit modern requirements, rendered the great majority of the old offices redundant. For instance, after the Civil War no royal castles were maintained in Wales, many of which had been abandoned to the ivy and owl in much earlier times, so that the office of constable fell into disuse.[2] When Lord Hereford tried to get his appointment confirmed as Constable of Carmarthen Castle in December 1660, a Whitehall clerk informed him, 'the castle of Carmarthen being now quite demolished, I conceive the constableship thereof to be unnecessary'. Better fortune attended Edward (Herbert) Lord Chirbury, when he petitioned for the offices of Chief Forester of Snowdon, Constable of Conway Castle,[3]

---

[1] Dodridge, pp. 67–76.

[2] e.g. 'Conway Castle, this ruin is the property of the Crown under which it is held on lease by Owen Holland, Esq, at the nominal rent of 6s 8d and a dish of fish to Lord Hereford as often as he passes through the town'—Grose, *Antiq.* vii (ed. 1773), p. 27. By the time of Queen Elizabeth, Haverfordwest castle was so decayed that Sessions could not be held in it— G. Dyfnallt Owen, *Elizabethan Wales*, Cardiff, 1962, p. 95.

[3] For a list of the Constables of the castles of Beaumaris, Caernarvon, Conway, and Harlech, which continued to modern times, see E. Breese, *Kalendars of Gwynedd*, London, 1873. Flint Castle also had a constable at the end of the last century.

Keeper of the Courts, and of the Manor of Bardsey, which had been granted to his father and grandfather by King James I, and in February 1660–1 they were confirmed to him by the restored monarch. Today there is no Captain of Aberystwyth, for its military significance has long since gone, and the government reposes in the hands of the red-robed mayor of that town. No stewards of commotes are necessary where commotes no longer exist. Today the Constable of Kidwelly Castle is the Ministry of Works, the Keeper of Penmaenmawr the County Council, the Governor of Milford Haven an oil company, and the Steward of Bardsey is the seagull. Where appointments persisted they were of an honorary nature, picturesque relics, carrying nominal or no duties or salary. Yet we welcome their survival, for the titles take us back to medieval romance and adventure, they perpetuate the memory of stirring events that influenced and shaped the destinies of our nation. When Mr. David Lloyd George, Constable of Caernarvon Castle, presented the key of that great fortress to the King on a memorable day in 1911, Welshmen saw in the act a continuity rather than a revival of ancient and honourable custom, while the appointment, a few years ago, of the Earl of Snowdon as Constable of the same castle gave further emphasis to that continuity.

4

REVENUES OF THE PRINCIPALITY

THE Princes of Wales derived their revenues from the Principality, the Duchy of Cornwall, and the Earldom of Chester, augmented by grants of additional territories and profits as well as sums of money from the Treasury granted and authorized by the monarch from time to time. The net revenues of the Principality were never very large, owing mainly to heavy establishment charges, for even after the conquest of 1282 the King could not afford to take chances, so that Wales remained a garrisoned land. The price of peace was heavy, for the constables of castles, royal officials from justiciars and chamberlains to local functionaries like the reeve, the cais, and ringild, archers, and men-at-arms, all had to be paid; castles had to be stocked with provisions and arms, buildings repaired, hostages and prisoners maintained, soldiers and levies paid, in addition to pensions, gifts, and incidental expenses.

The revenues of the Principality did not belong as of right to the Prince, neither did they come automatically to him when he became Prince of Wales. They formed part of the hereditary revenues of the Crown, and whenever the Princes have possessed lands and revenues in the Principality it has always been by virtue of a special grant from the Crown, entirely distinct from the patent by which the title and dignity were conferred. Moreover, such grants had to be further sanctioned by an Act of Parliament. The revenues were regularly granted to Princes of Wales during the Middle Ages, the last medieval prince to receive them being Prince Arthur, but they were withheld from his brother Prince Henry in 1504. The next, and indeed the last, time they were specifically granted occurred in 1715 when George I conferred them on the newly created Prince of Wales. This involved a special Act of Parliament[1] whose preamble stated that it was passed to enable the King to grant to his son 'the Regalities and Lands now remaining in the Crown in North Wales

---

[1] Public (General) Acts 1, Geo. I, c. xxxvii.

and South Wales and the County of Chester' in manner and form as the Principality and Earldom had been granted formerly to the Princes of Wales, and also to enable the Prince to make leases as necessary. The Act went on to describe the lands, castles, lordships, manors, commotes, forests, etc. in the counties of Flint, Denbigh, Montgomery, Caernarvon, Anglesey, Merioneth, Carmarthen, Cardigan, Pembroke, Brecon, Glamorgan, Radnor, Monmouth, and the County-Palatinate of Chester, 'notwithstanding great alienations made in former reigns', and which still belonged to the King as part of the ancient Principality and Earldom. The recital continued that the King by Letters Patent under the Great Seal, dated 27 September 1714, 'according to the ancient custom of the realm' had created his eldest son Prince of Wales and Earl of Chester, and that it had been 'usual' for the King to grant the land revenues to his son and Heir Apparent having been created Prince and Earl, but 'any grant so made must be Enacted by Parliament'. On the determination of that grant by the Prince's accession as King George II in 1728, the revenues merged again in the Crown, and so far as they concerned the Principality they have never since been granted by charter to a Prince of Wales.

The revenues within the Principality were derived from various sources—perquisites of the courts, fee-farm, quit and crown-rents, and rents of ancient customs such as 'cylch march', amobr, leyrwite, comortha, tunc, and mises. In some of these we recognize dues and renders that had been made to Welsh princes prior to 1282, and it is interesting to note that, commuted to money values, they survived for so long. All those specified above occur in Crown leases of lands in the Principality in 1787, and several of them continued to appear in leases to the beginning of the present century.

The *mise* was an investiture fee paid on the accession of a new lord in consideration of certain allowances and confirmation, peculiar to the Principality of Wales and the county of Chester. It had been paid in the first place to Welsh princes on their accession, and continued to be paid to the King, Prince, and lords-marcher throughout Wales.[1] In the Ministers' Accounts of 16 Edward IV (1476–7) the mises of the county of Carmarthen amounted to £533. 6s. 8d., those of the county of Cardigan £400, and in 4 James I the mises of those two counties amounted to

[1] See W. Rees, *South Wales and the March 1284–1415*, pp. 67–68, and references the e.

£495. 5s. 8d. and £355. 12s. 4d. respectively. The total mises for North
and South Wales, raised when James I came to the Throne, were assessed
at £5,653. 11s. 11d., those of Cheshire £2,000. A survey of Crown lands in
Bromfield and Yale[1] taken in 1620 provides some details relating to this
due. The jurors stated that when James I came to the Throne, the freeholders and leaseholders of forty years' tenure, within the lordship of
Bromfield and Yale, had rendered to him a mise of 600 marks (£400),
and rendered a mise of like value to the Princes Henry and Charles in
1610 and 1616 respectively, when the King had granted them the lordship on their accession as Princes of Wales,

upon the graunting and paying of which mizes in all former ages to the King's
most noble progenitors, Kings and Queens of England, and other the lords of
the said lordship, the said Tennaunts in lieu of the said mizes had all their
ancitient Customs, privileges and tenaunces confirmed And also white bookes
graunted to them, which was a pardon of all fines, amerciaments and forfeitures
in the Courtes, and also of suche Rents as were due to the said lords at the
graunting of the said mizes, insomuch as sometimes they had a wholle yeares
Rent and sometimes half a yeare's Rent and all fines remitted, As by the
Auntient Records of the said Lordship yet to be seene may plainely appeare.[2]

In addition to the customary dues and profits of the courts, special
sums were paid to the Princes on other particular occasions as well.
When the Black Prince was created Prince of Wales in 1343, the Crown
made an effort to persuade the tenants to pay a 'voluntary' sum towards
the upkeep and repair of Welsh castles, but as no precedence existed for
such a levy a marked lack of enthusiasm greeted the suggestion. On the
other hand, the counties of Cardigan and Carmarthen in 1473 voted a
tollage to the Prince of Wales in honour of his first visit to the country.[3]
Funds were also raised by direct taxation such as 'the fifteenth', a tax on
movables. In 1318–19 this subsidy was levied and collected by the
Chamberlains of the Principality of North and South Wales, as a contri-

---

[1] Palmer and Owen, *Ancient Tenures of Land in North Wales and the Marches*, p. 209.
Bromfield and Yale were granted by Edward I to the Earl of Surrey in 1282, and after passing
through several hands came to the Crown in 1495, which has held them ever since except
during 1534–6 when they were held by Henry FitzRoy, Duke of Richmond and Surrey,
illegitimate son of Henry VIII.

[2] Palmer and Owen, op. cit.

[3] *Antiquary*, vol. xvi; and Ministers' Accounts, quoted in Evans, *Wales and the Wars of the
Roses*, p. 37.

bution towards the war against the Scots.[1] The revenues of the Principality were acquired sometimes as special loans by the Exchequer, as in 1327 and 1331 when the Chamberlains of North and South Wales were instructed to forward all monies in hand to the Exchequer, part of which went to pay the advances made to the King by the Italian bankers, the Bardi. Occasionally parts of the revenues of the Principality were assigned to Dowager Queens and Princesses, as in 1376 when provision of one-third was made to the Black Prince's widow, Joan the Fair Maid, and again after the death of Henry V when revenues from Hawarden, Montgomery, Builth, Lleyn, Tabybolion, Malltraeth, Menai, Cemmaes, Newborough, Beaumaris, Aberffraw, Flint, Coleshill, Mostyn, Englefield, Caldecot, and Newton were assigned to Queen Catherine.[2]

Receipts varied from year to year, particularly during periods of internal troubles, the Wars of Glyndwr, the Wars of the Roses, and pestilences like the Black Death. They were increased as more lands fell to the Crown which were subsequently granted to the Princes. In post-medieval times they were considerably reduced due to alienations, and became less important as a result of the practice of providing for the Prince through the Parliamentary Vote to the Royal Family. The history of Welsh revenues is one of progressive decline. In 6 Edward II (1312–13) the receipts of South and West Wales amounted to £979. 13s. 11¼d. (of which £682. 13s. 5½d. came from Cardiganshire) and those of North Wales £3,182. 10s. 8¾d., making a total of £4,162. 4s. 8½d.[3] At this time there was no Prince of Wales, but the Household of the infant Edward, son of Edward II, was largely supported from an early date by drafts on these revenues.

An increase is shown during the principate of the Black Prince. After his death, special Commissioners examined the accounts of both the Principality and the Earldom for the three years 47, 48, and 49 Edward III, and a final analysis presented in great detail in 1376–7 showed the revenues were worth £5,986. 7s. 9d. per annum. The average issues from the Welsh lands for those years were: *The Province of North Wales*: The Prince's revenues from Caernarvonshire £1,134. 16s. 2¾d., Anglesey £832. 14s. 6¾d., Merionethshire £748. 11s. 5¾d., and with the Perquisites and Profits of Sessions of the Justice, the total revenues came to

---

[1] P.R.O., *Ministers' Accounts*, 1212/2, m. 1.
[2] *Rolls of Parliament*, 1 Henry VI, p. 203.   [3] *Pipe Roll*, 7 Edw. II, mm. 37, 40.

£3,041. 7s. 6d.: when the yearly fee of the Justice of North Wales was deducted, the net total came to £3,001. 7s. 6d. *The Province of South Wales*: The Prince's revenues from Cardiganshire £374. 11s. 3¼d., Carmarthenshire £406. 1s. 7d., the fee farm of the lordship of Builth £113. 6s. 8d., the lordship of Montgomery £56. 13s. 4d., Perquisites and Profits of Sessions of the Justice £738. 6s. 9½d., and with the Perquisites of the Courts of Haverford(west) £41. 5s. 3½d., the total revenues came to £1,730 4s. 11½d.: when the yearly fee of the Justice, £50, was deducted, the net total came to £1,680. 4s. 11¼d.

The net revenues of the Principality thus came to £4,681. 12s. 5½d. Those of Flintshire, amounting at that time to £242. 19s. 5d. per annum, were included in the accounts of the Earldom of Chester.

The activities of Owen Glyndwr materially disturbed the flow of revenue during the reign of Henry IV (1399–1413). Entries in Ministers' Accounts and other contemporary records tell of the melancholy devastation of those grim years—'there are no rents of profits as the Welshmen have destroyed the pasture and burnt the buildings', and so on. For example, from 2 February 1399 to 2 February 1400, the revenue from the Welsh estates of the Duchy of Lancaster came to £4,890. 4s. 8d., but in the year 2 February 1400 – 2 February 1401 fell to £2,643. 5s. 8½d. as a direct result of Glyndwr's enterprises: the Receiverships of Monmouth and Kidwelly, which brought in about £1,300 in the first of these two years, yielded nothing at all in the second. The Duchy of Cornwall alone remained undisturbed, and the only year of which we have any account, 1412–13, showed a gross receipt of £3,928, and net £3,050. If the receipts were light, the expenses were heavy. Thus the revenue of Henry of Monmouth came only to some £3,000, so that a subsidy from the exchequer became necessary to support him, and when he was appointed Lieutenant of Wales on 1 April 1403 he received an allowance of £8,102. 2s. 0d. for the maintenance of 500 men-at-arms and archers for operations against the insurgents.

These were exceptional times, and the accounts of the following reign show a steady return to more normal conditions. During the reign of Henry V (1413–22) the Duchy of Cornwall produced an average gross figure of about £3,744, a net sum of about £1,782: the accounts of Chester, though very fragmentary, indicate a gross annual receipt of about £1,000, net about £600. For the Principality, only the audited accounts for the three years 1413–16 have survived, and these show that annual sums of about £306 gross and £167 net were derived from North Wales, and £400 gross and £200 net from South Wales. The annual net figure for the whole Principality during these three years amounted, thus, to only £367—the fiscal epitaph of 'the wild and irregular Glendower'.

The reign of Henry VI, from 1422 to 1461, led to an improvement. During those years the average annual receipts from North Wales came to £1,300 (net £900), and from South Wales £1,585 (net £975), but as these sums were expended locally, nothing seems to have reached the Exchequer in London. The palatinate of Chester produced an annual average revenue of about £700, with a net figure of £330. The palatinate was liable by custom to give a mise of 3,000 marks (£2,000) on the creation of each new earl, and this sum was paid in 1453–4 on the birth of the Prince of Wales.[1]

The struggles of York and Lancaster had the effect of lowering the value of the Welsh revenues. The fluctuating fortunes of the contenders made the collection of revenues a complicated and often dangerous business. In October 1460, when Richard Duke of York was declared heir of Henry VI, he received the Principality, the counties of Chester and Flint, and the Duchy of Cornwall, which together were then worth £10,000 per annum.[2] An illustration of the incapacity of the government due to the civil turmoil is shown by the following declaration by Henry:

Whereas the lordships which came into the King's hands by the forfeiture of Richard, Duke of York, and Richard, Earl of Warwick, are detained from the King's possession by their adherents, and the revenues of divers lordships pertaining to the Prince of Wales are detained from his use by reason of such rebellion, the King, to repress the rebellion, has granted to the prince, by advice of the council, 500 marks yearly for life from the issues of the lordships of Uske, Caerlion, Glamorgan, Morgannok and Bergaveny.[3]

Receipts slumped heavily in the reign of Edward IV (1461–83), despite the fact that there were several consecutive years of peace. During these years the average annual receipts from North Wales were £1,000 (£25 net), South Wales £700 (£360 net), and the Earldom of Chester,

[1] Ormerod, *Cheshire*, ed. Helsby, ii. 875.
[2] *The Complete Peerage*. s.n, 'Cornwall' (Dukedom); and *D.N.B.*, s.n. Richard, Duke of York.
[3] *Cal. Patent Rolls*, Henry VI, vi. 576, 5 Feb. 1460.

including Flintshire, £750 (£300 net). The receipts of the Duchy also fell, producing only £3,100 (£2,300 net). During the first period of Edward's reign (1461–9) the freeholders and townsfolk of Anglesey gave an additional subsidy of 400 marks (£233. 6s. 8d.) to the King, received by the Exchequer on 26 April 1466. A similar additional grant, in this instance amounting to 800 marks (£533. 6s. 8d.), came from the counties of Carmarthen and Cardigan on 2 June 1466, the subsidy being described as a 'tollage of recognition' (*tallagium recognitionis*) in honour of the first visit made by the Prince of Wales into the Principality.

Despite the settled conditions of the Tudor period, a marked fall occurred in the Welsh revenues. In 44 Elizabeth (1601–2) the income was as follows: North Wales: Caernarvonshire £500. 3s. 0¼d., Anglesey £425. 10s. 9¾d., and Merioneth £263. 5s. 10¼d.; South Wales: Cardiganshire £299. 11s. 4d., and Carmarthenshire £376. 17s. 10½d.

The gross income amounted to £1,865. 8s. 10¾d., and after disbursements of £530. 6s. 7d. were deducted, only £1,335. 2s. 3¾d. remained. This figure continued virtually unchanged during the succeeding ten years, and when Henry was created Prince of Wales in 1610, his revenues from the Principality amounted to £1,008. 6s. 1¼d. and £320. 12s. 5d. from North and South Wales respectively, making a total of £1,328. 18s. 6¾d. from the Principality. From the Earldom of Chester, Henry received £252. 12s. 2½d., Flintshire £185. 5s. 0d., and fee farm rents £46. 1s. 6d., a total of £481. 10s. 8½d. In addition (not included in the Principality or Earldom) the King had granted to him Crown lands in North Wales worth £2,066. 2s. 2¾d. yearly, and lands in South Wales worth £1,317. 5s. 9¾d. Besides, he had the reversion of other lands in Wales valued at £507. 10s. 10½d. per annum, which had been granted to the Countess of Northumberland for life, without rent. The Prince also possessed 'diverse barren forestes in Wales, and some fewe parkes, but all the forestes deforested, and without deere, and the parties in lease, for a long time'.[1] Henry held extensive properties in England which, together with a grant of over £28,000 from the Exchequer, brought his annual income up to over £49,000. Of this, only some £1,300 derived from the Principality proper.

[1] *Ordinances and Regulations for the Government of the Royal Household*, Society of Antiquaries, London, 1790: see also *Archaeologia*, cv (1806), Wm. Bray 'An Account of the Revenues, etc. of Prince Henry', pp. 13–26.

Charles I made many alienations of Crown lands, and the value of the remaining properties continued to diminish throughout the seventeenth century. In 1689 the revenues derived from the *whole of the Crown lands in Wales* stood as follows: North Wales: receipts £3,399. 1s. 9d., disbursements £2,000. 14s. 6d.: and South Wales: receipts £3,599. 12s. 8d., disbursements £3,054. 9s. 10d. Thus from a total of £6,998. 14s. 5d., the net income amounted to only £1,901. 10s. 10d. In the reign of William III the net annual figure produced barely £1,900. That monarch's considerable alienations had a further adverse effect on the revenue-producing capacity of the Principality. On 9 June 1694 he made a grant of £2,000 per annum to Henry de Nassau, Seigneur d'Anverquerque and his heirs for ever, charged on lands, rents, and revenues of the Principality, namely £1,200 on North Wales and £800 on South Wales. As a result the revenues of the Principality fell further, so that in 1701 the receipts from North Wales amounted to £3,360. 6s. 0¼d., disbursements £2,952. 14s. 5d., and from South Wales £3,436. 4s. 6d., disbursements £2,699. 16s. 4d., the net figure being £1,143. 17s. 6d.

King William did not get everything his own way, and when he tried to grant the lordships of Denbigh, Bromfield, and Yale to the Duke of Portland the Welsh gentry acted with such explosive energy as not only to thwart but to humiliate him. This spirited action in defence of the Principality, together with the speech of a Welsh member in the Commons, became a *cause célèbre*, remembered for many a long day. It is worth recounting the affair in some detail.

William, naturally enough, had shown gratitude to his supporters by rewarding them with titles, offices, pensions, and lands. The Welsh, whose support of the Stuarts had been unswerving, were not particularly pleased when they found in 1694 that almost all the revenues of their former princes were being appropriated to foreign favourites. They voiced their displeasure, but this merely prompted the King to move with greater caution when next he rewarded his friends with lands of the Principality. Among those who had rendered valuable services to William was Hans Willem Bentinck who, in 1689, had been created Baron of Cirencester, Viscount Woodstock, and Earl of Portland. In 1695 the King decided that the time had come to reward him further, this time by a grant of the lordships of Denbigh, Bromfield, Yale, and other lands in the Principality, to be held by the grantee and his heirs for ever,

reserving to the Crown the trifling annual payment of 6s. 8d. The preliminary moves were carried out so discreetly that the docket for the
grant had been signed by the Lords of the Treasury and taken thence
to the Privy Seal without anyone knowing anything of the transaction.
However, some Welsh and border members of Parliament got wind of
the proceedings and immediately objected in vigorous terms. The lords
of the Treasury had no option other than to hear them, but gave them
only one day's notice to appear to state their case. On 10 May they
trooped to the Treasury and outlined their objections.[1] Sir William
Williams of Vaynol, Baronet, asserted that the lordships in question
were the ancient demesne of the Princes of Wales, and that the Welsh
were never subject to any but God and the King; he said that the Statute
governing the granting of fee-farm rents made an exception of those
belonging to the Principality which were inalienable; that when a Prince
of Wales was created there were many dues payable to him from those
lordships. Sir Roger Puleston then made the point that the revenues were
used to pay the salaries of the judges and other officers, and the alienation
might prejudice justice. Mr. Robert Price of Giler, the chief spokesman,
declared that the land earmarked for the grant covered five-sixths of the
county of Denbigh, which was more than a foreigner should receive, and
the people of the country were too great (i.e. numerous) to be subject
to any foreigner. Can it be, he asked, for His Majesty's honour or interest
that he daily gives away the revenues of the Crown, and what is more,
in perpetuity to a foreign subject? If the King gives away his lands like
this, then his successors will have nothing to live on; and as the deputation had received only one day's notice of attendance he hoped that their
lordships would appreciate that they were unprepared and that they
would improve on 'these hints and broken thoughts'. Lord Godolphin,
the first Commissioner of the Treasury, tried to discomfit them by
quoting a precedent. Was it not true, he asked, that the Earl of Leicester
had received a grant of these very lordships in Queen Elizabeth's time?
The reply came from a grim Sir Robert Cotton who said he could give
the best account of that case: the Earl of Leicester had received but one
of the lordships, namely Denbigh, but behaved so oppressively that the
gentry of the country took up arms against him, for which three or four
of Sir Robert's kinsmen were hanged; neither did the matter end there,

[1] See Cobbett's *Parliamentary History of England*, vol. v, London, 1809, pp. 978 ff.

for the quarrel was kept on foot until the Earl was glad to be in peace and to surrender the lordship to the Queen, since which it had remained vested in the Crown. Godolphin observed that they had offered many weighty reasons which he would represent to the King.

From the Treasury the members proceeded to attend the grant at the Privy Seal, where they again stated their case, and were heard with 'all candour and goodness'.

The King, when acquainted of these moves, used all the influence of his person and party to prevent the revocation of the grant, but finally in very bad humour agreed that it should be stayed. The Welsh members felt unable to accept this, insisting that the grant should not merely be stayed but recalled and utterly revoked, and decided to raise the matter in the House. Accordingly, Robert Price, Sir Robert Cotton, Sir William Williams, Sir Thomas Grosvenor, Sir Richard Middleton, Sir Roger Puleston, Sir John Conway, and Edward Vaughan, all descendants of ancient and distinguished Welsh houses, addressed themselves by petition to the Commons.

Robert Price, in what was described as 'a memorable speech', led the Cambrian attack.[1] The petition, he said, signed by a few had the approbation of thousands; if he could conceive that the glory and grandeur of England could be upheld by a poor landless Crown and a miserable necessitous people, then he would say the King was well advised to grant away all the revenues of the Crown; when kings had a landed interest coupled with their power, then the kingship was most stable and durable; the lordships or hundreds of Denbigh, Bromfield, and Yale for some centuries had been the revenues of the Kings of England and Princes of Wales, of which the petitioners and about fifteen hundred more freeholders were tenants: the lordships consisted of four-fifths of the best part of the county of Denbigh, being thirty miles in extent: the present rents to the Crown were by £1,700 per annum, besides heriots, reliefs, mises, wastes, estreats, perquisites of court and other contingent profits: there were also great and profitable wastes, several thousands of acres, rich and valuable mines, besides other advantages

---

[1] 'Gloria Cambriae or the Speech of a Bold Briton in Parliament against a Dutch Prince of Wales', London, 1702. Also printed in the *Somers' Tracts*, 1814, xi. 387–93. Robert Price, 1655–1733, second son of Thos. Price of Giler, qualified as barrister in 1679: became Baron of the Exchequer in 1702 and Judge of Court of Common Pleas in 1726. See *D.N.B.* and *D.W.B.*

which a mighty favourite and great courtier might make out of the country.

The petitioners, he said, had only heard casually that a grant to the Earl of Portland was at the Treasury in order to be passed, and upon examining it they found that not only the three lordships but also nearly £3,000 per annum of the ancient inheritance of petitioners and their countrymen were expressly granted; so that if all that comprised in the grant was passed it would have been a very noble, nay royal, gift, worth at least £100,000; furthermore, it was to be a grant in perpetuity reserving to the King and his successors only 6s. 8d. per annum; these facts were placed before the Lords of the Treasury by the petitioners, who were well heard, but it would have to be remembered that the docket signed by the Lords of the Treasury had been dated and carried to the Privy Seal a month before the Lords of the Treasury had ordered petitioners to attend them; as the next stage they had attended the grant from the Treasury to the Privy Seal, where their views were heard with all candour and goodness by the noble lord who had custody of the Seal, and who truly represented their views to the King, 'and that is the reason, at present that this grant halts, I suppose, till the Parliament rises, and then I doubt not but it will find legs and take its journey. Having made our application in the proper place to stop the grant, and without success, it becomes a grievance, and we hope that this honourable house will redress it.'

Robert Price went on. These lands are the lands of the Princes of Wales, he said. When Queen Elizabeth in the fourth year of her reign granted some parts of its revenues to a great favourite, so many lawsuits ensued that the freeholders gave large compositions for their peace which the Queen confirmed by charter; King James I settled these lordships on Prince Charles and his heirs Kings of England, who granted much of it to courtiers and favourites, so that the freeholders made another composition of £10,000 for their peace, confirmed by parliament in 3 Charles I. In later reigns there had been far more such grants. In the Long Parliament of King Charles, when they passed an Act for the fee-farm of rents, they excepted those of the Principality, since Parliament regarded them as inalienable. A great duty lay on the freeholders of those lordships—on the creation of a Prince of Wales they pay him £800 for mises, and that is a duty, service, or tenure not to be separated from the Prince of Wales. How can the payments be reconciled with this grant?

If we pay the mises to this noble lord, then he is quasi-prince of Wales, for such duty was never paid to any other; but if it is to be paid to the Prince of Wales and this noble lord too, then are the Welsh doubly charged. But I suppose that the grant of the revenues of the Principality is the forerunner of the honour too! The story goes that we were brought to entertain the nominee of Edward I by being recommended as one who knew not a word of the English tongue: how we were deceived is known. I suppose Bentinck, lord Portland, does not understand our language either; nor is it to be supposed that he will come amongst us to learn it, nor shall we be fond of learning *his*.

He then quoted many historical examples of the indignation of the English against greedy foreign favourites, and concluded:

By the old law it was part of the coronation oath of our Kings not to alienate the ancient patrimony of the Crown without the consent of Parliament. But now, when God shall please to send us a Prince of Wales, he may have such a present of a Crown made him as a Pope did to King John, made by his father, king of Ireland, surnamed Sans Terre or Lackland; the pope confirmed the grant, but gave him a crown of peacock's feathers in consideration of his poverty. I would have you consider we are Englishmen, and must, like patriots, stand by our country, and not suffer it to be tributary to strangers. . . . Yet do we see our rights given away, and our liberties will soon follow. The remedies of our forefathers are well known. Yet I desire not punishment, but redress.

This courageous speech, delivered with true Cambrian vigour and eloquence, so impressed the House that Price's motion, to stop the grant of the lordships of Denbigh, Bromfield, and Yale, and other lands in the Principality, was carried unanimously, and on 22 January 1695–6 the address was presented to the King by Mr. Speaker attended by the whole House. The King's answer reflects the measure of his anger at Parliament's remonstrance: 'Gentlemen, I have a kindness for my lord Portland, which he has deserved of me by long and faithful service; but I should not have given him these lands if I had imagined the House of Commons could have been concerned; I will therefore recall the Grant and find some other way of shewing my favour to him.'[1]

Had action of an equally courageous nature been taken in other cases of alienation, the value of the revenues of the Prince of Wales would not have declined so deplorably as they did.

[1] *Cal. Treasury Books*, 1693–6, pp. 1018–26, 1046–52; ibid. 1696–7, pp. 125–8. The petition and the King's answer appear in full in Cobbett, op. cit., and Wynne, *History of Wales*, 1697, pp. 303–4.

By the year 1701 the revenues had fallen further, and would have fallen considerably more had it not been for the timely intervention of the Welsh and border gentry. In that year they stood as follows: North Wales: receipts £3,360. 6s. 9¼d., disbursements £2,952. 14s. 5d.; South Wales: receipts £3,436. 4s. 6d., disbursements £2,699. 16s. 4d.; making a net sum of £1,143. 17s. 6d.

The accounts of 1761 contain some interesting details of the disbursements. Those rendered by Sir Lynch Salusbury Cotton, Baronet, Receiver-General for the counties of Anglesey, Caernarvon, Merioneth, Denbigh, Flint, and Montgomery show gross receipts of £3,339. 17s. 7d., among the disbursements being—to the Steward of Bardsey £3. 1s. 0d.; the Steward and the Recorder of Bromfield and Yale £20 and £3 respectively; the Steward and Receiver of Denbigh £40. 6s. 8d.; the Keeper of Penmaenmawr 6s. 8d.; the Constables of the castles of Caernarvon and Flint, £10 each; the Constable of Harlech Castle £50; the Constable of Beaumaris Castle £26. 13s. 4d.; the Keeper of the Gate of Flint Castle, £6. 1s. 8d.; the Chief Forester of Snowdon £11. 8s. 1d.; the Bishop of Bangor, a perpetual annual pension of £4, together with other payments connected with the North Wales circuit and legal fees. The account for the counties of Cardigan, Carmarthen, Pembroke, Brecon, Radnor, Glamorgan, and Monmouth, rendered by Henry Lord Holland and Richard Bateman, Receivers-General, showed gross receipts of £3,342. 13s. 11¼d., among the disbursements being: to the Steward of Pembroke £150; Steward of Cantref Maelienydd £100; Steward of Pencelli (for 6 months) 13s. 4d.; the Chamberlains of Carmarthen and Brecon, £100 each; the Bishop of St. David's, a perpetual pension of £5. 8s. 6d.; the Vicar of Walton East (Pembs.) £10; the Vicar of Strata Florida £5. 6s. 8d.; the Curate of Redberth chapel (Pembs.) £2; the Chantor of St. David's £10; the Master of Christ College, Cambridge, £6. 13s. 4d.; the Keeper of Ludlow Castle £30; while the Governor of Milford Haven had to be content with his title for he received nothing in cash.

In 1787 the gross receipts showed an increase: from North Wales £3,305. 6s. 1¼d., South Wales £2,976. 7s. 7¼d., and Comortha from South Wales £60. 7s. 6¼d., making a total of £6,342. 1s. 2¾d. The highest sum came from Denbighshire with £1,746. 19s. 4d., Pembrokeshire next with £1,137. 12s. 1¼d., the lowest Montgomeryshire with £56. 16s. 2d. The gross sum remained fairly constant, and on the face of it seems no inconsiderable figure, but when compared with earlier receipts in terms of money values it becomes clear that the revenues of the Principality had dwindled in a remarkable manner. In 1792 a Treasury official, greatly disturbed by the alienations that had taken place over the centuries, noted that the value of the Principality in 1376 had been £5,214, a sum, he said, that 'would be equivalent, at least, to £40,000 per annum, today'.[1]

Apart from alienations several other causes had contributed to this state of affairs, namely the diminution of business in the Great Sessions (abolished in 1830), the lapse of manorial dues and ancient incidents, and, in some places, gradual encroachments and appropriations. Thus the surviving revenues came to form a very minor item in the large budget of the Crown which derived its main income from English possessions and the Parliamentary vote.

The most valuable, by far, of the possessions of the princes was the Duchy of Cornwall. In 1610 the Duchy produced a revenue of £11,713 (when the Principality produced only £1,328), and by 1795 the income stood at £15,000 per annum. In 1841, when Edward Prince of Wales was born, they amounted to £16,000 per annum, and as a result of the careful administration under the Prince Consort's supervision had increased to £60,000 per annum by 1862. When Prince Edward came of age in that year, a very substantial private fortune had accumulated for him from the Duchy, amounting to £700,000 in capital value.

The revenues of the Principality, Duchy, and Earldom had never been sufficient to support the dignity of the Heir Apparent, and all princes from 1301 onwards received substantial grants from the King and later from the Parliamentary vote. Until the eighteenth century the princes, to a great degree, had to rely on the generosity of the King. Thus Prince Henry, whose annual income in the years of his principate, 1610–12, came to nearly £50,000, received over £28,000 of that sum out of the King's Exchequer. Owing to the dwindling value of the lands, the princes became more and more dependent on the King and on Parliament, and the increased expenses of the Hanoverian Princes of Wales, three of whom were married with children, together with the fact that they engaged actively in public, political, and social life, made the question of their finances an ever-present, and often pressing, one. The

---

[1] *12th Report of Commissioners on Crown Lands*, 25 May 1792.

parsimony of some monarchs, and the unsatisfactory father–son relationships as occurred in the time of George II for example, coupled with the extravagant tastes of some princes, 'Prinny' more notoriously, tended to aggravate the difficulties. From the reign of Queen Victoria onwards, these domestic embarrassments disappeared, and scenes such as bailiffs hammering on princely doors, and political wire-pulling to enable princely debts to be paid, became a thing of the past.

5

A GENERAL REVIEW OF THE PRINCES

SINCE the year 1301 twenty-one Heirs Apparent have borne the title of Prince of Wales. This covers a period of some 667 years, but we must remember that the principate has not been continuous by any means, for the accession to the dignity differs radically from the succession to the Throne. In British law the King never dies, for the Heir Apparent succeeds automatically the moment the monarch breathes his last: on the other hand, a Prince of Wales has to be created, this act being entirely in the will and pleasure of the sovereign. Some Heirs Apparent were created Princes of Wales while still in their swaddling clothes, others when in their 'teens', a few were approaching middle age, married and with families. Some monarchs had no sons on which to bestow it, and one, Edward II, deliberately refrained from granting the dignity to his heir. It follows therefore that there have been many years of vacancy so that the Princes of Wales have no continuous history as in the case of kings. Of the 667 years mentioned above, there have been some 374 years when no one bore the title, namely:

1307 July 7–1343 May 12	1625 Mar. 27–*c.* 1638–40
1376 June 8–1376 Nov. 2	1649 Jan.–*c.* June 1688
1377 June 21–1399 Oct. 15	1688 Dec. 11–1714 Sept. 22
1413 Mar. 21–1454 Mar. 15	1727 June 10–1728–9 Jan. 8
1460 Oct. 31–1471 June 26	1750–1 Mar. 20–1751 Apr. 20
1483 Apr. 9–1483 Aug. 24	1760 Oct. 24–1762 Aug. 17
1484 Apr. 9–1489 Nov. 29	1820 Jan. 29–1841 Dec. 4
1502 Apr. 2–1503 Feb. 18	1901 Jan. 22–1901 Nov. 9
1509 Apr. 21–1610 June 4	1910 May 4–1910 June 23
1612 Nov. 5–1616 Nov. 4	1936 June 20–1958 July 25

As we see, some of the vacancies were short, varying from a few months to a few years, others covered very long periods. Since Edward II did

PEDIGREE OF THE PRINCES OF WALES

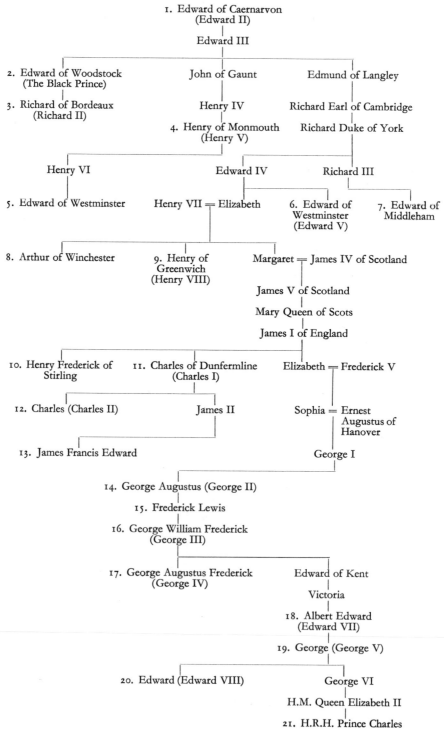

1. Edward of Caernarvon
(Edward II)

Edward III

2. Edward of Woodstock   John of Gaunt   Edmund of Langley
(The Black Prince)

3. Richard of Bordeaux   Henry IV   Richard Earl of Cambridge
(Richard II)

4. Henry of Monmouth   Richard Duke of York
(Henry V)

Henry VI   Edward IV   Richard III

5. Edward of Westminster   Henry VII = Elizabeth   6. Edward of   7. Edward of
Westminster   Middleham
(Edward V)

8. Arthur of Winchester   9. Henry of   Margaret = James IV of Scotland
Greenwich
(Henry VIII)

James V of Scotland

Mary Queen of Scots

James I of England

10. Henry Frederick of   11. Charles of Dunfermline   Elizabeth = Frederick V
Stirling   (Charles I)

12. Charles (Charles II)   James II   Sophia = Ernest
Augustus of
Hanover

13. James Francis Edward   George I

14. George Augustus (George II)

15. Frederick Lewis

16. George William Frederick
(George III)

17. George Augustus Frederick   Edward of Kent
(George IV)

Victoria

18. Albert Edward
(Edward VII)

19. George (George V)

20. Edward (Edward VIII)   George VI

H.M. Queen Elizabeth II

21. H.R.H. Prince Charles

not advance his son Edward (III) to the dignity, a vacancy of thirty-five years resulted, while from 1413, when Henry of Monmouth ascended the Throne, till his death in 1454, a period of forty-one years, the Principality had no Prince. The longest vacancy occurred during the Tudor period, from 1509 to 1610, a period of 101 years; the shortest in the reign of Edward III when a vacancy of some five months occurred in 1376.

Six dynasties have given princes to Wales. From the House of Plantagenet came seven, from Tudor two, from Stuart and Hanover four each, from Saxe-Coburg three, from Windsor one. Of these, only two of the Princes were born in the Welsh land, namely Edward of Caernarvon and Henry of Monmouth, although strictly speaking Monmouth lay in the Welsh marches: fourteen were born in England, two in Scotland, two in Hanover, one in France. Ten of them visited Wales, either as Princes or Kings, and thirteen succeeded to the Throne.

Fate dealt hardly with several. Five died of illnesses as Princes of Wales —Edward The Black Prince, Edward son of Richard III, Arthur son of Henry VII, Henry son of James I, and Frederick Lewis son of George II, while one, Edward son of Henry VI, fell on the field of battle. Four were murdered after succeeding to the Throne—Edward II, Richard II, Edward V, and Charles I, while one, James Francis Edward, was carried into exile, still in swaddling clothes, and died as a 'pretender' on foreign soil.

The ages at which they were created Princes of Wales varied considerably, the average being around 12 years. The youngest to be created was George (III) at the age of five days, the oldest George (V) at the age of 36 years. The longest holder of the dignity was Edward (VII) with 59 years, the shortest James Francis Edward, *de iure* and *de facto* Prince of Wales for five months. Two, Richard (II) and George (III), received the title as grandsons of the reigning king.

Precise dating is not easy to determine in all cases, particularly during the Wars of the Roses. Thus Edward son of Henry VI was created Prince of Wales on 15 March 1454; six years later the Yorkists gained ascendancy, and Richard, Duke of York, having obtained possession of the person of the infirm king, was declared by Parliament on 25 October 1460 to be Heir Apparent, appointed Protector of the Realm on 8 November, and early in December received, for the term of the King's life, the Principality of Wales—but *not* the title—the counties of Chester and

TABLE OF PRINCES OF WALES

Prince and birthplace	Date of birth	Date of creation	Age when created	Length of principate
1. Edward of Caernarvon	25 Apr. 1284	7 Feb. 1301	16 yrs. 9 m. 12 days	6 yrs. 5 m. (till July 1307)
2. Edward of Woodstock	15 June 1330	12 May 1343	12 yrs. 11 m.	33 yrs. 1 m. (till 8 June 1376)
3. Richard of Bordeaux	16 Jan. 1367	20 Nov. 1376	9 yrs. 10 m.	7 m. (till 21 June 1377)
4. Henry of Monmouth	9 Aug. 1387	15 Oct. 1399	11 yrs. 3 m.	13 yrs. 4 m. (till 21 Mar. 1413)
5. Edward of Westminster (Lancaster)	13 Oct. 1453	14 Mar. 1454	5 m.	(1) 16 yrs. (till 25 Oct. 1460) (2) 17 Feb. 1461–4 Mar. 1461 (3) 11 Apr. 1471 till 4 May 1471
6. Edward of Westminster (York)	2 Nov. 1470	26 June 1471	7 m. 3 w.	11 yrs. 9 m. (till 9 Apr. 1483)
7. Edward of Middleham	1473	24 Aug. 1483	9 yrs.	8 m. (till 9 Apr. 1484)
• 8. Arthur of Winchester	20 Sept. 1486	29 Nov. 1489	3 yrs. 2 m.	12 yrs. 4 m. (till 2 Apr. 1502)
9. Henry of Greenwich	28 June 1491	18 Feb. 1503–4	11 yrs. 2 m.	6 yrs. 2 m. (till 21 Apr. 1509)
10. Henry Frederick of Stirling	19 Feb. 1593–4	4 June 1610	16 yrs. 3 m.	2 yrs. 5 m. (till 5 Nov. 1612)
• 11. Charles of Dunfermline	19 Nov. 1600	4 Nov. 1616	15 yrs. 11 m.	8 yrs. 5 m. (till 27 Mar. 1625)
12. Charles of St. James	29 May 1630	c. 1638–41	c. 10–11 yrs.	18 yrs. 7 m. (till 30 Jan. 1649)
13. James Francis Edward of St. James	10 June 1688	c. 4 July 1688	c. 1 m.	5 m. (till 11 Dec. 1688)
14. George Augustus of Hanover	30 Oct. 1683	22/27 Sept. 1714	30 yrs. 11 m.	12 yrs. 8 m. (till 10 June 1727)
15. Frederick Lewis of Hanover	20 Jan. 1707	8 Jan. 1728–9	22 yrs.	22 yrs. 2 m. (till 20 Mar. 1750–1)
16. George William Frederick of London	4 June 1738	20 Apr. 1751	12 yrs. 11 m.	9 yrs. 6 m. (till 24 Oct. 1760)
17. George Augustus Frederick of St. James	12 Aug. 1762	17 Aug. 1762	5 days	57 yrs. 5 m. (till 29 Jan. 1820)
18. Albert Edward of London	9 Nov. 1841	4 Dec. 1841	1 m.	59 yrs. 1 m. (till 22 Jan. 1901)
• 19. George Frederick Ernest Albert of London	3 June 1865	9 Nov. 1901	36 yrs. 5 m.	8 yrs. 5 m. (till 4 May 1910)
20. Albert Edward Christian George Andrew Patrick David of Richmond	23 June 1894	23 June 1910	16 yrs.	25 yrs. 6 m. (till 20 Jan. 1936)
• 21. Charles Philip Arthur George of London	14 Nov. 1948	26 July 1958	9 yrs. 8 m.	

• Became Prince of W. after having been Duke of York.

Flint, and the Duchy o efield
on 30 December 1460 e essed.
For a brief period, 17 s were
supreme, so that duri rd son
of Henry VI as the *d*

On 4 March 1461, Edward
IV proclaimed King, became
fugitive. On the ne Act of
Attainder against s d, which
included the names Margaret
'late called Quene d Prynce
of Wales'. Edward y VI was
restored, so that th ual Prince
of Wales. The rest April 1471
it was Edward IV ian Prince
ceased to be Princ rian Prince
at Tewkesbury o the stormy
confused scene.

The period 9 hed by the
fact that the hig d, for there
existed two Kin On 25 June
1471 Edward c 1470) Prince
of Wales, a title he held until he succ one in 1483.
Lancastrians would regard Edward son of Henry VI as the *de iure* Prince of Wales—in so far as the term *de iure* can be applied during this ghastly interlude in our history—from 15 March 1454 to his death on 4 May 1471. The *de facto* Princes of Wales during this period were:

1. Edward son of Henry VI	15 March 1454–25 October 1460
	17 February 1461–4 March 1461
	11 April 1471–4 May 1471
2. Edward son of Edward IV	25 June 1471–9 April 1483

[1] *Rolls of Parliament*, v. 380–1. See *D.N.B.*, s.n. Richard, Duke of York. One chronicle states that Parliament ordained that Richard should 'be called Prince of Wales, Duke of Cornewayle, and erle of Chestre, and was made also by the sayde parlement protectoure of Englond' (*An English Chronicle* . . . , ed. Davies, p. 108); but we can be certain that he never received the title, only the lands as appanage of the Heir Apparent.

ESHER
~~173 Beecham's pills~~
~~176 THE FURRY BEAST~~
~~= J.M. Barrie~~
~~182 THE TRIUMVIRATE~~
~~225 THE MAGNIFICENT MILKMAN~~
~~= Alfred Watson~~
~~229 THE RUSHY~~
= L. Burgis
250 Catholic Government
~~262 MAN WITH A MILLION SECRETS = Hawkey~~
~~264 THE DOG AT THE FAIR = Esher~~
281 - Sassoon's wishes
~~291 THE BUTCHER = Haig~~
329 Death of Howard Sturgis
Thompson, Sir B.
Rumbold

Difficulties of precise dating also occur in the case of Charles (II) and James Francis Edward, since we do not know exactly when they were declared Princes of Wales. In the case of the former, all we know is that he received the title some time between 21 May 1638 and November 1641, and the latter in June 1688 within a month after his birth.

The upbringing of the Princes is a matter of prime importance and interest both to the nation as well as to the Royal Family. Most monarchs, particularly the Plantagenets and the Tudors, took especial care to entrust the education of the Heir Apparent to capable scholars and instructors. Tutors were generally appointed to attend them when they were between six and ten years of age, and the curriculum always included Latin, history, geography, navigation, mathematics, religious instruction, while music and the arts were given a prominent place. In much later days modern languages were added. This tuition was given privately, but in the nineteenth and twentieth centuries this cloistered education gave way to attendance at naval and military academies, universities, and public schools. Instruction in manly sports, games, equitation, hunting, and in military exercises like drill, archery, shooting, and study of tactics also found place in the programme. As they grew older, the princes were initiated into matters of state and government and in the performance of public duties and ceremonial. As no precise duties were laid down for the Princes of Wales or Heirs Apparent, their employment lay entirely in the decision of the monarch.

Most monarchs took a personal interest in the education of their sons, particularly Edward IV, Henry VII, James I, Charles I, and Queen Victoria. Royal fathers often compiled elaborate instructions for the guidance of tutors. James I composed the *Basilikon Doron* to instruct his sons in the business of ruling, a work which was translated into Welsh by two Pembrokeshire parsons, Robert Holland and George Owen Harry, and published in 1604. As a result of their careful upbringing many of the Princes were men of considerable culture, talent, and refinement, such as Richard II, Arthur of Winchester, and the Stuart brothers Henry and Charles; others like The Black Prince and Henry of Monmouth became eminent military commanders, while Henry VIII, Charles II, Edward VII, and George V showed superior capacity for government and diplomacy.

The choice of wives for royal personages has always been comparatively limited. Since European dynasties intermarried from early times it soon became impossible for a prince or princess to marry anyone to whom he or she was not related in near or remote degree. Edward I found it necessary to inform the Pope that he could not make suitable marriages for his children outside the prohibited degrees and accordingly asked for a general dispensation to be granted in the matter. Nationalist feelings rarely entered into the matrimonial calculations of royalty, so that marriages sometimes took place between dynasties hostile to, or even actually at war with, each other. In 1406 Henry IV tried to arrange a marriage between the Prince of Wales and 'the second daughter of our adversary', Maria daughter of the French king. Following the Reformation the European dynasties became divided into Catholic and Protestant, which narrowed the field still further, but even so, 'mixed' marriages occasionally took place. Charles I, as Prince of Wales, tried to marry a Catholic Infanta, and eventually married, as King, a Catholic daughter of France.

So far as 'blood' or 'race' was concerned, the royal genealogies of Europe present an experiment in internationalism. This is particularly true of the dynasties which have ruled in Britain since 1066. To describe a particular dynasty as English, Welsh, or Scots is invalid so far as 'race' is concerned. For instance, to describe the Tudor dynasty as Welsh is a clear misnomer, when we remember that the immediate ancestry of Henry VII shows him to be $\frac{1}{4}$ Welsh, $\frac{1}{4}$ French, and $\frac{1}{2}$ Anglo-Norman, and to be descended from Edward I, Edward III, and Henry III through different lines. Since his wife, Elizabeth of York, derived through three lines from Edward III, and through another from Henry III, we find the Plantagenets recurring again and again in the ancestry of their issue, especially as the mother of Queen Elizabeth of York was also descended from the Plantagenets. Thus in King Henry VIII, Queen Mary, and Queen Elizabeth the 'Tudors' scarcely had a look-in, and these three in fact provided an extension of the dynasty their father had supplanted. Indeed, it is fair to say that the House of Plantagenet never died out—it blossomed again in the nominal House of Tudor. These names are merely labels of convenience.

As a result of this endogamy, only four Princes of Wales—the sons of Henry VII and Elizabeth of York, of The Black Prince and Joan of

Kent, and of George V and Queen Mary—have been born in England of English-born parents.

There have been nine Princesses of Wales. The first three were left widows, and it is singular that although two of these were afterwards Queens of England neither derived that dignity from a Prince of Wales. Joan 'the Fair Maid', wife of The Black Prince, occupies a special place in Welsh hearts as a descendant of Llywelyn the Great. Poor Anne of Warwick, widow of the Lancastrian Prince of Wales slain in 1471, later remarried Richard, Duke of Gloucester, and the union, loveless as it may have been, ultimately brought her a crown. Catherine of Aragon, widow of Arthur Prince of Wales, became Queen by marrying her brother-in-law, Henry VIII. Over two centuries elapsed before there was another Princess of Wales. This was Caroline of Anspach, in 1714, who became Queen when her husband ascended the Throne as George II. Then came Augusta of Saxe-Gotha, who, although never Queen, lived as a Dowager Princess of Wales and the mother of a King, George III. Caroline of Brunswick, Princess of Wales for over twenty-five years, became Queen only in name, her husband, George IV, denying her the honour to which her marriage entitled her. The lives of the next Princesses of Wales, Alexandra of Denmark and Mary of Teck, were cast in happier mould, and both succeeded to the higher dignity.

In the table of precedence the Prince of Wales comes next to the Sovereign, and sits at the right hand of the Cloth of Estate in Parliament, and on the right of the King on all solemn occasions. He possessed no special prerogatives during the lifetime of his father, and during the Middle Ages he was, in practice, a great feudal lord with no privileges or powers to distinguish him from other magnates who held in chief. In more modern times the Prince has become the understudy of the monarch, a 'King in waiting' as he has been sometimes described.

A few words must be devoted to the titles borne by the Princes. The style *Prince of Wales*, although derived from the Welsh prince, was not particularly ancient. It is true that Llywelyn the Great had styled himself *Prince of North Wales*, and that this had been recognized by Henry III when the Welsh prince did homage to him at Worcester in 1218—*Rex omnibus &c Sciatis quod commisimus dilecto sororis nostro Lewelino principi Norwallie . . .*[1]—but in English state documents he was usually described

[1] *Patent Rolls*, Henry III, 1216–25, p. 143. For a note on this subject see Tout and Tait,

as *Prince of Aberfraw and Lord of Snowdon*, and, more occasionally, as *Princeps Norwalliae*.[1] His son, David, does not appear to have been regarded as the inheritor of the title, for official English records describe him as *David son of Llywelyn former Prince of North Wales*.[2] David's nephew, Llywelyn ap Gruffydd, did not rest so content, and in some of his earlier acts styled himself *Prince of Wales and Lord of Snowdon* (*Princeps Walliae et dominus Snaudon*), the earliest example of this usage being in 1258;[3] and when he formed an alliance in 1265 with Simon de Montfort, his title Prince of Wales and his claims to the Principality were recognized by that redoubtable baron on behalf of the English king, who, it must be remembered, was then under constraint.[4] Welsh chronicles of the day noticed this 'recognition' with satisfaction.[5] Finally the Crown acknowledged his right to the title by the Treaty of Montgomery (1267), which contained the clause: 'The lord King, wishing to magnify the person of the aforesaid Llywelyn and in him and his heirs by hereditary succession, from his own liberality and favour, and with the will and assent of the lord Edward, grants to Llywelyn and his heirs the Principality of Wales, so that Llywelyn and his heirs may be styled *Princes of Wales* who are Welshmen. . . .'

Such was the correct and legal style of Llywelyn ap Gruffydd from 1267 until his fall in December 1282. After his death the title was assumed by his brother David until his capture in 1283, and later by Madog ap Llywelyn, a cadet of the royal house of Gwynedd, when he rose in revolt in 1294–5. But so far as the Crown and English law were concerned, it had been extinguished with Llywelyn's death in 1282, and remained so until 1301 when Edward I conferred it on his eldest son. The only time a Welshman adopted it again occurred in the early years of the fifteenth century when Owen Glyndwr sought to re-establish the Welsh dynasty.

Although the title has to be conferred on the Heir Apparent, in the popular mind the eldest son of the King became automatically regarded as 'Prince of Wales' by virtue of his birth. Thus the burial of the eldest son of Charles I, an infant born and died on 13 May 1629, was recorded

Historical Essays, Manchester U.P., pp. 126 et seq, and also J. E. Lloyd, *History of Wales*, ii. 723–4, 736, 740.

[1] e.g. Rymer, *Foedora*, i. 196, 206, 214, 229–30, 236, 239, etc.   [2] Ibid., i. 242.

[3] Ibid., i. 339, 341.   [4] Ibid., i. 456

[5] e.g. *Brut y Tywysogion*, R.S., p. 537.

in the register of Westminster Abbey in the following form: 'Charles, Prince of Wales, was buried', while Sir Theodore Mayerne, physician to the Queen, announced the event to Lord Dorchester, Secretary of State, in these words: 'God has shewn us a Prince of Wales, but the flower was cut down the same instant that it saw light.'[1] On the day following the birth of Charles (II) in 1630, the British Ambassador in Paris received news that the Queen had become 'the happy mother of a Prince of Wales'.

The Prince also held several subsidiary peerage titles. Originally all dignities bestowed on the Heir Apparent were in the gift of the Crown, but in time some of them came to him automatically at his birth.

Prior to 1301 the Heir Apparent bore no title or dignity, being described simply as, for example, 'the lord Henry', 'the lord Edward', or 'son of the King'. The lord Edward son of Edward I received his first dignities in 1301, namely Prince of Wales and Earl of Chester. This earldom had been granted to the lord Edward (I) by Henry III in 1254, and with the exception of the short period 1264–5 when it was held by Simon de Montfort it has never been conferred on anyone save the Heir Apparent. The first Prince of Wales received further titles, Count of Ponthieu and of Montreuil in 1304, and Duke of Aquitaine in 1306.

The earliest title conferred on the second Prince of Wales, 'The Black Prince', was Earl of Chester in 1333. Four years later he was created Duke of Cornwall, the first time this dignity appeared in the English peerage. He became Prince of Wales in 1343, and Prince of Aquitaine and Gascony in 1362. The only other Prince of Wales to bear a 'French' title was Henry of Monmouth, created Duke of Aquitaine in 1399, but after this no further titles based on English possessions in France were bestowed on royal sons.

The three territorial titles—Wales, Cornwall, Chester—were borne by the princes throughout the Middle Ages, and although Edward of Middleham became Earl of Salisbury in 1477, before his father seized the Crown, and Edward of Westminster became Earl of March and Pembroke in 1479, these titles were borne by no other Princes of Wales.

The Tudors bestowed no additional dignities on their sons, but the accession of the Stuarts resulted in the introduction of further peerages

[1] See J. G. Nichols in *Her. et Gen.* iv (1867), pp. 515–25.

for the Heir Apparent. The Scottish king's eldest son, Henry of Stirling, bore the titles Prince of Scotland, Duke of Rothesay, Earl of Carrick, Baron of Renfrew, Lord of the Isles, and Steward of Scotland. After his father succeeded to the English throne, Henry was created Prince of Wales and Earl of Chester in 1610. The style Prince of Scotland had been long enjoyed by the heirs to the Scottish Crown, and continued to be borne by the Stuart Heirs Apparent in England until 1688, after which it was discontinued. A further addition was made when James I assumed the title King of Great Britain, and since that time the style of the son and Heir Apparent has been *Magnae Britanniae Princeps*.

Additional titles were bestowed on the first two Hanoverian Princes of Wales, but were withheld from their successors. Prince George (later King George II), in his own right Electoral Prince of Brunswick–Luneberg, was created by Queen Anne in 1706 Duke and Marquess of Cambridge, Earl of Milford Haven, Viscount Northallerton, and Baron of Tewkesbury. After his father's accession to the British Throne, George was created Prince of Wales, Duke of Cornwall, and Earl of Chester in 1714, and in the following year Duke of Rothesay. George I nominated his grandson, Frederick Lewis (later Prince of Wales), to be Duke of Gloucester on 10 January 1717–18, but the Patent was not proceeded with, and in 1726 he created him Duke of Edinburgh, Marquess of the Isle of Ely, Earl of Eltham, Viscount of Launceston, and Baron of Snowdon. The style Snowdon had been borne by the Welsh princes prior to 1282, and its royal association has again been revived in our time by the elevation of Mr. Armstrong-Jones to the dignity of Earl of Snowdon (1961). Since the reign of George II it has been customary when peerages were granted to members of the Royal Family to take titles from each of the three kingdoms. The titles Duke of Saxony and Earl of Dublin, borne by Prince Edward Albert (later King Edward VII), did not become permanent in his successors.

Another dignity that became hereditary in the Princes of Wales is the Most Noble Order of the Garter. The precise date of its institution is not known, but the best evidence seems to favour the year 1348. Originally, membership was confined to the Sovereign and twenty-five Companions, of whom the Prince of Wales (The Black Prince) was the first-named knight. All subsequent Princes of Wales, except Edward of Westminster (d. 1471), Edward of Middleham, and James Francis Stuart, have been admitted to the Order, the bestowal of the dignity being in the pleasure of the Sovereign. However, by virtue of a statute enacted on 10 January 1805, the Heir Apparent becomes automatically a Knight of the Garter from the date of his creation as Prince of Wales, the date of his installation being decided by the Sovereign.[1]

[1] For discussion on this Order see *The Complete Peerage*, vol. ii, app. B. See also G. F. Beltz, *Memorials of the Order of the Garter* . . . , London, 1841.

6

CREATION AND INVESTITURE

IN this chapter we shall discuss the ceremonial associated with the creation and investiture of the Princes of Wales, but before proceeding to do so a few words must be devoted to the insignia used in the ceremonies.

The insignia consisted of a coronet, a ring, a rod, and a mantle, to which, in Tudor times, a sword and girdle were added. The *sertum*, translated variously as chaplet, circlet, and coronet, was made of gold, with an open top, and raised by a series of four crosses pattee and four fleurs-de-lis arranged alternately around the rim.[1] It was used at the investiture of The Black Prince, and it is likely that a similar coronet had been used at the investiture of the first Prince of Wales in 1301. The Black Prince's coronet passed to his brother, Lionel of Clarence, whose will, dated 1388, mentions 'a gold circlet with which my brother and lord was created prince', as well as 'that circlet with which I was created duke'. When Lionel was created Duke of Clarence in 1362, the King girded him with a sword and placed on his head a fur cap and over it *un cercle d'or et de peres* (a coronet of gold and precious stones).[2]

The coronet appears in the form described above on the seals of the Princes of Wales down to the Stuart period.[3] The regalia of Henry (Stuart), invested in 1610, were elaborate and an inventory of his effects made after his death included 'a Crowne sett with Dyaments, Saphirs, and Emerandes'.[4] A sketch of this Prince drawn on his charter of creation shows him wearing a coronet of crosses pattee and fleurs-de-lis over a cap of estate turned-up ermine.[5] When ordering the Royal

[1] See Cyril Davenport, *The English Regalia*, London, 1897, p. 46 et seq., illustr.

[2] W. H. St. J. Hope, *Heraldry for Craftsmen and Designers*, London, 1913, p. 27. Originally confined to dukes, Richard II, when he advanced the Earl of Oxford to be Marquess of Dublin in 1385, invested him with a gold coronet and a sword.

[3] It occurs in the seals of The Black Prince in 1343. See Legge, *English Coronation Records*, and also *Gent. Mag.* xxxii (1762), p. 349.

[4] *Archaeologia*, xv (1860), p. 18.　　　　　　　　　　　[5] B.M. Add. MS. 36932.

regalia on 9 February 1660–1, Charles II added a single arch to the Prince of Wales's coronet, thereby making it into a crown. The only time that reference to the crown or coronet has been omitted was in the Letters Patent of George I, dated 22 September 1714, creating his son Prince of Wales, which speaks only of 'the delivering of a cap and placing it on his head', specifying no other traditional observances apart from the omnibus formula 'according to custom'. However, it is certain that this Prince did wear a crown on State occasions and it has been suggested it had formerly been the coronation crown of Mary of Modena, consort of James II.[1] His successor, Frederick Lewis, had a crown specially made for him as Prince of Wales. It was made of plain gold, with no jewels, with crosses pattee and fleurs-de-lis alternating around the rim, and had a single arch surmounted by a ball on which stood a cross pattee; this is still kept among the regalia in the Tower.[2] According to Mr. Holmes, guide-books of 1753 mention that this crown was placed before the Prince's seat when he attended Parliament. The latest coronet to be worn at the investiture of a Prince of Wales was the one made for Edward (VIII) from gold mined in the Welsh hills. Designed by Sir Goscombe John, it consisted of a jewelled coronet with crosses pattee and fleurs-de-lis around the rim, and without an arch, thus approximating more to the *sertum* used in the ceremonies of medieval days.

The cap of maintenance made its appearance in England during the first half of the fourteenth century, and appears on the seals of The Black Prince in 1343. Made of crimson velvet, indented, and turned-up ermine, with a tassel on top, it was worn also by Prince Henry in 1610 as shown in a contemporary sketch on his charter of creation.[3]

The gold rod or verge consisted of a plain wand without embellishment or decoration. The only variation in metal occurred at the investiture of The Black Prince, when the rod was of silver. No early example has survived, and the earliest drawing of one occurs in the charter of creation of Prince Henry, a plain wand, precisely similar to that shown in Selden's drawing of a Prince of Wales attired in full investiture robes

[1] M. R. Holmes, 'The Crowns of England', *Archaeologia*, lxxxvi (1937), p. 87.

[2] Ibid., p. 88 and pl. xviii, no. 5: Davenport, loc. cit., illustr. See also W. Jones, F.S.A., *Crowns and Coronations, A History of Regalia*, London, 1883, and Sitwell, *The Crown Jewels...*, pp. 54, 89, 106.

[3] Legge, op. cit.: *Gent. Mag.*, xxxii (1762), p. 349: B.M. Add. MS. 36932.

and insignia.[1] The wand provided for the 1911 investiture was more elaborate. Made of Welsh gold, two feet eight inches long, its head was composed of three amorini supporting a princely coronet, the cap of which was an amethyst, and below the amorini were fashioned the plume of ostrich feathers and the motto, 'Ich Dien', while the foot of the verge ended in a representation of a dragon.

No early example of rings in the ceremony has survived, and the drawing of Selden showing the ring on the third finger of the Prince's left hand is too small for any detail to be included. Camden describes the ring of Prince Charles (1616) as containing a diamond. The ring for the 1911 investiture was wrought in the form of two dragons grasping an amethyst.

The mantle and its long train was made of crimson velvet, doubled below the elbow, with ermine spots, and the drawing of the mantle worn in 1610 shows a collar with five bars of ermine set at equal distances, one above the other.[2] The mantle worn in 1911 was bordered with fleurs-de-lis, and secured at the breast with an elaborate brooch composed of gold and amethysts.

Medieval records make no mention of a sword in connexion with the investiture, and the earliest reference to it occurs in Tudor times. However, the girding on of the sword formed a normal part of the investiture of dukes, earls, and marquesses, and the charter creating The Black Prince to be Duke of Cornwall in 1337 contains the formula, 'we have girded him with a sword as is fitting' (*et gladio cinximus ut decet*). When Richard II promoted his uncle Edmund to be Duke of York, the Parliament Rolls record that the investiture was *per gladii cincturam et pillei ac circuli suo capiti impositionem maturius investivit*; and when the same monarch created Henry Earl of Derby to be Duke of Hereford, the ceremony included *per appositionem cappe suo capiti ac traditionem virgae aureae investimus*. Prince Charles was created Duke of York in 1604, 'by the girding of the Sword, Cap, and Circlet of Gold put upon his Head, and golden verge into his Hand . . .',[3] which closely resembled the investiture of a Prince of Wales.

The early Princes possessed ceremonial swords which may well have been used at their investiture. On 1 July 1463, 'a swerde garnysshed

---

[1] John Selden, *Titles of Honour*, p. 602.
[2] *Gent. Mag.*, xxxii (1762), p. 349.   [3] Sanderson, *A Compleat History . . .*, p. 322.

wit estriche fetherys of gold, some tyme beyng the Prynces of Wales'
was returned to the Treasury.[1] In January 1504 the Treasury issued a
sword girdle decorated with red roses, ostrich feathers, and 'man-
geretes', with buckle and pendant enamelled with roses and feathers,
'for the use of the Prince' (Henry of Greenwich, Prince of Wales).[2]
Henry of Stirling was certainly girded with a sword at his investiture in
1610, undoubtedly with that 'very riche cros sword all sett with Dyaments
with chap richelie sett, givin be hir Matie at his creation', described in
the inventory of his effects taken after his death two years later.

When creating his son Prince of Wales in 1911, the formula used by
the King ran as follows: 'We do Ennoble and Invest with the said
Principality and Earldom by Girding him with a Sword', followed by
the giving of the coronet, ring, and verge, in that order. The sword,
manufactured for the occasion, had a hilt of silver gilt, a pommel formed
of two dragons supporting a coronet, their collars inscribed *Ich Dien*,
the blade with the words *Iorwerth Tywysog Cymru* (Edward Prince of
Wales), and a scabbard and belt of a rich purple velvet ornamented with
gold bands.

So much, then, for the insignia. As I have said earlier the first stage
was the instrument of creation—royal charter or Letters Patent. In
a few cases it seems to have taken the form of a declaration by the
monarch, but little is known about this, which apparently consisted of a
verbal statement by the King. Charles (son of Charles I) was probably
'declared' Prince of Wales between the dates 21 May 1638 and November 1641: James Francis Edward, born 10 June 1688, was 'declared'
before the 4 July following: and finally, George, son of George I, who
was 'declared' Prince of Wales at the King's first Council on 22 September 1714, and formally created by Letters Patent five days later.

The investiture of most of the Princes, particularly the earlier ones,
was carried out on the date of the instrument of creation. A number
were invested some time later. Thus Edward of Lancaster, created
Prince of Wales on 15 March 1454, was invested on 9 June 1454, and
invested again on 9 July 1455 owing to the political difficulties of the
time and the illness of his father, Henry VI. Edward of Middleham,
created 24 August 1483, was invested on 8 September following: Arthur
of Winchester, created 29 November 1489 at the age of three years, was

[1] Palgrave, *Ancient Kalendars*, ii. 247.   [2] Ibid. iii. 399.

invested on 27 February 1490: Edward of Windsor, created on 23 June
1910, was invested on 13 July of the following year. The present Prince
of Wales was created on 26 July 1958, and announced at Cardiff on that
day, and awaits investiture.[1]

Prince	Date and place of creation	Date and place of Investiture
1. Edward	7 Feb. 1301. Parlt. at Lincoln	7 Feb. 1301
2. Edward	12 May 1343. Parlt. at Westminster	12 May 1343
3. Richard	20 Nov. 1376. Havering atte Bower, Essex	
4. Henry	15 Oct. 1399. Westminster	15 Oct. 1399. Parlt. at Westminster
5. Edward	15 Mar. 1454. Westminster	9 June 1454. Windsor
6. Edward	26 June 1471. Westminster	
7. Edward	24 Aug. 1483. Pontefract	8 Sept. 1483. York Minster
8. Arthur	29 Nov. 1489. Westminster	27 Feb. 1490. Westminster
9. Henry	18 Feb. 1503–4. Westminster	18 Feb. 1503–4. Westminster
10. Henry	4 June 1610. Westminster	4 June 1610. Westminster
11. Charles	4 Nov. 1616. Whitehall	4 Nov. 1616. Whitehall
12. Charles	[1638–41]. [? London]	
13. James	June–July 1688. St. James's	
14. George	27 Sept. 1714. Westminster	27 Sept. 1714. Westminster
15. Frederick	8 Jan. 1728–9. London	
16. George	20 Apr. 1751. London	
17. George	17 Aug. 1762. London	
18. Albert Edward	4 Dec. 1841. London	
19. George	9 Nov. 1901. London	
20. Edward	23 June 1910. London	13 July 1911. Caernarvon
21. Charles	26 July 1958. Cardiff (announced)	

It must be emphasized at the outset that the investiture of a Prince of
Wales was a parliamentary occasion, a constitutional act. He was invested by the King in Parliament, attended by the Lords and Commons,
archbishops and bishops, the great officers of state, certain officers
of the Royal Household, the Lord Mayor and the Livery Companies
of London, and numerous British and foreign guests, ambassadors,
etc. The Earl Marshal took a leading part in arranging the ceremonial,
and particularly Garter Principal King of Arms, who, according to
Dodridge, 'hath the manner and order of his Creation and Investiture
pointed' which would serve both as guidance to procedure and a record
of the event.[2] It was, as we shall see, very much a London occasion.

[1] Since this was written it has been announced that the Prince will be invested at
Caernarvon Castle on Tuesday, 1 July 1969.

[2] Dodridge, *An Historical Account of the . . . Principality of Wales, Dutchy of Cornwal, and
Earldom of Chester.*

From the descriptions that have survived (which will be examined in detail later on) it is possible to obtain a fairly faithful picture of the investiture proceedings. First of all, members of both Houses of Parliament, certain officials, and guests took their appointed seats. The King's procession then moved forward, and after the King had been enthroned, his retinue took position to the rear and the sides of the Throne. Shortly afterwards the Prince's procession advanced towards the Throne, the Prince bareheaded, attired in surcoat and knee breeches, accompanied by noblemen (usually earls) bearing the insignia—the mantle, coronet, ring, rod, and sword, while Garter Principal King of Arms carried the Patent of creation. Two earls supported the Prince, and, sometimes, as in the investiture of Henry of Stirling, the newly created Knights of the Bath formed part of the retinue.

Having made his obeisance, the Prince knelt on a cushion before the King, while a great Officer of State read the Patent which had been delivered by Garter, and as he read the relevant words '. . . by investing him with . . .', the insignia were handed to the monarch, who invested the Prince with them. After this, the Prince rose and the monarch kissed him on both cheeks.[1] He then occupied his seat on the right hand of the Throne, and on some occasions took the oath of fealty. The monarch departed in procession, and after a brief interval the Prince departed, also in procession.

After the ceremony, the Prince dined in state in the Palace of Westminster at which peers, prelates, officers of state, and guests were present, and the newly created Knights of the Bath dined in the same chamber at a table specially set aside for them. The King did not dine, but sometimes occupied a seat in the gallery to watch the proceedings for a little time. This banquet ended the Prince's day.

Although the ceremony varied in certain details, such as the venue, and the composition of the Prince's procession, the central and essential procedure as outlined above remained constant. New features were introduced at the investiture of Edward of Windsor in 1911 since this was a Welsh and not primarily a parliamentary occasion, one of the most attractive being the Presentation of the Prince to the people from the ramparts of Caernarvon Castle. The holding of the investiture on Welsh soil resulted in the presence of numerous representatives of Welsh life,

---

[1] The kiss is first mentioned in the case of Henry of Monmouth in 1399.

including a number of officers whose claim to attendance was grounded in ancient serjeanties that had slumbered for many centuries. Thus, apart from his parliamentary qualification, Mr. Lloyd George attended in his capacity of Constable of Caernarvon Castle. The attendance of Mr. Jasper More of More in Shropshire rested upon medieval serjeanty whereby the Lord of More was required to act as Constable of the King's host, to move with the vanguard and carry the Royal standard[1] whenever the King crossed the Welsh border in warlike array.

To mark the occasion, the King honoured certain of his subjects. Knights of the Bath were dubbed on the occasion of the investiture of Edward, Arthur, Henry of Greenwich, Henry of Stirling, and Charles, in 1475, 1489, 1503, 1610, and 1616 respectively. After 1616 the creation of Knights of the Bath was not specially associated with occasions concerning the Prince of Wales.[2] Higher dignities were sometimes bestowed, such as the baron and the two viscounts created, in addition to the Knights of the Bath, in 1616.

Fees were paid to officers of the Household on these occasions, for example, £30 to the Earl Marshal, £20 to the Serjeant Porter, £10 to the Cook of the Privy Kitchen—the last two receiving, in addition, £6 and £2 respectively from the Prince as Earl of Chester.[3] The strain on the royal coffers was lessened by the fact that the King was entitled by custom to levy a subsidy at such creation, while the Prince himself received a money gift, raised from his Welsh possessions.

Court and public celebrations accompanied the event. As might be expected the pageantry of the Londoners excelled all others and the records of livery companies contain numerous references to their participation on such occasions.

No details of the investiture of Edward, the first Prince of Wales, have survived, beyond the fact that he was created Prince of Wales and Earl of Chester by Letters Patent at the parliament held in Lincoln on 7 February 1301, and received a grant of the lands of the Principality and the Earldom.[4]

The next to receive the dignity, Edward son of Edward III, and better known as The Black Prince, received the titles that became associated

[1] *Trans. Shropshire Arch. Soc.*, xlix (1937–8), p. 71.
[2] See Shaw, *Knights of England*, vol. i.
[3] See John Chamberlayne, *Magnae Britanniae Notitia*, 1723.
[4] Enrolled on *Charter Roll*, 29 Edward I, m. 9 (36), 7 Feb. 1301.

with the Heir Apparent in somewhat piecemeal manner. On 18 May 1333 he was created Earl of Chester, and on 3 March 1337 Duke of Cornwall at a parliament in Westminster, being the first time that a duke had been created in England. Some six years later he became Prince of Wales. The charter of 12 May 1343 contains the earliest reference to the actual ceremony of investiture. In the preamble the King states, as the reason for conferring the dignity, that as the rays of light sent forth from the sun do not reduce its brightness, so the honour and eminence of the Throne are augmented in proportion as the inferior nobility receive honour, and the Royal Family strengthened; and so he created his dearly beloved eldest son Edward Duke of Cornwall and Earl of Chester to be Prince of Wales with the assent of the prelates, earls, barons *et comitatum in generali parliamento nostro apud Westm'*, and confirmed him in the dignity by placing the coronet (*sertum*) on his head, a gold ring on his finger, and a silver rod in his hand, according to custom (*iuxta morem*), and finally specified the lands accompanying the grant.[1] The formula *iuxta morem* in the foregoing grant makes it clear that the ceremonial of investiture was traditional, so that in all probability it had been observed in the case of Prince Edward in 1301.

In effect, the charter of 1343 was an Act of Parliament, for the sovereign acted 'with the consent of the prelates, earls, barons and comitatum in our general parliament assembled', the conferring of a dignity by Act of Parliament being a recognized procedure. A royal charter made with the assent of Parliament became essentially a parliamentary charter, whether recorded with the statute on the Parliament rolls or not. The grant of 1337 creating Edward Duke of Cornwall contained a similar clause of parliamentary assent, dated at the foot and expressed to be signed *Per ipsum Regem et totum consilium in Parliamento*. The Prince took his seat as a peer for the first time in the Parliament which commenced at Westminster on 7 July 1344.

The Londoners, then as now, always ready to acclaim a Royal occasion, celebrated the Prince's creation with joustings which went on for three

---

[1] For text see Originalia Roll 17 Edw. III, *Cal. Charter Rolls*, v. 14–15: Selden, *Titles of Honour* (2) 1631, 595–7: *Report Brought from the Lords on the Dignity of a Peer of the Realm*, London, 1829, v. 43–44: *B.M. Royal MS.* 18A, lxxvii, p. 276. Somewhat poetic introductions to charters occur often in medieval times, and Henry VI's charter creating his son Prince of Wales contains similar verbiage; for further examples see F. B. Palmer, *Peerage Law in England*, London, 1907.

days at Smithfield when 'the challengers came forth, one apparelled like
to the Pope, bringing with him twelve others in garments like to Cardinals', who we are told were opposed manfully by the Prince of Wales
'with manie erles, barons, knights, and esquires innumerable'.

The creation of the next Prince was made in unusual circumstances.
The death of Edward Prince of Wales on 8 June 1376 created a novel
situation, which had no precedent, and for which no provision had been
made. Richard of Bordeaux was the son of a Prince of Wales, and
grandson and heir of the reigning king. Richard was but nine years of
age, and of his father's brothers, John of Gaunt, Edmund of Langley,
and Thomas of Woodstock were still living, while the second son of
Edward III, the deceased Lionel of Antwerp, had left a daughter who had
married Edmund Mortimer, Earl of March. It seems that John of Gaunt,
the real ruler of England during The Black Prince's illness and his father's
senility, was disposed to contest his nephew's claim. However John,
avoiding a head-on collision, and looking to the future, tried to secure
the position of the future heir presumptive by a proposal to bar the
succession through female descent, which would thus disqualify the
Earl of March as descendant of the King's second son in the event of
Richard having no issue.

The Commons in Parliament were clearly in favour of the nine-years-
old Richard, and sent a petition to the King praying 'it should please
him, as a great comfort to the whole kingdom, if he would summon
Richard of Bordeaux, son and heir of Edward, to come before them, in
order that the Lords and Commons might see and honour him as the
very Heir Apparent of the kingdom'. Accordingly, Richard was presented
to them on Wednesday 26 June 1376, and after preliminary formalities,
the Prince expressed his will that the Bishop of St. David's, Chancellor
of England, should address the assembly and explain the cause for the
summons that had called the lords and commons together. This the
Bishop did in a long and cloquent speech. Parliament then agreed that
'the said Richard, who was the very Heir Apparent of the kingdom, in
the same way that his noble father the Prince was, ought to be held by
them and all other lieges of the king in great honour and reverence'.[1]

The Commons then went a step further. They prayed that Richard be
created Prince of Wales, to which the King answered that such a matter

[1] *Rot. Parl.* i. 330.

did not belong to the Prelates nor to the Lords to do this in Parliament or otherwise, but that this power belonged clearly to the King. On receiving this answer, the Prelates and Lords promised to mediate with the King for that purpose.[1]

The dignity was not long delayed. On 20 November 1376 the King 'out of his favour' and with the consent of the prelates, dukes, earls, and barons created his grandson Prince of Wales, Duke of Cornwall, and Earl of Chester, and granted him, by Letters Patent, all the possessions that The Black Prince had held together with the reversion of the dower of the widow Joan. The grant, dated at Havering atte Bower in Essex, was witnessed by the Archbishop of Canterbury, the Bishop of Lincoln, the Earls of Cambridge, Arundel, Warwick, Suffolk, and Salisbury, Henry de Percy, John de Nevyll (the King's Chamberlain), Roger de Beauchamp, and John de Ipre (Steward of the Household).[2]

The Londoners demonstrated their affection for the new Prince in picturesque and lively manner on the evening of Sunday, 1 February 1377. Over 130 leading citizens wearing various disguises, as popes, cardinals, emperors, knights, and as 'ambassadors from foreign parts', all on horseback, and accompanied by a band and torchlights, greeted the Prince who was staying with his mother at the manor of Kennington and gave him costly presents. They were afterwards entertained to wine and food in the house, enjoying some dancing and other games, before departing to their city dwellings well pleased with the evening's work.

The creation of the next Prince, Henry of Monmouth, was also attended with difficulties, for there were many who regarded his father as a usurper. When Richard II was formally deposed on 30 September 1399, Bolingbroke had been acclaimed king, and on 13 October following crowned as King Henry IV. This monarch required no prompting regarding his son's status. On the eve of the coronation he knighted his son and forty-four others. A few days later, on 15 October 1399, his eleven-years old son received the triple dignities reserved for the Heir Apparent.

The King first asked Parliament to assent to the proposed creation, to which 'the Lords and Commons gave answer and agreed that Henry

[1] *Rot. Parl.* i. 330.
[2] Charter 50 Edw. III, No. 10, *Cal. Close Rolls*, 1374–7, p. 420: *Rot. Parl.* 51 Edw. III 9. (m), I: Rymer, *Foedera*, 1065, 1067: B.M. Add MS. 15663: *Walsingham*, 321.

the said eldest son of the king should be made Prince of Wales, Duke of Cornwall, and Earl of Chester, and in the event of our said Lord the King's death before that of the said Prince, his eldest son, they would accept the said Prince as lawful heir to the Crown and Realm aforesaid, and that they would obey him as their king and liege lord . . .'.[1]

Three charters were executed by the King, each bearing the date 15 October 1399. By the first, the King created his son, 'of our special grace and of our certain knowledge, and with the counsel and assent of prelates, dukes, earls, barons, and commons of our Realm of England in our instant Parliament being assembled at Westminster', to be Prince of Wales, Duke of Cornwall, and Earl of Chester, *per sertum in capite ac anulum in digito aureum ac virgam auream investimus juxta morem*. By the second charter, having recited the foregoing creation, the King granted the lands of the Principality to him and by the third charter the counties of Chester and Flint.[2]

A contemporary chronicler noted: 'On the Wednesday the King promoted his son Henry, by five symbols, to wit, by the delivery of a golden rod, by a Kiss, by a belt, by a ring, and by letters of creation, to be prince of Wales. . . . And the King also granted and gave over to his eldest son the Principality of Wales, as well as the duchy of Cornwall, along with the county of Chester.'[3] Another stated: 'Sur quoi, mesme nostre Seigneur le Roy seant en son See roiale en plain Parliament myst un cercle sur le test le dit Henry son eisne fitz, et luy dona un anel d'or sur son dey, et luy bailla en sa mayne un verge d'or.'[4] And yet another account states: 'The election of the Prynce. And the same day Herry the kynges sone by assent of all the states in the parliament was chosyn and made prince of Walys Duke of Cornewaille and Erle of Chestre as heire apparant to the kyng and to the Crowne of Englond. That which prince was brought byfore the kyng, And the kyng sittyng toke a cornal of perry and putte on his head and kyssed and blessed hym and toke hym a Rodde of golde. And so he was made prince.'[5]

After the investiture, the Duke of York conducted the Prince to his

[1] *Rolls of Parliament*, iii. 425.
[2] Texts printed *in toto* in *Arch. Cam.* 6 Ser. xi, 1911, pp. 234–7.
[3] *Chronicon Adae de Usk*, 1377–1421, ed. E. M. Thompson, pp. 36–37, 90–91.
[4] *Rot. Parl.* iii. 426.
[5] *Great Chronicle of London*, ed. A. H. Thomas and J. D. Thornley, London, 1938, p. 75. 'Cornal of perry' means a coronet of precious stones and jewels.

place in Parliament, and the estates swore to observe 'the same faith and loyalty, aid, assistance, and fealty' towards him as to his father.

Further honours quickly followed. In the same Parliament, on 23 October, he was declared Duke of Aquitaine, and on 10 November Duke of Lancaster, when it was decided that he should be henceforth styled 'Prince of Wales, Duke of Aquitaine, Duke of Lancaster, and of Cornwall, and Earl of Chester'. He also received the knighthood of the Garter. On 3 November the 'Commons prayed that they might be entered on the record at the election of the Prince', probably from a desire to be officially associated with this popular act. To this the King assented. Another petition presented on the same day prayed 'forasmuch as the Prince is of tender age, that he may not pass forth from this realm, for we, the Commons, are informed that the Scots are coming with a mighty hand; and they of Ireland are purposed to elect a King among them, and disdain to hold of you'.[1]

But a foreign observer proved more astute than the faithful Lords and Commons, for it was not the Scots or Irish who raised 'a mighty hand'. The Frenchman, Creton, who attended the investiture, wrote: 'Then arose Duke Henry, his eldest son, who humbly knelt before him, he made Prince of Wales, and gave him the land; but I think he must conquer it if he will have it, for in my opinion, the Welsh would on no account allow him to be their lord, for the sorrow, evil, and disgrace which the English, together with his father, had brought upon King Richard.'

Events soon verified this shrewd prediction, so that Henry of Monmouth became the only Prince of Wales who had to recover by the sword the Principality whence he derived his title.

The creation of the next Prince was also attended by abnormal conditions. This was Edward, 'the child of sorrow and infelicity', son of Henry VI by Margaret of Anjou. When he was born, on 13 October 1453, the King was suffering from one of the fits of insanity that clouded his unhappy life. In addition, the rivalry of York and Lancaster was nearing breaking-point, and the birth of a prince to the Lancastrian king after some eight years of childless marriage was hailed with little joy by the Yorkists. The Queen, Margaret of Anjou, was alert to the situation and anxious that her son should receive as soon as possible the ensigns

[1] *Great Chronicle of London,* iii. 426–34.

of heirship from his father. However, the afflicted monarch showed no signs of recovery, and in March 1454 Richard of York was appointed Protector of the realm until such time as the King should be sufficiently recovered to resume his duties.

On 15 March 1454, during the Protectorate, the royal infant was created Prince of Wales and Earl of Chester by charter, confirmed by Parliament on the same day. He was then but five months old. He held one dignity already, for his father expressly stated that his 'first begotten sonne at the tyme of his birth was Duke of Cornewayle'.[1] A further ceremony was arranged, evidently for investiture, and reference to it occurs in a letter written on Saturday, 8 June 1454, by William Botoner to Paston, which stated that 'the Prince shall be created at Windsor upon Pentecost Sunday, the Chancellor Earl of Salisbury, the Duke of Buckingham, and many other lords of estate present with the Queen'.[2] The event duly took place on the following day, Whitsunday, 9 June 1454.

Owing to his illness, King Henry had taken no part in these proceedings, but towards the end of the year he suddenly improved, and by the Christmas of 1454 had recovered his faculties. The Prince's creation shortly received its third sanction, this time from the hands of the King. In Parliament, commenced at Westminster on 9 July 1455, the King ratified and confirmed the creation of his son as Prince of Wales and Earl of Chester, which had been done on his behalf in the previous year. This third transaction is recorded in considerable detail.[3] It opens with a recital of the Letters Patent, dated at Westminster 15 March 1454, whereby the King with the consent of the prelates, dukes, earls, viscounts, and barons in Parliament assembled, created and invested his son Prince of Wales and Earl of Chester 'by circlet (sertum) on his head, a gold ring on his finger, and a gold rod in his hand, according to custom' in the presence of the Archbishops of Canterbury and York, the Bishops of London, Lincoln, and Norwich, 'our beloved kinsmen' Richard Duke of York and Humphrey Duke of Buckingham, 'our beloved uterine brother' Jasper Earl of Pembroke, the Earls of Warwick, Salisbury, and Wiltshire, Ralph Bromwell, Chamberlain, William Fauconbridge and John Stourton, knights: now, with the assent of the

[1] *Rolls of Parliament*, v. 293.   [2] *Paston Letters*, i. 315.
[3] *Rolls of Parliament*, v. 290–5. The text has been printed in a rare work, *ΑΡΧΑΙΟΠΛΟΥ-ΤΟΣ containing ten following Books to the former Treasvrie of Avncient and Moderne Times* ... London, printed by Wm. Izzard, 1619, and reprinted in *Arch. Cam.* iv (1849), pp. 233 ff.

lords spiritual and temporal and the Commons in Parliament assembled, the King ratified, approved, and confirmed the said creation and the grant also made on 15 March 1454, together with the lands of the Principality.[1] The record proceeds to describe the provisions made for the upbringing and maintenance of the Prince who 'is tender of age'.

The next who demands our attention is Edward son of the Yorkist Edward IV who had become King in 1461. He was born at Westminster on 2 November 1470, when his father was a fugitive beyond seas. In the following March Edward returned and again secured the Crown which he held without interruption until his death in 1483.

The victorious monarch lost no time in conferring those dignities on his son that marked him as heir to the Throne. On 26 June 1471 he created the infant, Edward, Prince of Wales and Earl of Chester.[2] No descriptions of the grant and investiture have survived, but there was certainly some kind of ceremonial, doubtless similar to previous investitures, for we learn that the heralds and minstrels received a largess of £20 between them for their services on that occasion. On 3 July following, the King caused the lords in Parliament to acknowledge the Prince as Heir Apparent and to accept him as king in due course. The oath,[3] taken by ten spiritual and ten temporal peers, and twenty-six knights, describes him as 'Prince of Wales, Duke of Cornwall, and Earl of Chester'. However, it was not until 17 July that he was created Duke of Cornwall, by Patent, in Parliament, and on that day also received, by charter, the Principality of Wales and the counties of Chester and Flint.[4]

The next to succeed to the dignity was the son of the Yorkist Duke of Gloucester, namely Edward of Middleham, who had been created Earl of Salisbury on 15 February 1478.[5] When his father succeeded to the Throne as Richard III on 26 June 1483, the Prince automatically became Duke of Cornwall.[6]

On 24 August 1483 he was created Prince of Wales and Earl of Chester. Owing to his poor health the nine-years-old boy had been

---

[1] *Rolls of Parliament*, v. 293. These lands, specified in great detail, are identical with those granted to The Black Prince.

[2] *Rolls of Parliament*, vi. 9. [3] Ibid. vi. 234; Rymer, *Foedera*, xi. 714.

[4] *Rolls of Parliament*, vi. 9–16: *The Complete Peerage*, s.n. 'Chester' and 'Cornwall'; Nicolas, *Historic Peerage*, s.n. 'Prince of Wales'. [5] Nicolas, op. cit.

[6] See *The Complete Peerage*, s.n. 'Cornwall', where the title is discussed in detail.

unable to journey from Middleham Castle in Wensleydale to attend his father's coronation at Westminster.

In August the King and Queen progressed through England towards the city of York, having commanded the Prince to join them. The Prince and his retinue left Middleham about the 19th of the month, and travelling via Wetherby and Tadcaster met his parents at Pontefract Castle on the 24th. On that day the King formally created him, under the style of 'Edward, eldest son of the King', to be Prince of Wales and Earl of Chester.[1] The words used in the Patent indicate the monarch's opinion of his son, '. . . whose singular wit and endowments of nature wherewith, his young age considered, he is remarkably furnished, do portend, by the favour of God, that he will make an honest man'.

On Saturday, 30 August, the cavalcade arrived in York, the retinue including the Bishops of Coventry, Durham, Lichfield, Worcester, St. Asaph, St. David's, the Duke of Albany, the Earls of Lincoln, Huntingdon, Northumberland, Surrey, Warwick, the Lords Dudley, Morley, Scrope, Stanley, the Lord Chief Justice, the Lord Chamberlain, and many officers of the Household. At the head of the procession rode the two sheriffs of the city who had joined the King at Tadcaster. At Brekles Mills, the Mayor, and other leading citizens, greeted the royal visitors. The party entered the city by the Micklegate, to be cheered by enormous crowds. Three pageants were played at different points along the streets decorated with 'clothes of arras, tapistre werk and other'.

Delighted with the reception, the King decided to invest the Prince in this loyal and enthusiastic city. Arrangements had to be made quickly. Letters carried by galloping couriers reached the Keeper of the Wardrobe in London, instructing him to send garments and accoutrements suitable for the occasion, including gowns, doublets, cloth of gold, gilt spurs, four banners charged with religious devices, three coats of arms beaten with pure gold for the King, coats of arms for the heralds, one thousand pennons, and thirteen thousand of the King's own badges, the White Boar. Many yards of Holland cloth and other materials were handed to Sir James Tyrrel, Master of the King's Henchmen, and to seven of the Henchmen themselves. The preparations occupied a whole week, during which the citizens of York entertained the royal party with banquets and plays.

[1] Ibid.: Nicolas, op. cit.

The investiture took place in York Minster on Monday, 8 September 1483, as Polydore Vergil notes, 'a day of great state for York', there being present 'three princes wearing crowns—the king, the queen, and the prince of Wales'. The ceremony was performed by the King, who in the presence of the Archbishop of York and a large gathering invested his son with the gold circlet, gold ring, and gold rod. He also knighted the Prince, as well as the Spanish ambassador. After the ceremony the King and Queen, wearing their crowns, and the Prince his coronet, walked in procession through the thronged streets, to the 'great honour, joy, and congratulations of the inhabitants, as in show of rejoicing they extolled King Richard above the skies'. The little Prince walked sedately alongside the Queen, who held him with her left hand.[1]

The creation and investiture of the Tudor princes followed the traditional pattern. The first of these was the son of Henry VII, born at Westminster on 20 September 1486. On the Feast of St. Andrew, 29 November 1489, by the name of 'Arthur eldest son of the King', he was created by charter (delivered into Chancery on 1 December following) Prince of Wales and Earl of Chester, with the assent and advice of the peers in Parliament, and at the same time received the Knighthood of the Bath. He was invested with the Principality of Wales and the counties of Chester and Flint, by Signed Bill on 27 February 1490.[2]

On the day preceding the investiture the little Prince was led on board the King's great barge on the Thames, near Shere, which then sailed down river. Between Mortlake and Chelsea he met barges of the peers, spiritual and temporal, who, together with knights, esquires, Kings of Arms, heralds, pursuivants, trumpeters, and minstrels, boarded the royal craft. Shortly afterwards the gaily bedecked flotilla was joined by barges of the Lord Mayor and the crafts of the City, and at Lambeth by the barges of the Spanish ambassador and many Spanish merchants. On landing at 'the Brigge' the Prince was carried to the King's presence

---

[1] For the ceremonies at York see R. Davies (ed.), *Municipal Records of the City of York*, pp. 160–75, 280–8: Rymer, *Foedera*, xii. 200: P. Virgil, *Anglia Historia*, i. 190: *Chronicle of Croyland*, Contin: see also P. M. Kendall, *Richard the Third*; *V.C.H. Yorkshire*, iii (1913), p. 410. According to Jesse, *Memoirs of Richard III*, London, 1862, p. 148, the Prince carried the rod of gold in the procession following the investiture.

[2] *The Complete Peerage*, iii, s.n. 'Chester' and 'Cornwall'; 'Creations 1483–1646' in App. to *Forty-Seventh Report of the Deputy Keeper of Public Records*; Nicolas, op. cit., and Courthope, both s.n. 'Wales'.

in the Brick Tower, Westminster, the road being lined as far as the King's Bench by Members of the City crafts. As the King intended to create his son a Knight of the Bath as well as Prince of Wales, his bath was prepared that evening in the King's closet, while baths for the earls and lords who were to receive similar knighthood occupied the area between the Parliament chamber and the chapel, while the remainder were within the Parliament chamber itself.

After Mass on the following morning, Arthur was carried through St. Stephen's chapel to the end of the stair, where he was placed on horseback. His sword and spurs were carried by the Earl of Essex, and the remainder of the retinue, composed of knights who had been dubbed on the previous day, mounted their horses 'in the order of their Baynes'. The cavalcade headed by the Prince rode into Westminster Hall, dismounted before the King's Bench, and entered into Whitehall. A little later the King entered and took his seat. The Marquess of Berkeley and the Earl of Arundel led the Prince forward, and the King girded him with a sword and dubbed him knight. The Prince offered his target and spurs, and then retired into the King's closet where he donned his robes of state. He then returned, processionally, to the presence once again. The mantle, coronet, golden rod, and ring, were carried by the Earls of Arundel and Derby, and the sword, point upwards, by the Earl of Shrewsbury. 'And there he was created as accustomed. . . . Then the King departing, the Prince that day kept his state under the Clothe of Estate.'

A banquet followed. The newly made knights sat along one side of the chamber, and fell to after the Prince had 'licensed them' to eat their meat. 'After the minstrels had played, the officers of armes cried to the presence of the Prince, and Garter-kyng-of-Armes gave him Thankings in the name of all for his Largesse, which was XX^{ti} pounds.'

The only innovation on this occasion was the ceremonial voyage on the Thames, and the attendance in their own barges of the Lord Mayor and the City Companies. An entry in the accounts of the Carpenters' Company for 1490 reads, 'Payd for hyr of the barge when the Prynce was creatyd.'[1] The court poet, John Skelton, composed a poem to celebrate the occasion.

[1] E. B. Jupp and W. W. Pocock, *An Historical Account of the Worshipful Company of Carpenters of the City of London*, London, 1887, p. 37.

In the month following, the King granted him the castle, town, and honour of Wallingford, to be held as part of the Duchy of Cornwall. One of the Prince's officers of arms, Wallingford Pursuivant, derived his designation from this appanage.[1] On 8 May 1491 he was instituted Knight of the Garter.

The child-prince grew into a youth of great promise, but falling a victim to the sweating sickness died at Ludlow on 2 April 1502 at the age of sixteen. The next in succession was Henry, born at Greenwich on 28 June 1491, and created Duke of York on 31 October 1494. After his brother's death Henry became automatically Duke of Cornwall, and is so styled in a document under the Great Seal in October 1502.

Few details are available relating to his promotion to the Principality, but it seems reasonable to assume that the traditional ceremonials were observed. On 18 February 1504, by the style of 'the only son and heir of the King', Henry was created Prince of Wales and Earl of Chester.[2] A contemporary chronicler noted: 'In which yere 18 Henry VII the XVIII daye of February, the kyng at his palace at Westmynster, with all solempnite created hys onely sonne Henry prince of Wales, erle of Chestre, &c.'[3] As usual, a number of knights were dubbed, and an Act of Parliament, reciting the King's determination to create his son Prince of Wales, stated that 'for the encrease, honour, lawde, and tryumphe of the whiche creacion dyvers of the King's subjectts are commaunded by the King's Highnesse accordyng to his most honorable lawes to take upon them the honor and degree of knyghthode at the tyme of the said creacion'. However, the King withheld the usual grant of the revenues of the Principality and Chester which remained in the hands of the careful and penurious monarch, less one-third, the dower of the Princess of Wales, widow of Arthur.

A hundred and six years passed by before another creation took place. This was the creation of Henry Frederick of Stirling, eldest son of James I. Endowed with considerable talent, a questing mind, and creative energies, he was as accomplished in the arts as he was in the more robust fields of physical activity. A precocious child, by the time

[1] Noble, *History of the College of Arms*, p. 96.

[2] *The Complete Peerage*, s.n. 'Cornwall'.

[3] Hall, *Chronicle* (edn. 1809), p. 497. *The Complete Peerage*, s.n. 'Chester', citing Patent Roll, No. 130, 19 Henry VII, No. 10, says that the ceremony of his creation as Prince of Wales was to take place on 23 Feb.

he became Prince of Wales he had reached a standard of maturity well in advance of his sixteen years.

Henry was the only Heir Apparent who took steps to prompt his father's decision to advance him to the dignity. In addition to his Scottish titles, he had automatically become Duke of Cornwall on his father's succession on 24 March 1603. On 9 July of that year he had been instituted Knight of the Garter, and although only nine years old his 'quicke wittie answers and princely carriage and reverend obeisance at the altar' impressed those who attended the ceremony.

About the year 1609 Henry became interested in his future Welsh dignity. It all started when a Cornishman, Richard Connack, humbly begged him to pay a little more attention to the affairs of the duchy whence he derived his earliest English title. Far from showing offence, Henry reacted by making personal study of his rights connected with the duchy, and immediately exacted all arrears of rents and dues his agents had neglected to collect. The shrewd youth realized it might be possible to add still more to his coffers in due course. What about Wales, which one day would become his primary title? Accordingly he wrote to Connack instructing him to undertake detailed researches among state papers and other records to establish what action previous kings had taken in respect of honours and money grants to their eldest sons.

This request greatly alarmed Connack, who was anxious to please the Prince and at the same time not to offend the King. He carried out his task as discreetly as he could, and succeeded in amassing a formidable amount of data, and even contrived to 'prove' that Edward III and Edward VI had also been among the previous Princes of Wales. Connack's nervousness is revealed in the preface to his report, in which he prays the Prince to grant him the following indulgences:

First, that your Highness should be pleased to secrete these things to yourself until you find an inclination in the King's Majesty to create you Prince of Wales as others had been. Next, that his Majesty, upon the perusal thereof should allow the same, as I hope he will, I have my Desire. If otherwise, that then you would use your best endeavour to excuse me, and by my Humble Suit to his Majesty, obtain his gracious pardon for my boldness therein, and keep me from his Displeasure. For as in all duty I am bound to obey your lawful commands, so I ought to be careful not to give his Majesty just offence in the least degree, as in this I hope I do not.

The nervous suppliant need not have worried. At the end of 1609, the King announced his intention of advancing his eldest son to the dignity of Prince of Wales in the coming month of June. Whether Connack's memoranda hastened this decision in any way we know not. He certainly did not suffer on account of his uneasy researches, for, later on, he received the appointment of Auditor to the Prince's Household.

Detailed descriptions of Henry's creation have survived. As usual, it was a royal, parliamentary, and London occasion. By Letters Patent[1] dated 4 June 1610, the monarch declared that the creation of 'our first-born son Henry Duke of Cornwall and Rothesaye' as Prince of Wales and Earl of Chester was in accordance with the ancient customs of the kingdom, and done with the advice and consent of the prelates, dukes, marquesses, earls, viscounts, and barons assembled in Parliament; he now granted Henry 'the name, style, title, estate, dignity, and honour of the aforesaid Principality and Earldom, with authority to preside over, direct and defend it, investing him in this dignity by the girding on of a sword, the giving and placing of a chaplet on his head, a gold ring on his finger, and a gold staff in his hand, according to custom (ut est moris)'. The first witness to the charter was Charles Duke of York, and among others the Bishops of Chester, Bangor, and Llandaff, Edward Lord Bergevenny and George Lord Audeley.

This charter is a beautiful document. The opening initial, the letter J (Jacobus), encloses a painting executed in considerable detail, of the enthroned monarch handing the Patent to the kneeling Prince arrayed in a purple mantle turned ermine, wearing a gold coronet, and holding the rod in his left hand. Armorial shields of the Principality (the arms of Gwynedd), Duchy of Cornwall, and Earldom of Chester, all in their proper colours, decorate the margins; along the top the shield of Great Britain supported by leopard and unicorn is flanked by the arms of the Prince as Heir Apparent (Great Britain with a label), and by the three ostrich feathers placed upon a sun in splendour. It is a triumph of the herald's and scrivener's art.

Elaborate ceremonial, pageantry, and festivities attended the occasion. Contemporary accounts provide detailed descriptions of the ceremonies, which occupied nearly a week.[2]

---

[1] The original document is preserved in the British Museum as Add. MS. 36932.
[2] e.g. B.M. MSS. 66, 4483, 5176 (by Camden), and 6141; Stow, *Annales*, contin. Howes,

On 30 May the Prince attended by many young noblemen, together with his servants, rode from St. James's to Richmond, whence he was to return processionally to the capital. On the following day the Prince and his party embarked at Richmond, but owing to the low tide did not reach Chelsea until four o'clock in the afternoon, having first been entertained to a banquet at Barn Elms. There he was met by the Lord Mayor, aldermen, and liverymen of the City of London[1] who, earlier that morning, had sailed up the Thames in barges 'with banners, streamers, and ensigns, and sundry sorts of loud-sounding instruments', towing a large figure of a whale, on top of which perched a young woman 'Corniea queen of Cornwall', and a dolphin ridden by a young man representing 'Amphion genius of Wales'. The Lord Mayor and his party greeted the Prince with addresses of welcome, including one from the precariously perched Corniea.

The little armada, with flags flying and instruments sounding, the whale and the dolphin wallowing in its wake, sailed from Chelsea towards Whitehall. At Whitehall steps the Knight Marshal and the Earl Porter waited to receive the Prince. Having listened to a loyal farewell delivered by Amphion, 'a grave and judicious Prophet-like personage', the Prince landed and was escorted to the Great Hall where Lord Wotton, Comptroller of the Household, and Lord Knollys, Treasurer, received him. They conducted him into the Guard Chamber where the Viscount Fenton, Captain of the Guard, brought him to the Presence Chamber. From there the Lord Chamberlain conducted him to the Privy Chamber where his parents awaited him. Having taken a meal, he retired to an early bed.

On 4 June the Lords and Commons assembled in the Court of Requests which had been appointed and specially prepared as the Parliament house. Stages had been erected for members of both Houses, the Lord Mayor and aldermen of the City of London, the ambassadors, and other

p. 890 (edn. 1631); *London's Love to the Royal Prince Henrie* . . . , London, 1610; *Tethy's Festival* . . . , S. Daniel, London, 1610; *Court and Times of James I*, i. 111–15; Winwood, *Memorials*, iii; J. Budge, *The Order and Solemnitie of the Creation of* . . . *Henrie*, London, 1610; Williams, *Domestic Memoirs of the Royal Family and the Court of England*, 1860, ii. 275 et seq. and references there.

[1] The books of the Carpenters' Company, under 31 May 1610, record payment of 50*s.* for 'bardghyer', and £4. 5*s.* 7½*d.* for the liverymen's supper when they 'came home from the water when they attended in their bardge to bring the Prince from Richemond to Whytehall to be created Prince of Wales'—Jupp and Pocock, op. cit.

eminent ladies and gentlemen. At about half-past ten in the morning, the King and the Prince came by water to the Queen's Bridge, accompanied by members of the chief nobility and a band of pensioners. Prelates and peers attired in their robes and coronets met them at the bridge. The King was escorted to a robing-room at the north end of the Parliament house, and the Prince to the Court of Wards where he and his attendants robed themselves.

When all had taken their places in Parliament, the King entered, attended by Clarenceux and Norroy Kings of Arms, the Earl Marshal (Earl of Worcester), the Lord Chamberlain (Earl of Suffolk), the Serjeants at Arms, the Ushers, Garter Principal King of Arms, Lord Winchester carrying the cap of maintenance, Lord Arundel carrying the sword, and Lord Cranbourne carrying the train.

The King having seated himself on the Throne, the Lord Chamberlain, the Earl Marshal, and the Kings of Arms, withdrew and went to bring in the Prince. The Prince's procession then entered in the following order:

Clarenceux and Norroy

Earl Marshal and Lord Chamberlain

The new Knights of the Bath[1] in long robes of purple satin who were placed on both sides in the higher House, above the Bar. Garter Principal King of Arms, carrying the Prince's patent

Earl of Sussex, carrying the Prince's mantle of purple velvet

Earl of Huntingdon, carrying the train thereof

Earl of Cumberland, carrying the sword

Earl of Rutland, carrying the ring

Earl of Derby, carrying the rod of gold

Earl of Shrewsbury, carrying the cap of estate

THE PRINCE, bareheaded, in surcoat of velvet, assisted by

The Lord Privy Seal (Earl of Northampton) and the Lord Admiral (Earl of Nottingham).

The procession advanced through the chamber and made three deep bows to the King. Then the Prince knelt on a rich cushion. Garter kissed the Patent before handing it to the Lord Chamberlain who presented it to the King. He handed it to the principal Secretary and Lord Treasurer, the Earl of Salisbury, who read out the contents. At the words *fecimus et creavimus*, the Mantle was given to the King, who, rising,

---

[1] Twenty-five Knights of the Bath had been dubbed on 2 and 3 June.

delivered it to two assistants who robed the Prince. At the succeeding relevant words, the King girded him with the sword, and invested him with the circlet, gold ring, and gold rod. The Prince then rose, and with dutiful reverence kissed the King's hand, and the King kissed him on the cheek. Finally, the Earl Marshal and Lord Chamberlain placed him in his parliamentary seat, by the left side of the Throne.

The Deputy for the Clerk of the Crown, kneeling on the lower degree of the steps of State, read the names of the witnesses by their titles, omitting their Christian names, and finally, the Lord Chamberlain prorogued Parliament till the following Thursday, the trumpets sounded, and the lower House rose.

The procession left in the following order:[1]

Trumpeters
Masters of the Chancery
The King's Counsel and other law officers
The Judges
The Heralds
The Officers and Aldermen of London
The Knights of the Bath
The Barons
The Bishops
The Viscounts
The Earls
The Marquesses
The Lord Mayor of London
Clarenceux and Norroy Kings of Arms
The Archbishop of York
The Lord Treasurer
The Serjeants at Arms
THE PRINCE between his two Assistants
Earl of Huntingdon carrying the train
Gentlemen and Ushers
Garter Principal King of Arms
The Earl Marshal
The Lord Chamberlain carrying the Sword
THE KING
Viscount Cranbourne carrying the train.

[1] Minor differences occur in the order given by Stowe, op. cit., and B.M. Harl. MS. 6140, fols. 180 et seq.

They passed through the hall to the Westminster water-stairs where they embarked.

The party landed at the Whitehall steps, and the Prince entered the great hall where he was to dine.[1] The Prince was served by the Earls of Pembroke, Southampton, Montgomery, as sewer, carver, and cupbearer respectively, and by Lord Walden, eldest son of the Earl of Suffolk, who brought the glass of water. The Prince sat at the upper end of the table, and near him the Duke of York. Some three yards lower down sat the Lord Treasurer, Lord Privy Seal, Lord Chamberlain, Earl Marshal, Marquess of Winchester, the Earls of Salisbury, Northampton, Nottingham, Rutland, Shrewsbury, Derby, Cumberland, Huntingdon, and Sussex in their robes and coronets. The Knights of the Bath dined at a long side table where they were served by the Guard.

Throughout the banquet 'the hall resounded with all kinds of exquisite music'. At the second mess, Garter and the officers of arms, 'in a very reverend manner', advanced to the Prince's board, and proclaimed the King's style in Latin, French, and English, with three largesses according to custom, and the Prince's style, Prince of Wales, Duke of Cornwall and Rothesay, Earl of Chester, Knight of the Garter, with two largesses.

The banquet marked the close of the day's proceedings. The Lord Mayor and his brethren, well pleased with the occasion, sent a gratuity of £4 to the Clerk of the Council, and £5 to Garter who was 'to make a Recorde in his office of the whole buysines for the perpetuall honour of this citty'.

On the following day, 5 June, 'a most rich and Royall maske of Ladies' entertained the Court. In the first act, young Charles, Duke of York, appeared as Zephyr, while twelve little maidens, daughters of peers, danced around him. In the next act, the Queen appeared as 'Tethys, Mother of the Waters', attended by the Princess Elizabeth as 'the River Thames', and seven young ladies each representing a British river, among which were four Welsh rivers. One tableau showed a painted scene of Milford Haven and the fleet of Henry VII who had landed there in 1485. The 6th of June marked the close of official rejoicing. In the afternoon the King and Prince were amongst a 'world of people' at the Tiltyard to see noblemen and others in rich armour mounted on splen-

---

[1] The King dined privately elsewhere.

didly caparisoned horses running their courses. Aquatic events on the Thames, lit by fireworks and other illuminations, rounded off the evening. Boats and barges crowded with sightseers covered the river, while both banks were 'surcharged with people', to witness 'naval triumphs', the capture of a Turkish pirate, the storming of a castle built on the Lambeth shore, ships of war and galleys fighting briskly but 'without any manner of hurt to any person'. A spectacular display of fireworks provided a rousing finale. Poems were written in honour of Henry, and one by Ben Jonson included the names of all the previous Princes of Wales. The good burgesses of Chester seem to have 'beaten the pistol', for on St. George's Day 1610 they had already held an elaborate pageant entitled 'Chester's Triumph in Honor of her Prince' which included a poem to Henry written by 'her ill townsman Richard Davies'.

The tragic death of the Prince in November 1612 resulted in his younger brother Charles, Duke of York becoming Heir Apparent. On 25 February 1613 the King issued a declaration conferring upon him the title of Duke of Cornwall and the reversion of the office of Lord High Admiral. Three years later he was created Prince of Wales and Earl of Chester. The Patent is dated 4 November 1616, and the investiture took place on the same day.[1] A contemporary describes the occasion:[2]

Thursday the last of October 1616 viz All Saints Eve, Prince Charles came in great state by Barge from Barne Elmes to Whitehall accompanied and attended by divers great Lords, and others of honourable Rancke and quality, besides his owne traine, and was most joyfully met at Chelsey by the Lord Maior, Aldermen, and Citizens of London: each company in a several Barge,[3] and distinguished by their seuerall Armes in their rich Banners and Stately Streamers besides the Royall sound of Drum and Trumpet, and great variety of excellent Musicke, besides all which and the infinite number of people vpon the shoare and in Boates and Barges, to behold this joyfull day there was also at the Cities charge in honour of his highnesse creation, more particularly, pleasant Trophies and ingenious deuices met him upon the water then euer was at any former creation of any Prince of Wales.

[1] Rymer, *Foedera*, xvi. 792.

[2] Stow, *Annales*, contin. Howes, p. 1025 (edn. 1631); see also *Civitatis Amor the Cities Love, an Entertainment by Water at Chelsea and White Hall, &c.*, London, 1816.

[3] The expenses of twenty members of the Carpenters' Company who attended the Prince from Chelsea to Whitehall on 31 Oct. amounted to £3 for hire of the barge and 10s. 6d. 'for bread'—Jupp and Pocock, op. cit.

And vpon Monday, the fourth of November, at Whitehall where the King's Maiestie invested and crowned Prince Charles, Prince of Wales: at this solemne creation were present most of the Nobilitie of the Land: The Lord Archbishop of Canterbury and diuers other Bishops and reuerend Prelates, all the Judges of the Law: There were present also the Lord Maior and Aldermen of London in their scarlet Robes, as were the Judges (The Earle of Arundell was then Earle Marshall). In honour of this ioyfull Creation there were made fiue and twentie knights of the Bath. . . .

The investiture followed the same procedure as that of 1610, as shown by the detailed description made by the herald Camden.[1] The Prince entered London by water. At Chelsea he was met by the Lord Mayor and barges of City companies, when a young woman attired as 'the figure of London' sitting on a sea-unicorn, attended by six tritons, addressed the Prince, as 'the Glory of our day', after Neptune had 'silenced the river Thames so that her words might be heard. When he reached Whitehall steps, two Londoners dressed as 'Hope' and 'Peace' advanced. The former thanked London for waking her 'from the sad slumber of disconsolate fear', and the latter sang a song of welcome as the Prince stepped ashore.

The procession then entered the hall at Whitehall in the following order:

The Prince's Gentlemen according to their degrees
His learned Counsel
The Drums
The Trumpets
The Heralds
Clarenceux and Norroy
The Earl Marshal
The Lord Chamberlain
The Knights of the Bath, youngest foremost
Garter carrying the Patent
The following, bareheaded, carrying their caps of estate,
Earl of Sussex carrying the mantle of purple velvet
Earl of Huntingdon carrying the train
Earl of Rutland carrying the sword
Earl of Derby carrying the ring with a diamond
Earl of Shrewsbury carrying the verge of gold
Duke of Lennox, Lord Steward, carrying the cap of estate.

[1] B.M. Harl. MS. 5176, fols. 222a–25.

THE PRINCE in a surcoat of purple velvet girt to him, and a
feathered hat, assisted by
The Lord Treasurer and the Lord Admiral, and, finally,
The Principal Gentlemen of the Prince's Chamber.

The Prince knelt before the King. Garter delivered the Patent to the
Lord Chamberlain, who handed it to the King. Mr. Secretary Winwood,
receiving it from the King, then read the contents in a clear voice, kneeling. When he read the appropriate words, the King invested his son with
mantle, sword, coronet, ring, and verge, in that order. The Patent was
redelivered to the King, who handed it to the Prince. The monarch
kissed his son 'once or twice'. At the putting on of the mantle and at
the delivery of the Patent the trumpets and drums sounded.

This investiture, though popular and attended with due ceremony,
did not compare with that of 1610 so far as public celebrations were
concerned. This was because of 'the sharpness of the weather and the
prince's craziness'.[1] Not being in robust health, the Prince preferred
not to take part in too many processions, while the Queen's continued
grief for her eldest son precluded her attendance, which perhaps was as
well, for the Bishop of Ely, by an unfortunate slip of the tongue, prayed
for Prince *Henry*.

Nevertheless the usual observances were not ignored. After the investiture, the Prince dined at Whitehall with a large party of nobles
(wearing their robes and coronets), gentlemen, and official guests. The
Earl of Southampton (cup-bearer), the Earl of Dorset (carver), and Lord
Compton (sewer) were among the servers. At a side-table on the west
side of the hall the newly made Knights of the Bath dined according to
precedent.[2] The King did not dine, but viewed the proceedings from a
gallery, attended by Lord Buckingham and some foreign ambassadors.
The usual heraldic honours were rendered. At the second service, Garter
King of Arms proclaimed the styles of King and Prince in three languages, and received a fee of £40 and the Prince's upper garment, while
a similar sum was disbursed among the other officers of arms. Music
enlivened the banquet, and a song of forty parts was rendered by the
gentlemen of the chapel and others, who gave an encore at the command
of the King.

[1] i.e. indisposition. Letter from Chamberlain, 9 Nov. 1616, cited in *The Court and Times of
James I*, i. 434–6.
[2] *Diary of Sir Simonds d'Ewes*, edn. 1845, i. 91–92: B.M. Harl. MS. 5176.

On the evening of 5 November, a combat at barriers took place when forty gentlemen from the Inns of Court rode in the lists, but apparently gave a somewhat indifferent performance. Later a more lively incident occurred which gave the worthy citizens good cause to remember the occasion. The Lord Mayor and his fellows invited the new Knights of the Bath to a grand feast at the Drapers' Hall on Saturday. When the knightly guests arrived 'some were so rude and unmanly and carried themselves so insolently divers ways, but especially in putting citizens' wives to the squeak, so far forth that one of the sheriffs broke open a door upon Sir Edward Sackville which gave such scandal that they went away without the banquet, though it was prepared for them'.[1] The young blades then crowded into the Mitre Tavern and proved a sore trial to the apprehensive innkeeper.

More successful were the masques specially written for the occasion and acted in London playhouses. To remind the Prince of his connection with the Principality, live goats were led on to the stage where speeches in the Welsh tongue were delivered by men capable of such venture.

The provinces also rejoiced. The people of Ludlow celebrated in spectacular style, a detailed account of which appeared in a work entitled *The Love of Wales to their soueraigne Prince*[2] . . . by one Daniel Powel. In a prefatory letter to the Prince, Powel refers to 'your proper Meridian of Ludlow, the beautiful Seate of his Maiesties chiefe Castle and Counsell of Wales'. The proceedings were directed by that Council which arranged for the castle, court-house, and town to be decorated with the Prince's heraldic ensigns, and for processions, which included the Council and Ludlow's civic authorities, from the castle to the church. At various points in the streets, schoolboys recited Latin and English verses, the former composed 'vpon one dayes warning' by Humphrey Herbert, Master of the Free School, the latter by a rhyming alderman named Richard Fowler. After troops had fired a *feu de joie*, bonfires lit, and other demonstrations completed, banquets were partaken 'in all joyfull and joviall manner', and prayers were given in church for the Prince, and for the preservation of the King and the estates 'from the Papists' treasonable and horrible conspiracie' of 1605.

---

[1] Stow, op. cit., p. 1026.

[2] Reprinted by the Roxburghe Club in 1837; and by R. H. Clive in *Documents Connected with the History of Ludlow*, 1841, pp. 61–80.

The next prince to hold the dignity was Charles, later King Charles II. Research has failed to establish the date of his creation as Prince of Wales. After his birth on 30 May 1630 Lord Dorchester, Secretary of State, informed the British Resident in Paris—'Yesterday at noon the Queen was made the happy mother of a Prince of Wales',[1] but this was only a popular mode of expression for the King's eldest son. At his christening in the chapel at St. James on 27 June following we are told that the heralds stepped forward and that Garter King of Arms proclaimed the titles of the infant as 'Prince of Great Britain, Duke of Cornwall and Rothesay, Earl of Carrick, Baron of Renfrew, Lord of the Isles, and Great Steward of Scotland'. He became generally known as Prince Charles, and by the more formal style of 'Prince of Great Britain' which appeared on the medal struck to commemorate his birth. A legal document, dated 7 February 1633, refers to Sir John Walter, knight, 'Attorney General of the Prince of Wales',[2] but this may well have been a matter of courtesy as we have noticed earlier.

All authorities agree that Charles was 'declared' Prince of Wales, and not formally created. On his Garter stall place (he was installed on 21 May 1638) he is styled 'Prince of Great Britain, Duke of Cornwall and Rothesay', so it seems clear that he had not received the dignity at that time. One source asserts that an establishment was provided for him as Prince of Wales 'about 1638'.[3] It is true that a Household was established for him immediately after his installation as Knight of the Garter, and that an elaborate set of 'Orders for the Household of the Prince' was approved by the King in June 1638.[4] Nowhere in this latter document, initialled by the King himself, is he described as 'Prince of Wales', but always as 'the Prince' or 'His Highness'. One of the best authorities in these matters has stated that he was acknowledged as Prince of Wales 'probably before' November 1641, and 'certainly before' 4 April 1646.[5] Numerous warrants providing for the expenses of his Household up to 1644 describe him simply as Prince Charles, with one exception, dated

[1] Ellis, *Original Letters*, 2nd Ser. iii. 262. Neither Airy's statement that he became Prince of Wales 'at his birth', nor Jesse's that he was so created 'shortly after his birth', can be sustained.

[2] National Library of Wales, *Eaton-Evans and Williams Collection*, No. 1259.

[3] *D.N.B.* s.n. 'Charles II'.

[4] Ed. Francis W. Steer, *Orders for the Household of Charles, Prince of Wales*, 1959, from an original MS. in Lichfield Cathedral Library.

[5] *The Complete Peerage*, s.n. 'Cornwall'.

November 1641, when he is described as 'Prince of Wales'.[1] In communications with Parliament in 1645–6 he always appears as 'Prince of Wales'. We should note that he took his seat in the House of Lords in 1640, being ten years of age,[2] and although this did happen in some cases after the bestowal of the Principality, it cannot be regarded in itself as evidence for the promotion in dignity. It is easy to understand why no regular investiture took place if he was created *after* the Civil War opened in 1642, but it is less easy to understand such absence if the event took place before that date.

The next Prince of Wales, James Francis Edward, son of James II, was also 'declared', but in this case we are able to produce a much narrower date bracket. Born at St. James's Palace on 10 June 1688, the earliest official description as Prince of Wales occurs in a Gazette dated 4 July, so that he had been 'declared' before he was a month old.

The Stuart Princes of Wales had been born under unlucky stars. Henry died at the age of 17, the first Charles became King and was executed, the second Charles spent many years in exile before he sat on his father's Throne, and James Francis Edward was borne into permanent exile when but seven months old.

Although each Hanoverian monarch raised his Heir Apparent to the dignity, the former ceremonies were not revived. The pageantry became a mere memory of antiquaries. Gone were the days of solemn investiture. No gilded barges rode the Thames, no banquets were held in Whitehall, no junketings for the City fathers, no accolade for youthful aspirants. Until 1911 the people had to be content with a precise but prosaic statement that a Prince of Wales existed, and were given no opportunity to associate themselves with what had been a pre-eminently popular national act.

The eldest son of the first Hanoverian King, George Augustus the Electoral Prince, born in 1683, already held British peerage titles before his father's accession to the Throne. Queen Anne had conferred five dignities on him on 9 November 1706, namely Baron of Tewkesbury, Viscount Northallerton, Earl of Milford Haven, Marquess and Duke of Cambridge, all in the peerage of the United Kingdom, and in the same year appointed him a Knight of the Garter. The Queen's death on

---

[1] Quoted in Nicolas, *Historic Peerage*, s.n. 'Prince of Wales'.
[2] *D.N.B.* s.n. 'Charles II'; Bigham, *Kings of England*, s.n. 'Charles II'.

1 August 1714 radically changed the position of the Elector and his son.

When they landed at Greenwich on 17 September 1714 father and son were given a generous welcome by their British subjects. The Prince was especially popular for he had served with distinction against the Turks in eastern Europe, and had fought in 1708 under the great Marlborough at Oudenarde where he led a successful cavalry charge against the French army in which, ironically, the Jacobite Prince of Wales commanded a body of horse. So elated was the Prince with the welcome he received and with the prospects that now lay before him, that despite his fondness for studying German genealogies, he declared, 'I have not one drop of blood in my veins that is not English'. The father, more realistic and less genealogical, confined his enthusiasm about his new subjects to the terse remark 'All the King-killers are on my side'.

Among complications raised by the accession of the new king was the form in which the names of the Royal Family should appear in the liturgy of the Church of England. Should Sophia Dorothea, still behind the grey walls of Ahlden, be prayed for as Queen? Should the Heir Apparent be designated Prince of Wales? In the event the Queen's name was not mentioned, and after much discussion it was concluded that the Heir had automatically become Duke of Cornwall, but could not be styled Prince of Wales until formally created.

That dignity was not long delayed. At the first Council held by the King, on 22 September 1714, he declared his son Prince of Wales and Earl of Chester, and so created him by Letters Patent on 27 September. In the Patent, the traditional formula was used[1]—'Likewise we invest him, the said Prince, with the aforesaide Principality and county, which he may continue to govern and protect, and we confirm him in the same by these ensigns of honour, the girding on of a sword, the delivery of a cap and placing it on his head, with a ring on his finger, and a golden staff in his hand, according to custom, to be possessed by him and his heirs, King of Great Britain.' He afterwards took his place in the Lords. I have found no details of any ceremony in connection with the event.

Frederick Lewis, son and Heir Apparent of George II, born 20 January

---

[1] Printed *in toto* in the 2nd edn. of Dodridge, *An Historical Account of the . . . Principality of Wales, Dutchy of Cornwal, and Earldom of Chester*, London, 1714; which is dedicated to this Prince of Wales.

1706–7, spent his youth in Germany, and an unfortunate antagonism developed at a very early stage between father and son, which persisted throughout their lives. His grandfather, George I, however, bestowed high honours on him. Although popularly styled Duke of Gloucester from 1714 onwards,[1] the title was never formally granted, and was not recited at his installation as Knight of the Garter in 1718. On 26 July 1726 he received his first regular British dignities when George I created him Baron of Snowdon[2] in the county of Caernarvon, Viscount of Launceston, Earl of Eltham, Marquess of the Isle of Ely, and Duke of Edinburgh.[3] When his father ascended the Throne as George II on 11 June 1727 Frederick became automatically Duke of Cornwall and Rothesay.

He came to England for the first time on 7 December 1728. As if to get the formalities over as quickly as possible, the Prince was introduced to the Privy Council on 18 December and sat on the right of the monarch. On 8 January 1728–9 he was created Prince of Wales and Earl of Chester.[4]

Frederick died in his father's lifetime, on 20 March 1751, at the age of 44, leaving, among others, an eldest son, George William Frederick, a youth in his thirteenth year. Thus he became Heir Apparent to his grandfather, a state of affairs that had occurred but once previously, when the Black Prince had died in the lifetime of his father Edward III.

The King lost no time in advancing his grandson to the dignities enjoyed by Heirs Apparent. On 18 April 1751, less than a month after his father's death, a Household was appointed for him. Two days later, on 20 April, he was created Prince of Wales and Earl of Chester by Letters Patent. The notification in the *London Gazette* read: 'St. James's April 20 1751. His Majesty has been pleased to order Letters Patent to pass under the Great Seal of Great Britain, for creating His Royal Highness George William Frederick (the Prince of Great Britain, Electoral Prince of Brunswick Lunenburgh, Duke of Edinburgh, Marquis of the Isle of Ely, Earl of Eltham, Viscount of Launceston, Baron of Snaudon, and Knight of the Most Noble Order of the Garter)[5] Prince of Wales and Earl of Chester.' As in the case of his father and grandfather, there seems

---

[1] See *Complete Peerage*, s.n. 'Gloucester', dukedom.   [2] 'Snaudon' in the Patent.
[3] 'Edenburgh' in the Patent.   [4] *Complete Peerage*, s.n. 'Gloucester' dukedom.
[5] Instituted Knight of the Garter by proxy on 12 July 1748.

to have been no ceremonial of investiture. He was the first Prince of Wales of the Hanoverian line to have been born and bred on English soil.

George William Frederick ascended the Throne as King George III on 20 October 1760. His eldest son, George Augustus Frederick, was born on 12 August 1762, and when only five days old created Prince of Wales and Earl of Chester by Letters Patent dated 17 August. After reaching the age of 21 years, he was introduced into the House of Lords, and contemporary accounts enable us to follow the ceremony in detail.[1] Before entering the chamber, the Prince was robed, and wore the collar of the Order of the Garter. His procession was marshalled as follows: Gentleman Usher of the Black Rod (Sir Francis Molineux, Bt.), the Deputy Earl Marshal (Earl of Surrey), the Lord Privy Seal (Earl of Carlisle), Garter King of Arms carrying the Letters Patent creating him Prince of Wales, the Deputy Lord Great Chamberlain (Sir Peter Burrell), the Lord President of the Council (Viscount Stormont), a Gentleman of the Prince's Bedchamber (Viscount Lewisham) carrying the coronet on a crimson velvet cushion, and The Prince carrying the Writ of Summons, supported by the Duke of Cumberland and the Duke of Portland. The party proceeded through the chamber, with the usual obeisances. After the Writ and the Letters Patent had been delivered to the Lord Chancellor and read out by the Clerk at the table, the Prince was conducted to his chair on the right of the Throne, and the coronet and cushion placed on a stool before him. Shortly afterwards, the King entered in procession, and was enthroned with the usual solemnities. Having delivered his most gracious speech, he retired out of the House. Then the Prince, at the table, took the oaths of allegiance and supremacy, subscribed the declaration and the oaths of abjurations. And so the ceremony ended. Later in the day, by the King's command, the Prince was introduced into the Privy Council where he took his place at the upper end of the board, on the King's right hand.

The next Prince of Wales, Albert Edward, son of Queen Victoria and Albert, Prince Consort, was born on 9 November 1841. The Queen decreed, that in addition to holding British titles, he should be gazetted bearing one of his father's, namely Duke of Saxony, and that a coat of arms be designed for him quartering the arms of Saxony with those of Britain. No time was lost in promoting him to the highest dignity

---

[1] *London Gazette*, 15 Nov. 1783: *Gent. Mag.* liii (1783), p. 176.

enjoyed by Heirs Apparent. The Letters Patent, dated 4 December 1841, issued under the Great Seal, read 'Know ye that we have made our most dear son (Prince of the United Kingdom of Great Britain and Ireland, the Duke of Saxony, Duke of Cornwall) Prince of Wales and Earl of Chester. And him, our most dear son, we do ennoble and invest with the said Principality and Earldom by girding him with a sword, by putting a coronet on his head, and gold ring on his finger, and also by delivering a gold rod into his hand, that he may preside there and may direct and defend those parts.' No ceremony attended the event. The introduction of the Prince to the House of Lords on 5 February 1863 closely followed precedent. The procession entered the Chamber from the Robing Room in the following order: Gentleman Usher of the Black Rod, Garter King of Arms bearing the Prince's Letters Patent creating him Prince of Wales, the Lord Chamberlain of the Household, the Lord Steward of the Household, the Deputy Earl Marshal, the Lord Great Chamberlain, the Lord Privy Seal, the Lord President of the Council, R. H. Meade (one of the Prince's equerries) carrying the coronet on a crimson velvet cushion, The Prince carrying his Writ of Summons, supported by the Dukes of Newcastle and Cambridge, and attended by a Lord of the Bedchamber (The Earl of Mount Edgecumbe) and the Groom of the Stole (Earl Spencer). Following the usual reverences, the Letters Patent and the Writ were handed to the Lord Chancellor on the Woolsack, who handed them to the Clerk to read out, while the Prince and his procession stood near the table. Having taken the oath and subscribed the declaration, he was conducted to his chair on the right of the Throne. He then received the congratulations of the Lord Chancellor, and retired to be disrobed, after which the Lord Great Chamberlain, and Deputy Earl Marshal, Garter King of Arms, and Black Rod conducted him to his carriage.[1]

Albert Edward ascended the Throne as King Edward VII on 22 January 1901. On his 60th birthday, 9 November 1901, he issued Letters Patent creating his son George Frederick Ernest Albert to be Prince of Wales and Earl of Chester. He also sent a personal letter to him:

In making you today 'Prince of Wales and Earl of Chester', I am not only conferring on you ancient titles which I have borne upwards of 59 years, but

---

[1] *London Gazette*, 5 Feb. 1863.

I wish to mark my appreciation of the admirable manner in which you carried out the arduous duties in the Colonies which I entrusted you with. I have but little doubts that they will bear good fruit in the future & knit the Colonies more than ever to the Mother Country. God bless you, my dear boy, & I know I can always count on your support and assistance, in the heavy duties and responsible position I now occupy.[1]

There had been no ceremony of investiture since 1616, a period of nearly 300 years. Beyond carrying out the legal requirement, that is issuing the Patent of creation, no formalities had been observed. It had become an affair of seal and parchment.

The next creation witnessed a revival of traditional forms, and the enthusiastic, spontaneous, reaction of the British people revealed this national event to be as popular in the twentieth century as ever it had been in the heyday of the Plantagenets, Tudors, and Stuarts.

The nineteenth Prince of Wales ascended the Throne as King George V on 6 May 1910. His eldest son, Edward Albert Christian George Andrew Patrick David, automatically became Duke of Cornwall on his father's accession. On 10 June 1911, he was invested Knight of the Garter in the Garter Room at Windsor Castle, after which he walked in procession to the service in St. George's Chapel, a custom revived for the first time since the eighteenth century. On his sixteenth birthday, 23 June 1911, he was created Prince of Wales and Earl of Chester by Letters Patent, and on the 13 July following invested at Caernarvon Castle.

The investiture of the twentieth Prince of Wales at Caernarvon represented a complete departure from precedent so far as location was concerned. The suggestion that it should be held at Caernarvon came from Mr. David Lloyd George, and what had been a royal occasion with which Parliament, the Court, and the citizens of London had been intimately associated for centuries now became a royal occasion in a Welsh setting, amongst Welsh people. For the first time in history a Prince of Wales was to be invested within his Principality, and formally presented to the people. For the first time, too, the whole ceremony was to be held in the open air. And no more appropriate place could have been found than the birthplace of the first Prince of Wales, whose weathered effigy over the castle gateway was a reminder of the great Plantagenet's gift to the Welsh. The decision to go to Caernarvon evoked

[1] Harold Nicolson, *King George the Fifth*, London, 1952, p. 75.

history in dramatic fashion, and the whole country, England as well as Wales, recognized its validity.

Detailed accounts of the investiture exist in the journals and newspapers of the day, particularly in *The Times* newspaper. There are many people still living who witnessed or took part in the ceremony.

Arrangements were quickly made. The great castle was admirably suited for the ceremony. Its curtain walls and nine towers, in excellent state of preservation, and the interior, lent itself to pageantry. Apartments were prepared for their Majesties in the Eagle Tower, from which a processional way, carpeted with green cloth, led through the inner bailey to the centre of the outer bailey where the royal dais, with green and white canopy surmounted by a gilded effigy of St. David, had been erected. The interior was ablaze with heraldic insignia—the Royal Arms, the Arms of the Prince, of Cornwall and of Rothesay, of Chester, Carrick, and Renfrew, of the Royal House of Gwynedd, of the Five Royal and Fifteen Noble Tribes of Wales, together with the badges of the King and the Prince. In the Chamberlain's Tower, the Investiture insignia were to be laid out. Within the castle, seating accommodation existed for 7,637 persons, while seats for a further 2,550 were provided in the moats around the outer walls. A choir, 430 strong, distinguished by 200 women members in Welsh national costume, occupied a stand at the end of the outer bailey.

The ceremony was appointed for half-past two of the clock in the afternoon of 13 July 1911. At nine in the morning the guests began to arrive and by half-past twelve every seat was filled. Bands of the Royal Marine Light Infantry and the 2nd Battalion The Welch Regiment entertained the audience during the long hours of assembly.

The Prince arrived about half an hour before his parents. Leaving Griffith's Crossing shortly after one o'clock, in a carriage accompanied by an escort from the Denbighshire Yeomanry, the Prince, in the uniform of a midshipman, alighted at a platform in Castle Square where the Mayor and Town Clerk received him. His reply to their address of welcome, included several phrases in the Welsh language—'Môr o gân yw Cymru i gyd' (all Wales is a sea of song), 'Croesaw' (welcome), and 'Diolch o waelod fy nghalon i hen wlad fy nhadau' (Thanks from the depths of my heart to the old land of my fathers). The procession then passed by the Water Gate to the Eagle Tower, and a salute from twenty-one guns, followed by a fanfare of trumpets from the battlements, announced his arrival. The Prince's standard was broken over the Eagle Tower, and he was received by the Right Honourable David Lloyd George (Constable of the Castle), J. E. Greaves (Lieutenant), Thomas E. Roberts (Sheriff of Caernarvonshire), and Charles A. Jones (Deputy Constable of the Castle).

After this the Prince's procession moved through the inner bailey to the Chamberlain's Tower, in the following order: Two gentleman ushers, the Archdruid, Druids, Bards, Ovates, Pursuivants Extraordinary (Caernarvon and Fitzalan), Pursuivants (Rouge Dragon and Portcullis), Sir John Williams, Bart., Principal E. H. Griffith, Sir Alfred Thomas, Professor Edward Anwyl, Sir Vincent Evans, the Mayor of Chester and his Town Clerk with his Mace and Sword Bearers, twenty-nine Mayors of Welsh boroughs, the High Constable of Miskin Higher, the Lord Mayor of Cardiff with his Town Clerk, and Mace and Sword Bearers, twenty-four Welsh Members of Parliament, Chester Herald (deputized by Windsor Herald), The Prince, supported on the right by the Earl of Plymouth, on the left by Lord Kenyon; then came H. P. Hansell (the Prince's Tutor), the Rt. Hon. Sir W. Carington (Keeper of the Privy Purse), Captain B. Godfrey-Faussett, R.N., Lieut.-Gen. Sir James Hills-Johnes, V.C., Major H. G. Casson (South Wales Borderers), Lieut.-Col. C. H. Young (Welch Regiment), Col. H. A. Iggulden (Royal Welsh Fusiliers), and Major-Gen. the Hon. Sir Savage Mostyn (Colonel, Royal Welsh Fusiliers).

As this procession moved from the Eagle Tower, the Welch Regiment band played the first six bars of the National Anthem, and then changed to 'God Bless the Prince of Wales'. As the Prince reached the outer bailey, the massed choir sang a verse of the National Anthem in English followed by the Prince's anthem in Welsh. After he had entered the Chamberlain's Tower, two baronets, Sir Herbert Lloyd Watkin Williams-Wynn and Sir Marteine Owen Mowbray Lloyd, mounted guard at the entrance, the former bearing the standard of the Welsh Dragon, the latter the White Wolfhound.

The Prince then donned the traditional dress—white satin breeches, white silk stockings, black shoes with rectangular gold buckles, a purple velvet surcoat edged with ermine and slashed with black fur, with an outer edging of embroidery in mixed dull and bright gold. The surcoat was girt at the waist with a purple silk sash with cords fringed with purple and gold.

Meanwhile the King, in the uniform of an Admiral of the Fleet, and the Queen had been travelling from Griffith's Crossing, which they left at five minutes to two, escorted by a Sovereign's Escort of the 2nd Life Guards, the Royal Standard being borne behind the carriage. In the carriage with Their Majesties sat the Princess Mary and the Duke of Connaught. In the second carriage rode the Duchess of Devonshire (Mistress of the Robes), the Countess of Shaftesbury (Lady in Waiting), the Earl of Granard (Master of the Horse), and Winston Spencer Churchill (Home Secretary). At Caernarvon railway station, a detachment of Yeomen of the Guard fell in on either side of the carriage. In the Castle Square, Their Majesties were received by the Mayor and Corporation, and after alighting at the platform listened to addresses delivered in English by the Mayor and in Welsh by the Town Clerk. The King replied in a short speech reminding the audience 'that by his descent through the House of Tudor, My dear son derives a natural and intimate claim upon your allegiance'. He then knighted the Mayor of the town, and the Sheriff of the county. After several presentations had been made, the royal party continued towards the castle. A Royal Salute of twenty-one guns greeted them, the Prince's standard over the Eagle Tower was hauled down, and the Royal Standard run up in its place. A fanfare of trumpets sounded, and Mr. Lloyd George received Their Majesties at the Water Gate, and presented the key of the castle for the King to touch. They then passed into the Eagle Tower.

In the meantime the King's procession had formed up inside the castle grounds in the following order: four Gentlemen Ushers, six Welsh Members of Parliament, Bluemantle and Rouge Croix Pursuivants, York and Richmond Heralds, Lieut.-Gen. Sir Henry Mackinnon (the General Officer Commanding in Chief) and his staff of five officers, the Sheriffs of the Welsh counties, the Sheriff of Caernarvonshire on his own, eight Lieutenants of Welsh counties, the Lieutenant of Caernarvonshire on his own, a group of peers consisting of one duke and eighteen earls and barons. These members of the procession moved forward and arranged themselves around the royal dais. Waiting in the open space between the Black and the Granary Towers stood the Cabinet Ministers and Welsh dignitaries—Mr. H. H. Asquith in the uniform of an Elder Brother of

Trinity Corporation, Mr. Harcourt, Mr. Birrell, Mr. John Burns, Mr. Buxton, the Bishops of St. Asaph, St. David's, Bangor, and Llandaff, the Chairman of the Welsh Congregational Union, the Moderator of the General Assembly of the Welsh Calvinistic Methodist Connexion, the Presidents of the Welsh Baptist Union and of the Welsh Wesleyan Methodist Assembly, Bishop Mostyn of Menevia, the Revd. J. W. Wynne Jones, Vicar of Caernarvon (said to be a descendant of a nurse of the first Prince of Wales), the Arch-Druid, and Sir John Rhys.

Then came the main King's procession in the following order:

Home Secretary (*Rt. Hon. W. S. Churchill, M.P.*)	First Lord of the Admiralty (*Rt. Hon. R. Mckenna, M.P.*)	Constable of the Castle (*Rt. Hon. D. Lloyd George, M.P.*)
Norroy King of Arms		Clarenceux King of Arms (represented by Somerset Herald).

Peers to bear Insignia

Lord Mostyn

Earl of Powis	Marquess of Anglesey
Lord Dynevor (representing Marquess of Bath)[1]	Duke of Beaufort

Garter King of Arms

The Earl Marshal (*Duke of Norfolk*)	Lord Great Chamberlain (*Earl Carrington*)

Sword of State,[2] borne by Earl Beauchamp

H.M. THE QUEEN	H.M. THE KING
H. R. H. Princess Mary	H.R.H. The Duke of Connaught

Master of the Horse (*Earl of Granard*)	Lord Steward (*Earl of Chesterfield*)	Acting Lord Chamberlain (*Lord Hamilton of Dalzell*)
Lady of the Bedchamber (*Countess of Shrewsbury*)	Mistress of the Robes (*Duchess of Devonshire*)	Lord in Waiting (*Lord Annaly*)
Captain of Yeoman of the Guard (*Lord Allendale*)		Captain of the Gentlemen at Arms (*Lord Colebrooke*)
Lord Chamberlain to the Queen (*Earl of Shaftesbury*)	Woman of the Bed-chamber (*Lady Bertha Dawkins*)	Private Secretary of the King (*Rt. Hon. Sir Arthur Bigge*)
Crown Equerry (*Hon. Sir C. Wentworth Fitzwilliam*)	Master of the House-hold (*Sir Chas. Frederick*)	Comptroller, Lord Chamberlain's Department (*Sir Douglas Dawson*)
Equerry in Waiting (*Major Clive Wigram*)	Groom in Waiting (*E. W. Wallington, Esq.*)	Equerry in Waiting (*Hon. Sir Harry Legge*)

1 Absent through illness.

2 It was discovered at the last moment that owing to an oversight the Sword of State had not been brought. The fifteenth-century ceremonial sword of the Earldom of Chester was borrowed, and it was this that Lord Beauchamp bore.

Assistant Comptroller, Lord Chamberlain's Department (*Hon. George Crichton*)

Equerry to the Duke of Connaught (*Capt. T. Bulkeley*)

Deputy Master of the Household (*Hon. Derek Keppel*)

Silver Stick in Waiting (*Col. A. V. Vaughan Lee*)

During the movement of the procession the band of the Welch Regiment played the National Anthem, afterwards sung by the choir. Their Majesties then took their seats. The King commanded the Earl Marshal, who stood at the foot of the dais, to direct Garter Principal King of Arms to summon the Prince to the Presence. Then Garter, accompanied by four peers deputed to bear the Insignia, walked to the Chamberlain's Tower. The Prince's procession moved towards the dais in the following order:

Carnarvon and Fitzalan Pursuivants Extraordinary

Portcullis and Rouge Dragon Pursuivants

Chester Herald

Garter King of Arms, bearing the Letters Patent

Lord Mostyn, bearing the Mantle

Earl of Powis bearing the Sword	Marquess of Anglesey bearing the Coronet
Lord Dynevor bearing the Ring	Duke of Beaufort bearing the Verge

Lord Kenyon	H.R.H. THE PRINCE OF WALES	Earl of Plymouth
H. P. Hansell, Esq.	Rt. Hon. Sir W. Carington (Keeper of the Privy Purse)	Capt. Bryan Godfrey-Faussett, R.N.

Lieut.-Gen. Sir James Hills-Johnes, V.C.

Major H. G. Casson (The South Wales Borderers)	Lieut.-Col. C. H. Young (The Welch Regiment)	Col. H. A. Iggulden (The Royal Welsh Fusiliers)	Maj.-Gen. the Hon. Sir Savage Mostyn (Col. The Royal Welsh Fusiliers)

The Prince, bareheaded, waited while the officers of arms made three separate obeisances, and Garter delivered the Letters Patent to the Lord Great Chamberlain who, kneeling, presented them to the King who handed them to the Home Secretary. The Prince, with Lord Plymouth on his right and Lord Kenyon on his left, then passed between the peers bearing the Insignia, and having made three separate obeisances, knelt upon a cushion in front of the King. Mr. Winston Churchill read the Patent:

George the Fifth by the Grace of God of the United Kingdom of Great Britain and Ireland and of the British Dominions beyond the Seas King, Defender of the Faith—To all Archbishops, Dukes, Marquesses, Earls, Viscounts, Bishops, Barons, Baronets, Knights, Justices, Provosts, Ministers, and all other Our faithful Subjects Greeting—Know Ye that We have made and created and by these Our Letters Patent do make and create [*here the King invested the Prince with the mantle*] Our Most Dear Son, Edward Albert Christian George Andrew Patrick David, Prince of the United Kingdom of Great Britain and Ireland, Duke of Cornwall and Rothesay, Earl of Carrick, Baron of Renfrew, Lord of the Isles, and Great Steward of Scotland, Duke of Saxony and Prince of Saxe-Coburg and Gotha, PRINCE OF WALES AND EARL OF CHESTER, and of the same Our Most Dear Son Edward Albert Christian George Andrew Patrick David have given and granted And by this Our present Charter do give grant and confirm the Name, Style, Title, Dignity, and Honour of the Same Principality, and Earldom, And Him Our said most Dear Son Edward Albert Christian George Andrew Patrick David, as has been accustomed, We do Ennoble and Invest with the said Principality and Earldom by Girding Him with a Sword [*here the King invested him with the Sword*], By putting a Coronet on His Head [*here the King placed the coronet on the Prince's head*], And a Gold Ring on His Finger [*here the King placed the ring on the third finger of the Prince's left hand*], And also by delivering a Gold Rod into His hand [*here the King placed the rod in the Prince's right hand*], That He may preside there and may direct and defend those parts To Hold to Him and His Heirs Kings of the United Kingdom of Great Britain and Ireland and of the British Dominions beyond the Seas for ever. Wherefore We will and strictly Command for Us, Our Heirs and Successors, That Our said Most Dear Son Edward Albert Christian George Andrew Patrick David may have the Name, Style, Title, Dignity, and Honour of the Principality of Wales and Earldom of Chester aforesaid unto Him and His Heirs Kings of the United Kingdom of Great Britain and Ireland and of the British Dominions beyond the Seas as is above mentioned.

In Witness whereof We have caused these Our Letters to be made Patent.

Witness Ourself at Westminster the twenty-third day of June in the first year of Our Reign.

As each item was required, its bearer moved forward and, kneeling, offered it to the King, who took it from its crimson gold-fringed cushion, and invested his son. The bearer then bowed and retired backwards from the dais.

Having been invested, the Prince, still kneeling, offered his homage in these words: 'I, Edward Prince of Wales, do become your liege man of life and limb and of earthly worship and faith and truth I will bear unto you to live and die against all manner of folks.'

The King stepped forward, and raising the Prince from his knees, kissed him on either cheek, and placed the Letters Patent in his left hand. The Prince took his seat on the right hand of the King. This completed the investiture.

Sir John Rhys, supported by the Archdruid, read the address from the people of Wales to their Prince. The Prince answered in a speech which included several Welsh phrases, including the ancient motto, 'Heb Dduw heb ddim, Duw a digon' (Without God nothing, God and enough). The choir and the people sang the hymn, 'O God our help in ages past', after which the Revd. Evan Jones, past-President of the National Free Church Council, read the lesson (Ephesians vi. 10–18). The Bishop of Bangor, accompanied by the choir, read the Lesser Litany, the Lord's Prayer, and a specially written Collect, and finally the well-known collect beginning 'Almighty and Everlasting God by whose spirit the whole body of the Church is governed' was recited. The Welsh hymn 'Marchog Iesu yn llwyddianus' was rendered by the choir, after which the benediction was pronounced in Welsh by the Bishop of St. Asaph, the senior bishop present. The first verse of the National Anthem, sung by choir and people, followed by a salute of twenty-one guns from the naval vessels in the straits and by units of the Royal Field Artillery, ended this part of the ceremony.

The final act, the Presentation of the Prince to the people of his Principality, now took place. The procession, led by two Gentlemen-at-Arms, consisted of the Earl Marshal, the Lord Great Chamberlain, the Earl Beauchamp bearing the Sword of State, the King leading the Prince by the hand, the Queen, and Lord Mostyn carrying the Prince's train. On the balcony at Queen Eleanor's Gate, overlooking the Castle Square, the Prince of Wales was presented to the cheering people. The choir and the people within and without the castle sang the Welsh National Anthem with great fervour. The procession moved to the King's Gate where he was again presented to the people without the walls, and finally presented to the assembly within the inner bailey. The procession reformed and the choir singing the National Anthem accompanied by the band, King,

Queen, and Prince, passed into the Eagle Tower. The memorable and moving ceremony was over. The clock stood at twenty minutes to four. The ceremony had taken one hour and forty minutes.

The troops assembled for the occasion, apart from the Household troops and the saluting battery of the Royal Field Artillery, were provided by Welsh units, Regular and Territorial, and units with Welsh associations or bearing the Prince of Wales's ostrich feathers as their badge or his name in their designations.

The Investiture Medal, designed by Goscombe John, was struck to commemorate the day. The obverse showed the head and shoulders of the Prince, wearing his coronet, with the collar of the Garter over his robe: and the legend, 'Investiture of Edward Prince of Wales K G'. The reverse contained a representation of Caernarvon Castle, with sun-rays as background, and above, the ostrich feathers badge within the Garter surmounted by the Prince's coronet, and in base the dragon badge. The inscription, a translation into Welsh of that on the obverse, ran, 'Arwisgiad Iorwerth Tywysog Cymru M G'.

The investiture at Caernarvon had been a triumph. Those with a feeling for history could reflect on the genealogical combinations and the constitutional vicissitudes that had resulted in the appearance at this ancient town of a twentieth-century prince whose ancestors, Gwyneddan and Plantagenet, some seven centuries before, had held court on this very spot. The King and Queen shared the unrestrained joy of their subjects: the former recorded in his diary: 'The dear boy did it all remarkably well and looked so nice'; the latter wrote: 'It was a most picturesque and beautiful ceremony and very well arranged. David looked charming in his purple and miniver cloak and gold circlet and did his part very well.'

The announcement of the creation of the present Prince of Wales provides an illustration of the way that our monarchy identifies itself with contemporary developments and trends.

Born at Buckingham Palace on 14 November 1948, he was christened Charles Philip Arthur George on 15 December following. When little over three years of age he became Heir Apparent to the Throne. As the years passed by, speculation arose as to when the Prince would be advanced to the hereditary dignities enjoyed by Heirs Apparent. The Welsh people, to whom his birth, in addition to its constitutional significance, was an emotional event, looked forward eagerly to the day when they would have a Prince of their own once more. The long-awaited words came in unexpected manner, not on the cold page of a *Gazette* but in live and human way made possible by the techniques of the twentieth century.

The announcement, when it came, was as dramatic as it was unexpected. Saturday, 26 July 1958, a breezy summer's day, marked the end of the sixth British Empire and Commonwealth Games held at Cardiff Arms Park in the modern capital of Wales. His Royal Highness the Duke of Edinburgh attended the closing ceremony, alone, because of the Queen's illness. In course of his speech to a gathering of some 36,000 people, the Duke said that the Queen had recorded a closing message. This message was then relayed by B.B.C. engineers over the public address system to the attentive crowd, and was heard also throughout the world by millions of listeners to radio and television broadcasts.

After expressing regret at her inability to be present, and congratulating the athletes on their achievements, the Queen went on to say:

I want to take this opportunity of speaking to all Welsh people, not only in this arena, but wherever they may be.

The British Empire and Commonwealth Games in the capital, together with all the activities of the Festival of Wales, have made this a memorable year for the Principality.

I have, therefore, decided to mark it further by an act which will, I hope, give as much pleasure to all Welshmen as it does to me.

I intend to create my son, Charles, Prince of Wales, today. When he is grown up I will present him to you at Caernarvon. . . .

A tremedous surge of cheering, lasting for about two minutes, greeted the announcement, and as the Duke made his final drive around the arena a chorus of Welsh voices rose jubilantly to sing the anthem 'God bless the Prince of Wales'. The news was received with enthusiasm and satisfaction throughout Wales and beyond. How appropriate it was that this royal and constitutional act had been made on Welsh soil and in the presence of young athletes from all countries bound by allegiance to the Crown; for the Prince of Wales as Heir Apparent belongs to all loyal peoples.

The Prince himself had listened to the broadcast at Cheam school in Berkshire, where he had been a pupil for the past year. The land of

Wales was already known to him for he had accompanied the royal visit to Brecon, Haverfordwest, and Tenby in August 1955. His first visit to the Principality after his creation was made a few weeks afterwards, in August 1958.

The *London Gazette*, dated Saturday 26 July 1958, contained the following statement: 'The Queen has been pleased to order Letters Patent to be passed under the Great Seal for creating His Royal Highness Prince Charles Philip Arthur George, Duke of Cornwall and Rothesay, Earl of Carrick, Baron Renfrew, Lord of the Isles, and Great Steward of Scotland, Prince of Wales and Earl of Chester.'

The act had been made. The Prince was aged nine years and eight months when he received the senior dignity conferred on the Heir Apparent. He is the twenty-first Prince of Wales. His creation had once more emphasized the unity of Crown and Principality, a happy union established so long ago as 1301.

7

THE HERALDRY OF THE PRINCES

THE heraldic insignia of the Princes of Wales fall into two classes, namely those with Welsh associations and those borne by the Heir Apparent. The former consists of a coat of arms first used by the Princes of Gwynedd which became extended to represent the Principality of Gwynedd, and, later, the Principality of Wales, and so belongs to that class known as 'arms of dominion'; and also the Red Dragon badge. In this group too we have to consider the ascription of the spurious 'lions coward' shield, which, I shall show, has no connexion whatsoever with Wales. The latter contains the heraldry of the Heir Apparent, consisting of the arms of England differenced with a label, and the badge of the Plume of Ostrich feathers, popularly called 'The Prince of Wales' Feathers'. It will be convenient to discuss these classes separately, during which I shall try to trace the origin of the symbols and the manner in which they became part of the heraldry of our princes.

Since the Princes of Wales sometimes possessed special heraldic officers it will be convenient to place on record such evidence as I have found concerning them, and also reference to heralds whose special jurisdiction included the Welsh land.

Finally, a list will be given of the actual arms and badges as borne by each Prince of Wales since 1301.

I. ARMS WITH WELSH ASSOCIATIONS

(a) *Arms of the House of Gwynedd*

It is not known when the Prince of Gwynedd first adopted a coat of arms. The earliest surviving seal of those rulers is attached to a letter written in 1212 or 1214 (probably the latter), from *Leolinus princeps Norwallie* to Philip (Augustus) King of France, confirming a treaty arranged between them.[1] A conventional equestrian seal, it shows a galloping horse,

[1] T. Matthews, *Welsh Records in Paris*, Carmarthen, 1910, pp. 3–4, 119, where there is a good photograph of the deed and seal.

carrying a man in armour, with a shield slung over his shoulder. All that remains of the legend are the words SIGILLVM LOELI[NI]. . . . This was Llywelyn ap Iorwerth, generally known as Llywelyn the Great.

Another seal of the same prince is attached to the marriage contract executed in 1222, between Elen daughter of Llywelyn the Great and John the Scot, nephew of Ranulph Earl of Chester, an instrument to which Llywelyn was a witness. This again is an equestrian seal, and possibly the same matrix was used in both cases. The prince is represented mounted on a horse, holding a raised sword, while a shield is slung by a strap over his shoulder; the secretum contains a lion, or perhaps a boar, passant beneath a tree, and the words SIGILLVM SECRETVM LEWELINI.[1]

Other contemporary references are found to seals of this prince. Soon after 2 May 1230 Llywelyn, described as Prince of Aberffraw and Lord of Snowdon, wrote to William Marshall, Earl of Pembroke, explaining that he was sealing the letter with his *secret seal* because he had not got his *Great Seal* with him at the time.[2]

The earliest example of an armorial seal of a Gwyneddan prince is attended by unsatisfactory features. Between August 1241 and the end of 1242 David son of Llywelyn the Great executed a deed whereby he agreed to surrender certain possessions to Henry III and covenanted to obey that King in all things in the future. The seal attached to the document is fragmentary and the legend has disappeared. On the obverse a man is represented seated, holding a sword in his right hand, while the left arm is also extended but the hand is missing; the reverse shows a man mounted on a horse carrying a shield charged with what appears to have been a lion rampant. However, careful examination has revealed that the lion did not form part of the original impress, but that it had been cut in subsequently with a knife or some such instrument. In all other respects the seal seems identical with the Great Seal of Henry III, and the suspicion arises that the lions of England had been pared away and a single lion rampant substituted.[3] Whatever occurred, it is clear that this shield did not display the arms normally attributed to the house of Gwynedd.

[1] Birch, *B.M. Catalogue of Seals*, no. 5547. The seal is contained in B.M. Cotton Charters, xxiv. 17.

[2] J. G. Edwards, *Calendar of Ancient Correspondence concerning Wales*, p. 51.

[3] See Owen and Blakeway, *A History of Shrewsbury*, 1825, i. 118, and engraving: the deed was preserved in the archives of the Earl of Bridgwater.

Those are the only examples of the seals of the princes of Gwynedd known to me. That other princes of the dynasty possessed seals is certain, but no descriptions of them have survived. For example, following the death of Llywelyn ap Gruffydd, the Archbishop of Canterbury wrote on 17 December 1282 to inform the Bishop of Bath and Wells that Edmund Mortimer had obtained Llywelyn's *privy seal* (called also his *small seal* elsewhere in the same letter) which had been found on the body of the slain prince.[1]

We have to turn to English sources for the earliest description of the armorial bearings of the Welsh princes, and it is ironical that the only contemporary evidences are contained in the records of the race that destroyed the dynasty that bore them.

The lively pen of Mathew Paris has preserved the information we seek. That chronicler, who died about 1256, made a sketch of the tragic Gruffydd son of Llywelyn the Great, falling to his death while attempting to escape from the Tower on St. David's Day 1240. At the side of this sketch is drawn the shield of arms of Gruffydd, namely, quarterly, *or* and *gules* four lions passant counterchanged.[2] Paris has also recorded two other coats of arms which he attributes to that David whose suspect seal we have already discussed. One of these[3] is identical with that of his brother Gruffydd described above; and the other, *or* three roundels *vert*, 2 and 1, on a chief dancetty of the second a lion passant *sable*, has a peculiarly un-Welsh air about it, and is not assigned to David in any other known source, English or Welsh.

In a recension made about 1310 of a work composed about 1260, the quarterly shield is described as being that of Iorwerth Drwyndwn (died about 1174), father of Llywelyn the Great[4]—'A tawnt vynt Yervard armee, dont les armes furent de or e de goules quartyle e un chescun quarter un leopart'.[5] Although this cannot be accepted as proof that the coat was actually borne by that prince, it is a valuable reference inasmuch as it shows that by the middle of the thirteenth century this coat had become recognized as that of the rulers of Gwynedd.

---

[1] J. G. Edwards, op. cit., p. 129.

[2] Mathew Paris in *Walpole Society Publications*, vol. xiv, pl. xvii. Note that the lions in this drawing are looking to their front, and are *not* shown as guardant.

[3] Mathew Paris, p. 468.

[4] Chetham MS. 6712, fol. 185 verso (M. Paris original MS.).

[5] *Foulk Fitz Warin*, ed. Brandin, p. 25, l. 28.

English officers of arms had no doubt at all on the subject. According to *Walford's Roll* (compiled *circa* 1275) Llywelyn ap Gruffydd bore 'escartelle d'or et gules four lions d'lun et l'autre'.[1] *Planche's Roll* (*circa* 1280) gives the arms of 'Le Prince de Gales' as quarterly *or* and *gules* four lions passant guardant counterchanged.[2] *Smalepece's Roll* (*temp.* Edward I) and the *Camden Roll* (*circa* 1280) both assign similar arms to the Prince of Wales, the animals being described as leopards, i.e. lions guardant.[3] The *St. George Roll* (*circa* 1285) records that 'Th' lin ap Griffith' bore quarterly *or* and *gules* four lions passant guardant counterchanged,[4] while his brother David (executed 1283) is said to have borne the same coat differenced by the substitution of *azure* for *gules*, which, if correct, provides an example of differencing by a younger brother. According to the *Lord Marshall's Roll* (*circa* 1300) the same David is said to have borne the quarters *argent* and *azure*, the lions being counter-coloured. Since these sources provide David with four different coats, it would seem that some uncertainty existed, and one may be forgiven for suspecting that the English armorists were 'assigning' coats to him.

Succeeding armorists, like the compilers of the *Nobility Roll* i (*circa* 1370), *Jenyns' Ordinary* (*circa* 1380), the *Sherborne Missal* (*circa* 1405), and the *Bradfer-Lawrence Roll*, ii (*circa* 1446), all unite in attributing the quarterly coat of lions passant to the native princes of North Wales.

Welsh dynastic history ceases when the truncated remains of Llywelyn were laid within the precincts of sequestered Abbey Cwm Hir in 1282. But his heraldry was not buried with him, and, as we shall see, re-emerged in the sixteenth century and again in the twentieth, to occupy a position of particular honour.

A word must be said, in passing, about the arms of Owen Glyndwr whose sword brought him the temporary sovereignty of the land over which his ancestors had once ruled. After he had assumed the title of Prince of Wales, shortly after 1400, a Great Seal was manufactured for him, and on this his shield of arms showed quarterly, four lions rampant, an arrangement based, seemingly, on the old coat of Gwynedd.[5] The

---

[1] *Archaeologia*, xxxix. 381: see A. R Wagner, *Catalogue . . .* p. 8, and *passim* for dating of the rolls.

[2] *The Genealogist*, N.S. vols. 3, 4, 5.   [3] *Vide* Wagner, op. cit., p. 16.

[4] *St. George Roll*, i. 7, which also assigns these arms to *William* ap Griffith, but no man named William (or Gwilym) occurs in the genealogies of the House of Gwynedd.

[5] T. Matthews, op. cit., pp. 120–1: A. R. Wagner, *Historic Heraldry*, 1939, p. 56.

tinctures of this coat are not known from contemporary evidence, but in view of certain lines written by Iolo Goch, it is not unlikely that they too were adapted from the Gwyneddan arms. In a poem addressed to Owen, then a fugitive, Iolo refers to his quarterly shield and urges him to voyage overseas with a fleet to rally to his support, amongst others, the Irish, for, says Iolo, the emblem most welcomed by that people is 'the gold and red upon the sail', and he then tells Owen 'to dignify the pensel[1] of Llywelyn' with those two colours:

> Gorau arwydd gan Wyddyl
> Melyn a choch ymlaen chwyl
> Urdda bensel Llywelyn
> Arddel hwy a'r ddeuliw hyn.[2]

Since Glyndwr claimed sovereignty by virtue of his descent from the Houses of Powys, Deheubarth, and Gwynedd, all of whom had borne lions and the gold and red colours in their arms,[3] he may have adopted the tinctures and the charges associated with the traditions of Welsh sovereignty.

The early armorists whose works we have noted, and later heralds such as Ballard (*circa* 1480) and Le Neve (*circa* 1500), all considered these arms to belong to the Princes of Wales, and that Wales in this context meant North Wales, that is, ancient Gwynedd. The compiler of a Tudor armorial, about 1520,[4] who assigned the quarterly coat to 'Gladius the Prynce of Wales's doughter', did so because he knew that King Henry VIII was the representative of Llywelyn the Great by virtue of the descent of his mother (Elizabeth of York) from Gwladys Ddu[5] wife of Roger Mortimer. The sixteenth-century Welsh armorials are consistent in their descriptions of the arms of the thirteenth-century Gwyneddan princes—'Efo a dduc maes o gowls ac aur yn chwarteroc llew aur passant yn y gowls a llew o gowls passant yn yr aur a'u kynffonnau oddiwrthynt' (He bears a field of *gules* and *or* quarterly, a gold lion passant in the *gules*,

---

[1] Pensel, an old word meaning a pennant.   [2] Ashton, *Gweithiau Iolo Goch*, pp. 212, 215.
[3] Powys, *or* a lion rampant *gules*: Deheubarth, *gules* a lion rampant *or*, a border engrailed *or*: Gwynedd we have described. These colours and the lions appear in the arms of the royal houses of England, Scotland, Normandy, Flanders, Holland, Denmark, Norway, etc. Were the colours and the lions regarded as pertaining to royalty in early times? Did the Welsh princes model their arms on those of the Plantagenets?
[4] De Walden, *Two Tudor Books of Arms*, p. 230: also De Walden, *Banners, Standards, and Badges from a Tudor MSS*, p. 22.
[5] Daughter of Llywelyn the Great.

and a red lion passant in the *or*, their tails (pointing) away from them).[1]
At a later period they came to be accepted as the arms of the whole of
Wales, that is, of the Wales of the thirteen counties.

The Tudors were the first to make official use of the Welsh arms that
had slumbered since 1282. Among the coats of arms of Henry VIII,
depicted on folio 90 of 'Prince Arthur's Book', preserved in the College
of Arms, is a shield quarterly (*or*) and (*gules*) four lions statant guardant
(counterchanged).[2] Another Tudor manuscript preserved at the College
contains a royal armorial shield on which is placed, in pretence, an
escutcheon quarterly, 1st and 4th, *argent* three lions passant coward *gules*;
2nd and 3rd, quarterly *gules* and *or* four lions passant guardant counterchanged.[3] The old coat of Gwynedd, described as 'The Banner of Wales',
was borne by Lord Bindon at the funeral of Queen Elizabeth,[4] and it
appeared on a shield at the base of her monument in Westminster Abbey.

The Stuarts also used the Gwyneddan coat, which was painted on
the charter of King James I, dated 4 June 1610, whereby he created his
son Henry Prince of Wales,[5] and at that Prince's funeral in 1612 Sir
John Wynn of Gwydir bore a banner of the same arms. Banners repre-
senting Wales were borne at royal funerals in later times. For instance,
the directions governing the funeral of Queen Mary in 1695 contained
the following instructions concerning the carrying of her ensigns: 'The
Banner of Chester by a Baron, *The Banner of Wales* by a Viscount. The
Banner of France and of England, Quarterly, by an Earl. The Banner of
England singly, by an Elder Earl of a Marquis or a Duke. The great
Banner of England, Scotland, France, and Ireland, by a Duke. . . .
Ordered that the Banner of Chester, Cornwall, and *Wales* be carried
in the State and precede the Scotch and Irish Nobility, by a Baron,
an Earl's Eldest Son, and a Viscount, and *the Banner of Wales* in the
Middle. . . .' Unfortunately the 'Banner of Wales' is not described in
detail in these instructions, but it seems reasonable to conclude that it
displayed the lions of Gwynedd.

[1] N.L.W. Peniarth MS. 138, fol. 99: Peniarth MS. 135, fol. 320: Mostyn MS. 149.

[2] *Heralds' Commemorative Exhibition*, London, 1936, No. 108. 'Prince Arthur's Book' was
mainly written temp. Henry VII, with later additions.

[3] *Archaeologia*, xxxix. 407–13, citing College of Arms MS. 2 G 4.

[4] *Vetusta Monumenta* (Soc. of Antiq.), vol. iii (1796), pl. xviii, drawn by Camden: this
banner is also reproduced on the frontispiece of vol. ii of Dwnn's *Heraldic Visitations of
Wales*, ed. Meyrick, Llandovery.

[5] B.M. Add. MS. 36932.

After that time they disappeared from royal heraldry until 1911, when they were placed, by the order of King George V, in an inescutcheon on the arms of Edward Prince of Wales, being then specifically described as 'the arms of Wales'.[1]

(b) The 'Lions Coward'

At one period three lions coward seem to have been regarded as the arms of Wales, and since such arms have been engraved on the seals of at least two of the Princes, it becomes necessary to investigate their history in some detail.

The seal of Edward Prince of Wales, 1471–83, shows on the obverse the Prince mounted on a charger, bearing on his shield and horse trappers three lions regardant coward in pale; and on the reverse the same arms occur on a shield surmounted by a prince's coronet, while two crouching lions each holding an ostrich feather do duty as supporters.[2] On the sword of state of the same Prince, preserved in the British Museum, are engraved six shields, of which five can be accounted for. The sixth shield, charged with three lions coward as described in the preceding seal, has been considered to stand for Wales since none of the others on the sword represent that country.

The seal of Arthur Prince of Wales (1489–1502) contains identical lions, the supporters being two dragons.[3]

The only other example of their use on an official seal which has come to my notice, is the seal for Wales of King James I, manufactured in 1603. This contains a shield of the royal arms, supported by two lions sejant guardant with their tails between their legs.[4]

Prior to the time of Prince Edward and Prince Arthur the royal arms differenced with a label had done service for the Prince of Wales. Whence came this new coat? Why was it adopted?

It seems safe to assume that the coat was intended to represent Wales, an assumption which is strengthened by the literary evidence. According to a manuscript compiled during the reign of Henry VI (1422–61) the arms of the Prince of Wales are *argent* three lions passant reguardant coward in pale, *gules*; the same arms are superscribed 'Armys de Walys'

---

[1] *Vide infra*, pp. 196–7.
[2] Engraved in *Archaeologia*, vol. xx, and discussed further in vol. xxix.
[3] Ibid.   [4] B.M. *Catalogue of Seals*, Birch, No. 5564: B.M. Seal, xlviii. 155.

in *Creswick's Roll* (*circa* 1445–6); and in the *Vermandois Roll* as 'dargent a iii leons de geules passans savoin lun sur lautre a queue entortillu dedans lune des jambes du leon de derriere'.[1]

The herald, William Ballard, who wrote about 1480, describes the following coats: (i) 'Prins of North Wallis', *argent* three lions passant reguardant coward in pale, *gules*. (ii) 'The Prynce of Sowthe Wallis', *gules* three chevrons *argent*, in chief two lions rampant facing inwards *or*. (iii) 'The Prynce off Walys', *or* and *gules* four lions rampant counterchanged.[2] From this it is clear that (i) and (ii) were regarded as the arms of native Welsh princes, and (iii) as those of the Princes of Wales. About 1460, another herald attributed the coward lions to 'the Prynce of Wales', alongside which a later hand has added the words 'Howel Dda',[3] a Welsh ruler who lived nearly two hundred years before the introduction of heraldry. *Writhe's Book* (*circa* 1530) attributes them to 'the Prince of North Wales', and in another shield a baton *azure* bruises the lions.

According to T. W. King, sometime Rouge Dragon Pursuivant, the lions coward, described as those of Rhodri Mawr (d. 877), occur in a number of armorials in the College of Arms. One of the manuscripts cited by King (College of Arms MS. 2 G 4) contains a shield of Queen Elizabeth charged with the arms of Saxon princes, on which is placed an escutcheon of pretence, quarterly, 1st and 4th *argent* three lions passant reguardant coward *gules*; 2nd and 3rd the arms of Gwynedd (*or* and *gules* four lions passant counterchanged).[4] The Tudor armorists certainly noticed this coat, and were in no doubt as to its ownership. For instance, one writer in a British Museum manuscript[5] recorded: 1. *argent* three lions passant reguardant coward *gules*—'Prince of Wales'; 2. France and England quarterly, a label of three points *argent*, each file charged with three torteaux—'The Prince'.[6]

The same attribution occurs at the end of the Tudor period, and a manuscript compiled in 1604 by (Sir) William Segar, Garter, and in possession of Sir Samuel Rush Meyrick in 1841, contained the shield of the lions coward said to have been borne by 'Brute' (Brutus, the

---

[1] See S. V. L. Collins, 'Continental Medieval Rolls', *Antiquaries Journal*, xxi (1941), p. 205.
[2] See B.M. Harl. MS. 6085.
[3] *R.H. No.* 523: I have to thank Mr. T. D. Tremlett for this reference.
[4] *Archaeologia*, xxix. 407–13.
[5] Harl. MS. 6163: see De Walden, *Two Tudor Books of Arms*, p. 131.
[6] Ibid.

eponymous ancestor of the Britons). After this time they are discontinued in English armorials as also in the arms and seals of Princes of Wales.

In this matter the Welsh evidence must be considered decisive. We have searched in vain for the coward lions in the great Welsh heraldic compilations in the National Library of Wales, at the Cardiff Free Library, in the British Museum, and in journals produced by Welsh learned societies. H. R. Hughes of Kinmel, eminent in the last century as an authority on Welsh heraldry, stated that the coat of the lions coward was never assigned to, nor borne by, any of the Welsh princes. With that view the present writer concurs. Anarawd ap Rhodri Mawr, Howel Dda, Iago ap Idwal, and Gruffydd ap Cynan are said to have borne *argent* three lions passant regardant in pale *gules* (the colours being sometimes transposed),[1] but in no case are the animals shown as coward. The only example of a Welsh coat containing a lion coward is the one occasionally assigned to Llywelyn Aurdorchog, a chieftain of Ial, namely, 'arian, llew passant wyneb gyfan o aur ai arveu or gouls ai gynphon druy ei afl tros ei gefn tu ai din'.[2]

The available evidence indicates that somewhere around 1450 English heralds originated this coat and attributed it to certain Welsh dynasties. It is an egg laid by an English cuckoo. No historical basis whatsoever exists for it, and one regrets that E. A. Ebblewhite thought fit to recall from limbo this heraldic pretender to decorate the casket presented by the Welsh people to the Prince and Princess of Wales at Caernarvon on 11 July 1894.[3] It occupied no place in the heraldic decorations of Caernarvon Castle, designed by the better-informed E. E. Dorling on the occasion of the investiture of the Prince of Wales in 1911.

(c) *The Red Dragon*

What is the origin of the dragon emblem? Was it ever borne on banners that waved over the Ancient Britons and the fighting men of medieval Wales? Did it appear on the ensigns of their princes? When did it become the national emblem of Wales? Was it exclusively a Welsh symbol? These are some of the questions asked from time to time, and in this brief review an effort will be made to answer them.

[1] e.g. Golden Grove MS., Peniarth MS. 138, Mostyn MS. 149, Cardiff MS. 4, 265.
[2] Mostyn MSS. 113, 149.
[3] See his unconvincing remarks in *Arch. Cam.*, 1895, pp. 191–2.

In early times the dragon appeared variously as a winged serpent of aggressive appearance, possessing two or four legs, and, during the Middle Ages, with very small wings or none at all. Prior to the Tudor period both its tongue and tail were blunt-ended, but during that period these extremities became barbed or spiked while the wings developed into large enveloping bat-like members. In time a distinction, possibly heraldic in origin, arose between two varieties—the two-legged animal came to be known as a wyvern, the four-legged one as a dragon.

A ubiquitous creature, the dragon is found in the myth and legend of all countries in Europe and Asia, and occupies no inconsiderable place in the literature and art of Antiquity.[1] In Classical legends, in addition to fearsome and destructive dragons, such as the hydra and chimaera, there were also beneficent ones like the dragon that guarded the apples of the Hesperides, and the serpents of the temples of Aesculapius.

The Romans used it as an emblem of war, and Flavius Vagitius towards the close of the fourth century of our era mentions among the Roman military ensigns the *draco* which had been adopted from the Parthians after Trajan's conquest.[2] The standard-bearer of the cohort was called the *draconarius*, the symbol being attached to a gilded staff.

Archaeological evidence reveals that brooches and pins, fashioned in the form of a stylized dragon-like animal, were worn by continental Celts during the La Tène period (*circa* 500 B.C.–A.D. 1), and fibulae, richly enamelled 'dragon brooches', Celtic in form and origin, were worn by the island Britons during the Roman occupation.[3] Later, Christianity helped to perpetuate its memory, for the 'great red dragon' appears as the fearful monster of the Revelation, in the legends of the saints, such as that of St. George, and in other ecclesiastical lore, always as a symbol of evil. Since it occupied a prominent place in the art, literature, and mythology of Greece and Rome, of Norse and Teuton lands, there were several channels by which it could have been introduced into Britain—migrating Celts, invading Romans, conquering Anglo-Saxons, Norse settlers, or Christian missionaries, for the dragon belonged to them all.[4]

[1] See Du Cange, *Glossarium*, s.v. 'Draco'; *Encyclopaedia Britannica*, s.v. 'Dragon'. 'Serpent Worship'; G. Elliot Smith, *Evolution of the Dragon*, London, 1919; and J. Vinycomb, *Fictitious and Symbolic Creatures in Art*, London, 1906.   [2] *De Re Militari*, iii. 5.

[3] F. Haverfield, *The Roman Occupation of Britain*, Oxford, 1924, p. 24.

[4] It has survived in English folk-lore in the 'Lambton worm' and the 'dragon of Wantage',

There is every likelihood that the *draco* and the *draconarius* of the Romans were familiar to the Britons, particularly as we know that the Welsh used the word *draig/dragon* figuratively to denote a leader, warrior, hero, chief, ruler, prince. But this does not mean that the Romans introduced it into British imagery; the Britons may well have brought it with them from their continental homelands.

Several references to the animal occur in the works of the sixth- and seventh-century poets collectively known as Cynfeirdd. A line in the Gododdin of Aneurin alludes to a *red* dragon:

> Ar *rud dhreic* fud pharaon,

being probably a reference to the imprisoned dragons at Dinas Emrys,[1] and in another part of the same poem both *dreic* and *dragon* are used for leader or chief. Thus we learn that

> Gwernabwy, son of Gwen, after the wine feast
> Was a dragon in battle (at) the strife of Cattraeth,[2]

and the poet also refers to the feast of a leading dragon (*o gwyn dragon ducaut*).[3]

The sixth-century Gildas castigates the North Wales prince Maelgwn Gwynedd as *insularis draco*, words meant to indicate the qualities that distinguished that vigorous ruler,[4] and in no way to be interpreted as a 'title' as some modern writers would affect to believe. Nennius, writing about the year 800, describes the famous combat in a deep pit between the *white* and *red* dragons, representing the English and Welsh respectively,[5] a story repeated by Geoffrey of Monmouth *circa* 1136. This is set forth in the Welsh version of Geoffrey's *History* as follows: 'Gwae hi y *dreic coch*, kanys y haball yssyd yn bryssyaw. y gogofeu hi aachub y *dreic wen* yr hon a arwydockau ysaeson . . . y *dreic coch* a arwydockaa kenedyl y brytanyeit'.[6] A more literary form occurs in the tale of Lludd and Llevelys.[7]

---

for instance, and in numerous Welsh legends. See further M. Trevelyan, *Folk-lore and Folk-Stories of Wales*, London, 1909, ch. xiii.

[1] *Canu Aneirin*, ed. Ifor Williams, Cardiff, 1938, p. 36, l. 1432, and n. on p. 379.

[2] Ibid., p. 12, ll. 289–9; cf. also l. 297, *dreic ehelaeth*.

[3] Ibid., p. 10, l. 243.   [4] Gildas, *De Excidio*, chs. 33–36.

[5] Nennius, *Hist.*, ch. 42. See also Zimmer, *Nennius Vindicatus*, Berlin, 1893, p. 268, n.

[6] *Hist. Reg. Brit.*, Book vii cap. 3.

[7] *The Mabinogion*, trans. G. and T. Jones, 1949, p. 89.

Thus the view that the red dragon represented the Welsh is certainly as old as A.D. 800, perhaps as old as the sixth century if the *rud dhreic* of Aneurin means *draig rhudd* (ruddy dragon). As a result of the introduction of heraldry into Britain the dragon assumes a new significance. Anglo-Norman writers of the twelfth century associated dragons with the Welsh. Wace, in 1155, describes King Arthur's helm,

> . . . ensom ot portrait un dragon . . .[1]

while Robert of Gloucester describes the same king,

> Wyth helm of gold on ys heued, (nas nour hym ylych)
> The fourme of a dragon thereon was ycast.

Of course this is no proof that Arthur ever bore a dragon emblem, but merely that twelfth-century writers were assigning such an emblem to him.

All the earliest Welsh references associate the dragon with war-leaders and with fighting. The compositions of the Court-poets, the Gogynfeirdd,[2] contain numerous examples of the use of the word *draic/dragon*, also associated with war. The princes and nobles are said to defend Wales with the strength and tenacity of the dragon. Meilir Brydydd (*circa* 1137) calls Gruffydd ap Cynan the 'dragon of Gwynedd'; to Gwalchmai (*circa* 1140–80) the prince Madoc ap Maredudd was the 'dragon of Powys'; Cynddelw Brydydd Mawr (*circa* 1155–1200) says that Owain Gwynedd opposed 'the white dragon from the east' (i.e. the English), the household troops of Prince Madoc ap Maredydd of Powys appeared to him as 'a dragon-wall', the Lord Rhys as 'the lion-dragon, prince of dragons', Hywel ap Owain as 'penn dragon'. The prince-bard Owain Cyfeiliog (*circa* 1140–97) speaks of 'the dragon of generous Owain ap Cynfyn's line'; to Prydydd y Moch (*circa* 1173–1220), Llywelyn the Great is 'Pendragon' and 'Dragon of Britain'; in an early fourteenth-century poem by Einion Offeiriad we are told that Sir Rhys ap Gruffydd is a 'swift dragon' (*rugldhraig*) in battle.[3] An early Welsh hero, Uthir, is usually accorded the description 'pendragon', and he appears in the *Black Book of Carmarthen*[4]

[1] *Roman de Brut*, ed. Roux de Liney, 1838, l. 9521.
[2] *Llawysgrif Hendregadredd*, ed. J. Morris Jones and T. H. Parry-Williams, Cardiff, 1933: *The Poetry of the Gogynfeirdd*, ed. E. Anwyl, Denbigh, 1909.
[3] Poem edited by (Sir) Ifor Williams in *Y Cymmrodor*, xxvi (1916), p. 134.
[4] Edited by J. Gwenogvryn Evans, Pwllheli, 1907, p. 94. 7.

as *uthir pen dragon*, but its conversion into a 'title' lacks any historical basis.

The poetry of fourteenth-century Iolo Goch bristles with references to the animal. Between 1395 and 1398 he wrote an ode to Mortimer Earl of March, descendant of the dynasty of Gwynedd, calling him 'our dragon', 'dragon of the islands', 'the dragon-heir', and reminding him that 'the blood of the *red* dragon (y ddraic koch) is the sinobr in your veins'.[1] He describes the tinctures in Mortimer's armorial achievement, the gold representing France, the white England:

> Yn achen y ddraig wen wiw
> Rawnllaes y mae'r arianlliw,

the red representing Wales, for the blood of the red dragon runs in the Earl's veins,

> Gwodrudd cerdd, gwaed y ddraig goch
> Yw'r sinobr ysy ynoch,

and the blue representing Ireland.[2]

The illustrious ancestry of the young Earl of March, Heir Apparent of Richard II, was one to conjure with, his pedigree a political document of decisive import. Iolo was not the only contemporary to proclaim and emphasize those antecedents, for Adam of Usk, before his conversion to Bolingbroke's cause, proved himself a stout propagandist of the genealogical claims of Mortimer. A manuscript compiled at Wigmore Abbey towards the end of the fourteenth century contains a detailed genealogy of the Mortimers, tracing them to Norman and Saxon kings, through Gwladys Ddu to the House of Gwynedd, Cadwaladr the Blessed, and ultimately to Brutus. Laid out in codex form, it is prefaced with the traditional chronicle of the founding of Britain by Brutus, illuminated with Mortimer heraldry, and on folio 55 with a two-legged dragon, a long sinuous blunt-tailed creature, red head and pointed ears, red legs, the top of its blue wing and its underparts being pale red. Although displayed in decorative rather than heraldic form, there can be little doubt that it was intended to symbolize the Welsh connexion which occupies so prominent a place in the manuscript.[3] In the fifteenth

---

[1] H. Lewis, T. Roberts, I. Williams, *Iolo Goch ac Eraill*, Cardiff, 1937, p. 45. The Earl of March was descended from Gwladys Ddu daughter of Llywelyn the Great. 'Sinobr' (*recte* sinobl), an old heraldic word for 'red'.   [2] *Iolo Goch ac Eraill*, p. 47.

[3] *Studies in Chaucer and his Audience*, by Mary Giffin, Associate Professor of English, Vassar

century, Tudur Aled describes Sir Rhys ap Thomas as 'Draig Urien',[1] and refers to the red and white dragons of the Lludd and Llyvelys tale.[2]

Many more examples could be cited,[3] for there are few poems composed by medieval Welshmen which did not contain some reference to the dragon, but sufficient have been called to bear witness to its position in Welsh tradition. So far, our examples have been confined mainly to literature and bardic vocabulary; I now turn to its appearance in the heraldry of medieval Wales.

Owen Glyndwr, provider of themes for poets and orators, moralists, historians, and dramatists, was well versed in heraldry, particularly its military usages, having served in the campaigns of Richard II, and testified in the celebrated case of *Scrope* v. *Grosvenor* relating to the disputed ownership of the coat with a golden bend on a blue shield. Glyndwr's Great Seal, made in the heyday of his success, in 1404 or thereabouts, shows a wyvern statant with wings raised, on his helm and on his charger's head, and also appears as a sinister supporter to his shield of arms.[4] We do not know the colours of these wyverns, but when he attacked Caernarvon in 1401, a contemporary tells us 'there in the midst of a great host (he) unfurled his standard, a golden dragon on a white field'.[5] This is the only contemporary evidence we have of a Welshman displaying a dragon in heraldic form in the Middle Ages. As already indicated the red dragon had been accounted a Welsh beast many centuries previously, and the line penned by a fifteenth-century bard, *Y Ddraig Goch ddyry cychwyn*,[6] came to be adopted as a motto of the Welsh nation in later

College, Quebec, Canada, 1965, for private distribution, p. 94 et seq.; fol. 55 of Wigmore MS. (now in the University of Chicago Library) is reproduced in colour (pl. vii). See also M. E. Giffin, 'A Wigmore Manuscript at the University of Chicago'. *N.L.W. Journal*, vii (1952), pp. 316–25.

[1] *Tudur Aled*, i. 78. Urien Rheged was an ancestor of Sir Rhys.

[2] Ibid. ii. 395.

[3] e.g. *Howel Swrdwal a'i Fab Ieuan*, and *Gruffydd ab Ieuan*, Bangor, 1908 and 1910, both edited by J. C. Morris. See especially, J. Lloyd-Jones, *Geirfa Barddoniaeth Gynnar Gymraeg*, Cardiff, 1946, s.n. 'dragon', 'dreic'.

[4] For this seal see *Archaeologia*, xxv. 616; Gilbert Stone, *Wales*, London, 1915, p. 378: *Arch. Cam.* N.S. (1851), ii. 121–2, iv. 193–201; *Trans. Shropshire Arch. Soc.* Series 3, iii (1903), p. 163: T. Matthews, *Welsh Records in Paris*, Carmarthen, 1910, pp. 120–1: A. R. Wagner, *Historic Heraldry*, 1939, p. 56.

[5] *Chronicon Adae de Usk*, ed. E. Maunde Thompson, 1904 (R.S.), p. 71. No rule prohibiting the use of 'colour on colour' and 'metal on metal' existed in medieval times.

[6] It occurs in a poem by Deio ab Ieuan Du (fl. 1460–80). See *Gorchestion Beirdd Cymru*, Shrewsbury, 1773, p. 177.

times. The tendency to see heraldic significance in bardic references must be resisted, for 'dragon', as we have seen, formed only a conventional description, part of the stock-in-trade of a myriad bards.

Curiously, the animal never became popular in Welsh heraldry, and with one exception is never found in Cymric shields until the present century. None of the numerous landed families who derived from the Five Royal and Fifteen Noble Tribes, and from other great chieftains, adopted the dragon as an heraldic charge. Despite its close association with Welsh tradition, with Owen Glyndwr, and with the Tudors, it never found general favour. Only during this present century has the dragon become established in the heraldry of Wales.

The dragon reached its noontide glory during the sixteenth century when it became very much a Tudor animal. Why did the Tudors give such prominence to it? Did they consciously revive it as a symbol of their connexion with Wales, or were they continuing English usage? As we have seen, the red dragon was common to both nations, and since the Tudors descended from Celt and Plantagenet they could claim, with perfect propriety, the heraldic honours of both ancestral groups. In 1902 Fox-Davies in a long and singularly unconvincing paper[1] sought to prove that Henry VII derived it from the Lancastrians and that it had no connexion with Wales. Our leading heraldic authority, Sir Anthony Wagner, in a letter to me (dated 14 April 1953) says that the herald Anstis quotes European writers as stating that the English dragon supporter of Tudor times derived from St. George's dragon. However, as the beast slain by the national patron of Englishmen represented evil, it is difficult to imagine that a personification of it should have been elevated to an honourable position in any arms, royal arms least of all. The whole question is not without difficulties, but the impression that I have gained is that the Tudors displayed the dragon as a compliment to their Welsh ancestry and a gesture to their Welsh supporters. Indeed Henry VII created a special officer of arms whose name perpetuates its memory, namely Rouge Dragon Pursuivant, an appointment that continues to be made in the Heralds' College.

The Tudors did not derive the animal from their Welsh ancestors who had lived in heraldic days. They traced to the chieftain Marchudd, whose assigned arms were *gules* a giant's head erased at the neck proper,

[1] *The Genealogical Magazine*, vi. 235 et seq.

which Ednyfed Fychan (died 1246) a descendant of Marchudd, is said to have changed for *gules* three Englishmen's heads in profile, to commemorate a battle during which he slew three English captains. A popular story relates that later on, when Maredudd father of Owen Tudor[1] settled in London, he deemed it inadvisable to exhibit arms that might have aroused tempestuous emotions in the breasts of even phlegmatic Englishmen, and rather than tempt Providence he replaced the gory heads with three closed helmets. However, there is evidence that these helmets were borne on the shield of Gronw Fychan (died 1382) uncle of Owen Tudor, in the late fourteenth century,[2] but I have seen no example of its use by Maredudd or by his son Owen Tudor. Statements by modern writers that Owen discarded the helmets and adopted the red dragon are without warrant.[3]

The earliest known connexion between the Tudors and the dragon occurred when Edmund and Jasper Tudor adopted it as a crest and supporter to the modified version of the royal arms granted to them by their half-brother Henry VI. Those arms were, quarterly 1st and 4th, France (modern) but the lilies arranged 1 and 2; 2nd and 3rd, three lions passant guardant; the whole being enclosed within a border semee of martlets.[4] The tails of the dragon's supporters and crest were blunt, the spiked extremities being a later development. At Bosworth one of the standards of Henry VII was 'the red fierye dragon beaten upon white and greene sarcenet', afterwards offered at the altar of St. Paul's Cathedral as a thanksgiving for the victory.[5] Another of his standards showed the same animal, passant, breathing flames, placed on a field divided horizontally green and white, the background being powdered with flames, white and red roses, and golden fleur-de-lis.[6] He further introduced the dragon as a dexter supporter to the royal arms and the animal was carved on his tomb in Westminster Abbey.

[1] Owen Tudor's agnatic descent runs as follows: Owen Tudor ap Maredudd ap Tudur Fychan ap Gronwy ap Tudur hen ap Gronwy ap Ednyfed Fychan, and so back to Marchudd.

[2] The monument of Gronw Tudor at Penmynydd has a shield charged with a chevron between three tilting helms. See *Anc. Mon. Anglesey*, pls. 85 and 86.

[3] One of the banners borne at the funeral of Elizabeth, queen of Henry VII, charged with the head of a warrior enclosed in a helmet, may have been a badge derived from the Tudor coat. See also Willement, *Regal Heraldry*, p. 64.

[4] Arms of Jasper Tudor, Duke of Bedford, B.M. Seals, lxxx. 77, 78: see also *Archaeologia*, xviii. 429, and *Journal of the British Archaeological Association*, xiv (1858), pp. 56–60.

[5] Hall, *Chronicle*.   [6] De Walden, *Banners*, etc., pp. 78, 80.

It is likely, then, that the Tudors adopted the dragon to demonstrate their Welsh connexion, for they were not indifferent to their antecedents. Henry VII ordered an inquiry into his agnatic ancestry by expert genealogists, resulting in a magnificent pedigree in which the name and fame of the seventh-century king, Cadwaladr the Blessed, occupied a position of prominence.[1] Two manuscripts compiled *circa* 1520 contain a picture of a two-legged red dragon with golden underparts, supporting a blue banner charged with a gold cross formy fitchy, assigned to 'Le Roy Cadwalader'.[2]

The Tudor descent from Ednyfed Fychan and Marchudd was no passport to sovereignty, the former being a competent servant of a Welsh prince, the latter one of the many chieftains of whom nothing is known beyond their names. Marchudd himself did not trace to Cadwaladr, but one of his descendants married a princess of South Wales, and her descent from Cadwaladr was carefully outlined in the pedigree drawn out for Henry VII.[3] This distaff connexion enabled the Tudors to place their feet on steps that led to the royal dais. The traditions and legends of Cadwaladr had never been forgotten, the bards had seen to that, so that descent from him constituted a potent political force in Wales and the Marches. The acquisition of the dragon was the Tudor way of symbolizing descent from early Celtic royalty. Theirs was the dragon of Cadwaladr, not only the dragon of Wales or of the Welsh. The Tudors were not merely Welshmen who had 'made good'; they were the heirs of Cadwaladr. Such was the outlook of this astute dynasty which strove to find legality for its actions even in legends.

The dragon served as a supporter in the arms of every Tudor sovereign except Mary. At Prince Arthur's wedding in 1501 'a red dragon dredfull' appeared on flags, decorations, and in other forms of display that accompanied that event;[4] among the drooping pennons borne at the obsequies of the same prince were 'the arms of Wales' and 'the arms of Cadwalader', and a dragon supports his shield on the tomb in Worcester. At the funeral of the last Tudor monarch, the standard carried by Lord Bourchier displayed a red dragon passant with raised wings and a barbed tail.[5]

---

[1] L. Dwnn, *Heraldic Visitations*, ed. S. R. Meyrick, Llandovery, 1846, i, preface.
[2] De Walden, *Banners*, etc., p. 33, from MS. I. 2. fol. 3 in the College of Arms. It also occurs in 'Prince Arthur's Book', p. 95, cited by H. S. London in *Royal Beasts*, p. 44.
[3] L. Dwnn, op. cit., i, p. xvi.
[4] *Antiquarian Repertory*, p. 241; Leland, *Collectanea*, iv. 225.
[5] *Vetusta Monumenta* (Soc. of Antiquaries), vol. iii (1796), pl. xviii, drawing by Camden.

A few words about the colour of the dragon becomes necessary here, in view of a change said to have taken place by the end of the Tudor period. We know that the red dragon of the English at Hastings was garnished with gold, the one ordered by Henry III being red 'sparkling with gold', while the 'fiery' dragon borne at Crécy may have presented a similar appearance. Henry Tudor's flag at Bosworth was 'the red fiery dragon'. The underparts—the breast and belly of the red dragon of Cadwaladr—were shown as gold, and this combination of colours seem to have been the normal method of presenting the animal during Tudor times. The red dragons shown in 'Prince Arthur's Book' (*c.* 1520) and in the Tudor manuscripts printed in De Walden's *Banners*, all have golden underparts, and it would appear that this had become an established convention by, or in, the reign of Henry VIII. It may have been an effort to produce a naturalistic effect, for the underparts of reptilean creatures are generally of yellowish colour, and the fifteenth-century poet, Lewis Glyn Cothi, in one of his poems actually speaks of

> A gold brigandine like the casting of a dragon's skin.

Another bard, Rhys Goch Eryri, between the years 1385 and 1448, describes the dragon's colour as similar to a hearthful of fire in a smithy, a significant comparison for such a fire is not composed of lambent flames, but of a golden-red glow. In the same poem in which he sends a 'red dragon' to Sir William Thomas (Herbert) of Raglan to collect certain presents he says:

> Y ddraig bob arynaig bobl
> Olau son o liw sinobl
> Gefail deg oreufail dan
> Gwrelbais gu o'r Alban.
> I'r Brytaniaid lle caid cawdd,
> Y'th rodded, egni a'th ruddawdd
> Llafn marwor briw ffriw dy ffrwyn,
> Unllif aur, yn llawforwyn. . . .
> I genedl. . . .
> Gamber. . . .
> Cywir dy lwybr uwch wybrwynt.[1]
> Y ddraig goch oedd rywiog gynt.

[1] *Cywyddau Iolo Goch ac Eraill*, 1937, p. 173.

There seems to have been a dragon of gold also, not one merely garnished with that metal. Owen Glyndwr's war standard in 1401 showed a golden dragon, and the bard Dafydd Nanmor in a poem to the two sons of Owen Tudor says that the *draig velen* (the yellow or golden dragon) will overthrow the white dragon.[1] The only other examples known to me concern Queen Elizabeth I, whose arms in B.M. Harl. MS. 6096 contain as sinister supporter a golden dragon depicted with red colour along its back-scales, breast, belly, and legs,[2] and a later writer states that she 'changed' the dragon from red to gold.[3] But these sources are of uncertain value, and I myself have seen no conclusive evidence for the change attributed to 'Gloriana'.

With the death of Queen Elizabeth I, the dragon disappeared from the royal arms. Nevertheless, the animal remained on departmental seals,[4] such as those for the King's Bench, the Court of Wards and Liveries, Exchequer and King's Bench seals for Ireland, and for the Great Sessions of Wales. Numerous examples of seals of the Great Sessions (1542–1830) have survived, and a fine one, attached to a document dated 1619, preserved among the archives of the county of Carmarthen, shows the dexter supporter to the royal arms as a dragon gorged with a prince's coronet, a chain attached thereto reflexed over the animal's back, the sinister supporter being a goat. Dragon supporters, each holding an ostrich feather, continued to appear on the seals for the earldom of Chester.[5]

Early in the nineteenth century the dragon once more received royal attention. In 1807, after the union of the parliaments of Great Britain and Ireland, it was declared, *inter alia*, that a red dragon passant standing on a mound should be the King's badge for Wales. About a hundred years later, King Edward VII assigned this badge, differenced with a silver label, to the Prince of Wales. Today it forms one of the badges of His Royal Highness Prince Charles, Prince of Wales.

[1] T. Roberts and Ifor Williams, *The Poetical Works of Dafydd Nanmor*, Cardiff, 1923, poem xiii, lines 57–59.

[2] See Willement, *Royal Heraldry*, p. 81.

[3] Sylvanus Morgan, *Armilogia*, p. 189.

[4] See H. Jenkinson, 'The Great Seal of England: Deputed or Departmental Seals', *Archaeologia*, lxxxv. 293–338, and A. B. Tonnochy, *Catalogue of British Seal Dies in the British Museum*, 1952.

[5] e.g. seal of Charles, Prince of Wales, as Earl of Chester, in 1616, *B.M. Catalogue* (Birch), No. 4809. The dragon occurs in the present arms of the Carmarthenshire County Council.

This dissertation would be incomplete without mention of the flag of Wales. The earliest reference to a dragon standard borne in war by Welsh troops is Adam of Usk's description of Owen Glyndwr's white standard charged with a golden dragon which he bore before the walls of Caernarvon in 1401. The next, in point of time, is to the red dragon on a ground of white and green borne by Henry Tudor at Bosworth in 1485, and this is the first example we possess of a *red* dragon being borne by a Welshman, if so we may term the first Tudor king.

Some four centuries elapsed before the Welsh raised this standard again, but when it did reappear it was hailed everywhere as 'the flag of Wales', and there can be no doubt, that, historically, the adoption of the dragon ensign is in perfect accord with the ancient traditions of our land. When the Prince of Wales was invested at Caernarvon Castle in 1911, his standard bearer, Sir Watkin Wynn, bore a red dragon passant on a plain white field.

There are two versions of the flag—(1) *argent*, on a base *vert*, a dragon passant, wings raised, *gules*; and (2) a dragon as above, placed on a field parted fessways *argent* and *vert*.

The College of Arms did not recognize these manifestations, and in 1914 Garter King of Arms stated, '. . . There is no authority for it: it is clearly the invention of some flag-maker. Ancient Welsh poets and chronicles assert that King Cadwaladr bore a dragon upon his fighting banner, a red dragon rampant upon a white field—but such a flag is not the National Flag of Wales. Quarterly *or* and *gules*, four lions passant guardant counterchanged is the proper authorised national Flag for Wales.' This pronouncement, however, did not prove sufficient to deter the display of the dragon flag, in both its forms, on public occasions.

In 1953 Her Majesty by an Order in Council, dated 11 March, decreed that the badge should be augmented 'for the greater honour and distinction of Wales'. This took the form of a shield divided fesseways white and green, charged with a red dragon passant, the shield encircled by a white band bearing in letters of green the legend '*Y Ddraig Goch Ddyry Cychwyn*. The augmented badge in its entirety was placed on a white flag and on appropriate occasions flown over government buildings. While welcoming the mark of Royal favour so graciously bestowed the form of the augmented badge failed to find general approval. In 1958 the Gorsedd of the Bards passed a resolution in favour of recognizing the

Red Dragon flag as the national flag of Wales instead of the augmented badge so displayed. Accordingly, in February 1959, Her Majesty was pleased to command that in future 'only the Red Dragon on a green and white flag, shall be flown on Government buildings in Wales, and, where appropriate, in London'. This was announced on 23 February 1959, in the House of Commons by the Minister of Welsh Affairs, who added that the augmented badge would continue in use for 'other purposes'[1]—the words 'other purposes' presumably meaning its display as a *badge* in accordance with established heraldic procedure. The Chairman of the Council of Wales and Monmouthshire conveyed a message of gratitude to the Queen for her direction in the matter, and in April 1959 Her Majesty informed the Council that she was very glad that her decision about flying the Red Dragon flag had given pleasure.[2]

This, then, is the final answer, the correct flag of Wales—per fess *argent* and *vert* a dragon passant *gules*.

From time to time letters appear in the press complaining that Wales is not represented in the royal arms,[3] and representations are made for the inclusion of an appropriate emblem. In this omission the Welsh find themselves in good company, for neither are the English represented, because the leopards are those of Anjou, the tressured lion belongs to Scotland, the harp to Ireland. However, the excluded Welsh and English may console themselves with the knowledge that the one still possesses the dragon and the other the cross of the saint who slew it.

II. THE PLUME OF OSTRICH FEATHERS

Before I go on to discuss the arms borne by the individual Princes of Wales I propose to review the history of the Plume of Ostrich Feathers, often referred to as 'The Prince of Wales's Feathers' and 'The Prince of Wales's Crest'.

The use of ostrich feathers in royal heraldry is first found during the reign of Edward III, and from that time onwards were widely used by members of the royal house. They are shown singly, in pairs, in threes,

---

[1] *The Times* newspaper, 24 Feb. 1959.

[2] The *Western Mail* newspaper, 20 Apr. 1959.

[3] Viz. quarterly, 1st and 4th *gules* three leopards passant in pale *or*; 2nd, *or* a lion rampant within a tressure flory counterflory *gules*; 3rd, *azure* a harp *or*, stringed *argent*.

as badges, and as decorations, and many years were to pass before they assumed the form with which we are all familiar.

The circumstance of their adoption by the Plantagenets is obscure, but the best evidence suggests that they derive from the heraldry of the house of Hainault, probably from the county of Ostrevant appanage of the eldest sons of Hainault. The first association of the Plantagenets with that dynasty occured in 1329 when Edward III married Philippa daughter of William, Count of Holland and Hainault.

The earliest reference to the feathers appears in a Wardrobe Account, describing the royal plate at Windsor shortly after 1369–70. The plate was engraved with the arms of England and of Hainault, and one large alms-dish, belonging to Queen Philippa, was enamelled with 'a black escutcheon with ostrich feathers'.[1] One of Edward III's seals contained two ostrich feathers, one on either side of the shield of arms.[2] They were used heraldically by the Prince of Wales, who, in his will dated 7 June 1376, instructed his executors to place on his tomb 'our badge of peace', namely the ostrich feathers, and in the same document mentions black tapestry and vestments decorated with similar feathers. Accordingly the 'badge of peace' surmounted by the word *Houmont* was placed on the monument, the feathers being arranged singly, two and one, on a shield. Sir N. H. Nicolas cites seven of the Prince's seals, on four of which single ostrich feathers appear, seemingly as a form of decoration.

The Princess of Wales also adopted them. In her will, dated 1385, 'The Fair Maid' bequeathed a new bed of red velvet 'embroidered with ostrich feathers of silver' and other emblems to her son Richard, later Prince of Wales. They were used by some, if not all, of Edward III's sons, such as John of Gaunt whose descendants continued to display them, and also by the Black Prince's illegitimate son, Sir Roger de Clarendon, who bore *or* on a bend *sable* three ostrich feathers *argent*, the quills fixed through scrolls of gold.[3] The seal of Edward of York, son of Edmund of Langley, who fell at Agincourt, is decorated with a single feather with the words *Ich dien* on the scroll.

[1] Sir N. H. Nicolas, 'Observations on the Origin and History of the Badge and Mottoes of Edward Prince of Wales' in *Archaeologia*, xxxi (1846), pp. 350–84; and see 'Contemporary Authority for the popular idea that the Ostrich Feathers of the Princes of Wales were derived from the Crest of the King of Bohemia' in *Archaeologia*, xxxii. 332–4.

[2] *Archaeologia*, xxxi. 361, engraving.

[3] James Parker, *Glossary of Heraldry*, London, 1894, p. 238.

Richard II, when Prince of Wales, used a seal which showed a single feather engraved at the end of the legend,[1] and after he ascended the Throne occasionally used the same device. The Great Wardrobe Accounts for 1383–5 refers to one of his gowns embroidered with white ostrich feathers, and to a bed similarly decorated. Richard made a grant of two feathers, together with the assigned arms of Edward the Confessor, to his cousin Thomas (Mowbray) Duke of Norfolk, Earl Marshal of England.[2] A medieval French metrical history describing the deposition of Richard contains a coloured sketch which shows the King standing with a group of knights, one of whom bears the Royal pennon semée of ostrich feathers, and the housings of the King's charger are powdered with the same device.[3]

The foregoing examples show that the feathers were popular with the Royal Family in the second half of the fourteenth century, and although borne by two Princes of Wales during that period were by no means confined exclusively to them.

The House of Lancaster continued the use of the feathers in the next century. Henry IV placed a feather on either side of his shield in his armorial seal, and feathers are occasionally shown in the paws of crouching lions in some of his seals. His son, Henry of Monmouth, when Prince of Wales, used a single feather and scroll upheld in the beak of a swan on either side of his shield of arms,[4] and also used feathers as Duke of Cornwall and Earl of Chester. The cook of King Henry VI was inspired by the device and produced at that monarch's coronation feast a succulent dish of 'frytour garnished with a leopard's head and ii estryche feders'.[5] Feathers also occur in a list of Henry's banners and pennons in 1454–5, and a contemporary writer described one of his badges as *sable* three ostrich feathers *argent*, penned and labelled *or*.[6] His son, Edward, Prince of Wales (died 1471) used a seal of arms which contained a feather and scroll,[7] while the 'sword garnished with ostrich feathers in gold, and sometime of the prince of Wales', valued at

---

[1] Sandford, p. 190: Dinely, *Progress*, 262, sketch of seal attached to a deed dated at Carmarthen, 16 Apr. 1376.
[2] Fox-Davies, *Complete Guide* . . . , 1951 edn., p. 465, citing College of Arms MS. R 22, 67.
[3] *Archaeologia*, xx. 371, printed from B.M. Harl. MS. 1319.
[4] Sandford, p. 190.
[5] *Chronicle of London*, pp. 168–9.   [6] B.M. Harl. MS. 6163.
[7] Sandford, p. 240.

£13. 6s. 8d., mentioned in a list of Henry VI's crown jewels, had probably been borne by his son.

Although popular and widely used in the Royal Family the device as yet had not achieved a fixity of form and conformed to no rigid convention in the style of presentation. For instance the seal of Edward (V) as Prince of Wales represented the feathers with a freedom that suggested artistic rather than heraldic feeling. On the obverse of one of his seals, a single feather is affixed to the head of his charger, while the diapered background contains a sprinkling of roses and feathers: on either side of the shield of arms on the reverse is a large feather with a scroll inscribed *Ich Dien*.[1]

In the representation of Edward IV and his family shown in the window of the north transept of Canterbury Cathedral, the Prince of Wales stands before an arras divided per pale *argent* and *vert*, semee of feathers complete with scroll and motto. Perhaps the most interesting heraldic relics of this prince are his swords of state as Earl of Chester. One of the swords is engraved with six shields of arms and on one side of the pommel are three feathers rising from a coronet, the earliest-known example of the grouping of the feathers within a coronet.[2] This sword belongs to the period of Edward's principacy, 1471–83.

With the accession of the Tudors two developments are to be noted— the feathers have become exclusively a badge of the Heir Apparent, and their grouping as three feathers ensigned by a coronet becomes standardized. Several seals of Arthur, Prince of Wales contain feathers in various form. One seal shows the Prince mounted, a plume of three feathers affixed to the horse's head, and the background decorated with single feathers and crosses, and on the reverse the shield of arms is flanked by a single feather.[3] Another of his seals, attached to a deed dated at Carnarvon 20 September 1495, contains a dragon holding a single feather with a label inscribed *Ich dien*.[4] On his tomb in Worcester Cathedral the feathers occur several times, singly, in twos and in threes.

During the early Tudor period, when grouped in three, the feathers are enfiled by a label with the words 'Ich dien', an example of which occurs in a stained glass window of the time of Henry VIII in the

[1] *Archaeologia*, xx. 379, engraving.
[2] *Vetusta Monumenta* (Society of Antiquaries pubn.), vol. v (1833), pl. L.
[3] *Archaeologia*, xx. 379–82.　　　　　[4] *Cambrian Journal*, iii (1856), pp. 199–200.

Porter's Lodge in the Tower of London.[1] Edward (VI), although never Prince of Wales, was the first to add the princely coronet to the badge. In St. Dunstan's church the three feathers ensigned with the inscribed scroll are shown on a roundel per pale *sanguine* and *azure*, flanked by the initial letters P[rince] E[dward], the whole being enclosed within a wreath of leaves and roses and surmounted by a coronet.[2] On another piece of glass, made before Edward's accession, the badge is shown as follows—on a circle *argent*, rayonated *or*, three feathers *argent*, quilled *or*, ensigned with a gold coronet, and around the quills below the coronet, a scroll with the usual legend, the whole flanked by the initial letters P.E.[3] A similar illustration appears in *The Prince's Primer*, printed by Richard Grafton in London in 1546. The feathers ensigned by the coronet also appear as one of the devices on the dragon standard borne at Queen Elizabeth's funeral.[4]

We have now arrived at a stage when the badge had assumed its final form and become the exclusive possession of the Heir Apparent. Henry, Prince of Wales sometimes bore the badge placed on a sun, and on the charter granting him the Principality in 1610 a second coronet is shown resting on the top of the sun.[5]

From the time of the first Stuart monarch the device appears on royal seals relating to Wales. A judicial seal for the counties of Pembroke, Carmarthen, and Cardigan, of the reign of James I, shows the royal arms supported by a dragon and a goat, and below the shield the feathers badge in its standard form, and the seal of Charles I for the same counties is very similar. The judicial seal of George III for the counties of Caernarvon, Merioneth, and Anglesey, and another for the counties of Denbigh, Montgomery, and Flint show the badge beneath the royal arms.[6] The seal for the Council of Wales and the Marches in the reign of Charles II included the Plume of Feathers surmounting the royal arms.

The badge also appeared as a provenance mark on coins minted in Wales or minted from Welsh silver. Towards the end of the reign of James I, after 1621, all crowns, half-crowns, and shillings, so minted,

[1] *Archaeologia*, xxxi. 370, illustr.
[2] B.M. Lansdowne MS. 874, fol. 97.   [3] *Archaeologia*, xxxi. 370, illustr.
[4] *Vetusta Monumenta* (Society of Antiquaries pubn.) vol. iii (1796), drawing.
[5] B.M. Add. MS. 36932.
[6] A. B. Tonnochy, *Catalogue of British Seal-Dies in the British Museum*, London, 1952, p. 18.

bore the feathers badge above the royal arms on the reverse side of the coins. All coins minted at Aberystwyth bear the feathers above the royal arms on the larger denominations, and it forms the whole reverse design on the half-groat, penny, and halfpenny; they were also placed before the King's head on the shilling, sixpence, groat, and threepence, and behind his head on the half-crown. When the mint moved from Aberystwyth to Shrewsbury and then to Oxford in 1642, the plume continued to appear, as well as on some coins minted at Bristol during that period.[1] The badge decorated some of the coins minted from Welsh silver in the reigns of Charles II, James II, William III (after 1694), and Queen Anne. Their last appearance is on the shilling of George I, known as 'The Welsh Copper Company Shilling'. It is clear that the badge was included as a compliment to Wales, and the foregoing examples could be cited as precedents, with historical justification, by Welsh people of our time who are anxious to see some emblem representing the Principality included in the British coinage.

It is understandable that the emblem came to be regarded as 'The Prince of Wales's badge', and the term sometimes occurs in official documents. This is illustrated in the story of the somewhat unusual visit made to the Principality by George, Prince of Wales, later George IV. In September 1806 he stayed at Loton Park, the Shropshire seat of Sir Richard Leighton, a short distance from the Welsh border. It was suggested that he should set foot in the land whence he derived his title, and Sir Richard Puleston of Emral, the only Welshman in the house party, was deputed to escort him. Accordingly on 9 September he crossed the border into Montgomeryshire, and planted an oak sapling near a road-side cottage, which was known ever after as 'The Prince's Tree'. In testimony of 'the regard and esteem' which the Prince held for Puleston, and 'in commemoration' of the event, he granted him 'a Crest of honourable augmentation . . . an Oak Tree, pendant therefrom an Escutcheon [gules] charged with three Ostrich Feathers within a Coronet in allusion to the Badge of His Royal Highness as Prince of Wales'. Seven years later Sir Richard Puleston requested a written confirmation of the honour, and on 5 July 1813 the Rt. Hon. John McMahon, P.C., Keeper of the Privy Purse and Private Secretary to the Prince Regent, wrote to him from Carlton House confirming the royal approbation.

[1] R. Seaby, *Story of the English Coinage*, London, 1952, illustr.

Accordingly, on 15 May 1815, the crest was exemplified to him by the Kings of Arms, in whose records the Plume is specifically described as 'the Badge or cognizance of the Prince of Wales'.[1] This is an extremely interesting example, and also a very rare one, of an heraldic augmentation made in modern times.

I have not considered it necessary to discuss the various legends, all modern and groundless, relating to the origin of the Feathers badge. The earliest reference to the story that the Black Prince acquired the plume and motto from the device of the blind King John of Bohemia who fell at Crécy occurs in the works of the antiquary Camden towards the end of the sixteenth century. Not to be outdone, Camden's contemporary, Randle Holme of Chester, boldly stated that the badge was derived from 'the auntcient Brittaines or Welsh' who used the three white feathers 'upon all their warlike colours'.[2] The recent suggestion that 'Ich dien' is derived from the Welsh words 'Eich dyn', meaning 'your man', provides us with an example of what can be achieved when a lively imagination and romantic patriotism combine to provide a dainty dish for nationalistic palates.

The Feathers badge acquired Welsh associations only because they were borne by the Heirs Apparent, who, normally, also became Princes of Wales. It is an attractive badge and was adopted, both officially and casually, by Welsh folk and Welsh organizations. The title-page of Dineley's account of the Duke of Beaufort's Progress through Wales in 1684 bears the feathers placed on a shield. The shield of arms of the Cymmrodorion (the 1751 foundation) was surmounted by the feathers and motto, because the Prince of Wales (later George IV) was patron of the society. It is the badge of the Welch Regiment, the Pembrokeshire Yeomanry, and several other military units raised in Wales. They appear in civic arms, on football jerseys, and school badges, and generations of Welshmen have quenched their thirst in alehouses called 'The Plume of Feathers'.

Although the badge is non-Welsh in origin, and is primarily that of the Heir Apparent, it has become, by extension, intimately associated with Wales, and no one but a very pedant could object today to the description 'Prince of Wales's Feathers'.

[1] College of Arms Records, *Grants*, xxix.
[2] B.M. Harl. MS. 2035.

III. ARMS OF THE PRINCES

In this section the arms of the Princes of Wales, from 1301 to our own times, are given. The descriptions are based on contemporary evidence, particularly on seals where such exist. They conform to the accepted heraldic practice of using the father's arms, differenced by a three-pointed label to represent the eldest son. There are no emblems representing Wales in the shields of the medieval princes, and the only reference to their senior territorial dignity occurs in the legend inscribed on the seals. The earliest introduction of a Welsh emblem is found in the dragon supporters on the seal of Arthur of Winchester (No. 8 *infra*). The peculiarly Welsh coat of the old dynasty of Gwynedd occurs in a marshalled achievement of Henry of Greenwich (No. 9 *infra*), but from the nature of the document in which it is found this may well have been the *obiter dicta* of a herald, for there is no evidence of its inclusion in a seal or some other example of user. The arms of Gwynedd were certainly associated with Henry of Stirling (No. 10 *infra*), and in the 'baner of ye Principality of Wales' borne at his funeral in 1612 they were actually *quartered* with the royal arms.

The arms of the Hanoverian princes included those of their continental possessions, and further continental arms were introduced in the arms of Prince Albert Edward (No. 18 *infra*). The continental quarterings were discontinued in 1910, when the arms of Prince Edward (No. 20 *infra*) contained the quarterly shield showing England, Scotland, and Ireland, with the arms of Wales (Gwynedd) on an inescutcheon of pretence. These are also the arms borne today by His Royal Highness, Prince Charles, Prince of Wales. That the ancient coat of the Principality has been incorporated in the arms of the Prince of Wales is a matter of deep satisfaction to Welsh people whose loyalty to the Crown has been one of the most enduring features of their long history, and the display of this coat is particularly appropriate in view of the fact that His Royal Highness Prince Charles is a descendant of Llywelyn the Great.

A manuscript armorial of the arms of the Princes of Wales, compiled by Sir George Naylor, Garter Principal King of Arms 1822–31, was presented by H.M. King George VI to the National Library of Wales in 1937.

1. EDWARD OF CAERNARVON

(Son of King Edward I. Prince of Wales 7 February 1301–7 July 1307.)
Seal—*obverse*: The Prince in armour, mounted, a shield charged with the
arms of England and a label of three points, the horse caparisoned with
the same arms; legend, EDWARDVS ILLVSTRIS REGIS ANGLIE FILIVS:
reverse, within a carved rosette of eight semicircular cusps, with a sunken
trefoil in each spandril, and suspended by a guige from an oak-tree, a
shield of arms of England with a label of five points, and legend, EDWARDVS
PRINCEPS WALLIE COMES CESTRIE ET PONT. IVI.[1] [Prince of Wales, Earl of
Chester, Ponthieu, and Montreuil.]

2. EDWARD OF WOODSTOCK, THE BLACK PRINCE

(Son of King Edward III. Prince of Wales 12 May 1343–8 June 1376.)
Seal—*obverse*, figure of the Prince seated under an elaborate canopy: in
the field on each side an ostrich feather labelled, over them the initials
E.P. Legend, S' EDVARDI PRIMOGENITI REGIS ANGL'. P'NCIPIS AQVITANNIE
ET WALLIE DVCIS CORNVBIE ET COMITIS CESTRIE. *Reverse*—the prince in
armour mounted, on his shield, quarterly, France ancient and England, a label of three points; crest, the lion statant of England, tail extended, the horse trappings decorated with similar heraldry. Legend,
as on the obverse.[2] In his will the Prince directed that two distinct
armorial compositions were to be displayed at his obsequies—'for war'
his quartered coat as primogenitus (as above), and 'for peace' three silver
ostrich feathers, 2 and 1, on a black shield.

Examples of seals of the wives of the Princes are rare. One belonging
to the widow of the Black Prince, Joan, Dowager Princess of Wales,
attached to a deed dated 1380, has survived. This shows—party per
pale, quarterly 1st and 4th France ancient, 2nd and 3rd England with a

[1] *B.M. Catalogue of Seals*, Birch, ii. 220–1, nos. 5549, 5550, Ancient Deeds, 1305. See
Sandford, *Genealogical History* . . . , p. 122. Edward was created Count of Ponthieu and
Montreuil in 1304. According to *Glover's Roll*, the colour of the label in the Prince's arms was
azure.

[2] *B.M. Catalogue of Seals*, Birch, ii. 221, no. 5551: other seals of the same prince, nos. 5552
(A.D. 1360), 5553–4 (A.D. 1350), 5555 (A.D. 1360), 5556–7 (A.D. 1361) and 5558: for further
examples and discussion see Sandford, op. cit., p. 125, figs. 1, 2, and p. 188; Stothard,
Monumental Effigies, ii; and especially A. R. Wagner, *Historic Heraldry of Britain* and references
there. He was created Earl of Chester 18 May 1333, Duke of Cornwall 3 Mar. 1336–7, Prince
of Wales 13 May 1343, Prince of Aquitaine and Gascony 19 July 1362.

label of three points, impaling, England with a border (Edmund of Woodstock, Earl of Kent). Legend, s' IOH'E P'NCIPISSE . . . IE & WALL' DVCISSE CORNVB' & COMITISSE CESTR' & KANCIE.[1]

3. RICHARD OF BORDEAUX

(Son of Edward, Prince of Wales (the Black Prince). Prince of Wales 20 November 1376–21 June 1377.)

Seal—*obverse*, The Prince mounted; on his shield, quarterly 1st and 4th France ancient, 2nd and 3rd England, a label of three points; these arms appear also on his surcoat and horse trappings: crest, a lion passant. Legend, SIGILLVM RICARDI PRINCIPIS WALLIE DVCIS CORNVBIE ET COMITIS CESTRIE, followed by a single ostrich feather. *Reverse*, a shield, quarterly, as above. Legend, SIGILLVM RICARDI PRINCIPIS WALLIE DVCIS CORNVBIE ET COMITIS CESTRIE PRO OFFICIO SVTHWALLIE.[2] During the lifetime of his father, the centre point in the label is said to have been charged with the cross of St. George.[3] A separate seal made for Richard as Earl of Chester showed quarterly France and England, a label of three points: legend, SIGILLVM RICARDI COMITIS CESTRIE.[4]

4. HENRY OF MONMOUTH

(Son of King Henry IV. Prince of Wales 15 October 1399–21 March 1413.)

His seal as Prince of Wales shows quarterly France ancient and England, a label of three points; on either side of the shield two chained swans ensigned with a crown and holding in their beaks a single ostrich feather. Legend, s' HENRICI PRINCIPIS WALL' DVCIS AQVITAN CORNVB COMITIS CESTR.[5] Another of his seals in 1404–5 is the same as above, with crest, on a chapeau turned-up ermine a lion statant guardant, a label of three points around its neck.[6] A seal of the Prince, from St. John's

[1] *B.M. Add. Charter*, 27, 703.

[2] Dineley, *Progress* . . . , p. 262, illustr.: T. Nicholas, *County Families*, ii. 855, illustr.; Sandford, op. cit., pp. 191–2.

[3] *Sandford*, loc. cit.

[4] *Journal of the Architectural, Archaeological and Historical Society for . . . Chester*, i. 180, sketch.

[5] P.R.O. Loose Seals G 6 described in *Archaeoolgia*, lxxiv. 115: for other of his seals in P.R.O. see *Archaeologia*, lxxiv. 115: see also Sandford, op. cit., p. 245, engr. The Swan, a Bohun badge, was derived from his mother, Mary Bohun. He was created Duke of Lancaster and of Aquitaine in 1399.   [6] Sandford, op. cit., p. 277.

College, Cambridge, and dated by Sir Anthony Wagner as 1404, shows a quarterly shield of France modern and England.[1]

Seals 'for his lordship of Carmarthen' have survived. One shows the Prince mounted, his horse standing on a rocky mound: his shield, quarterly, 1st and 4th England, 2nd and 3rd France modern, a label of three points; crest, on a chapeau the lion statant of England crowned: the background is decorated with sprigs of the broom (Plantagenet). Legend, s' HENR PRINCIPIS WALL DVC ACQVIT' LANCASTR' [ET] CORNVB COMES CESTR DE DMIO DE KERMERDYNE.[2] This was the Prince's seal for the Chancery of Carmarthen, intended for use in matters concerning the Principality of South Wales.

His second Great Seal, as Henry V, contained in panels, the arms of the Principality of Wales, the Duchy of Cornwall, and the Earldom of Chester.[3]

5. EDWARD OF WESTMINSTER (LANCASTER)

(Son of King Henry VI. *De facto* Prince of Wales 15 March 1454–25 October 1460, 17 February 1461–4 March 1461, 11 April 1471–4 May 1471.)

He bore quarterly, France modern and England, with a label of three points argent. His livery consisted of 'a bende of crymesyn & blacke, with esteryge is fetherys'.[4]

6. EDWARD OF WESTMINSTER (YORK)

(Son of King Edward IV. Prince of Wales 25 June 1471–9 April 1483. He succeeded on the latter date as King Edward V, and was shortly afterwards murdered in the Tower.)

Seal (A.D. 1476): *Obverse*: The Prince mounted; on his shield three lions passant regardant coward in pale, and these arms are repeated twice on the horse trappings: crest, a lion statant, and from the horse's head issues a single ostrich feather; the background is lozengy, in each lozenge a single ostrich feather and scroll. *Reverse*: A shield with arms as above,

---

[1] *Archaeologia*, cxvii, pl. XXXIVb.

[2] *B.M. Catalogue*, ii. 228, nos. 5573, 5574: *Archaeological Journal*, xii (1856), pp. 189–90: Nicholas, *County Families*, i. 244–6: *Cambrian Journal*, iii (1856), p. 289.

[3] *Catalogue of Heraldic Exhibition, Birmingham*, 1936, no. 205.

[4] Gregory, *Chronicle*, p. 212.

the shield surmounted by the Prince's coronet; supporters, two lions couchant guardant, their backs to the shield, each holding an ostrich feather in raised forepaw.[1]

The sword of state of this Prince, as Earl of Chester, was decorated with several coats of arms and badges. He possessed two of these swords. The first, known only from Catherall's description of it in B.M. Harl. MS. 1988, had the following shields of arms engraved on one side of the blade:

i. Three lions passant guardant, a label of three points (the Prince).
ii. Three lions passant reguardant in pale (NOT coward).
iii. Eighteen roundels, 4, 4, 4, 3, 2, 1 (Cornwall).

On the other side of the blade were:

iv. Mortimer quartering De Burgh (Earldom of March).
v. Three garbs, 2 and 1 (Chester).
vi. Party per fess (*azure* and *argent*).

On the pommel are two small shields: one charged with a cross, the other with three ostrich feathers issuing from a coronet.

The other sword, preserved in the British Museum, contains similar arms except that (i) above has been substituted by a shield containing the arms of France and England quarterly, a label of five points, and in (ii) the lions are shown as coward.[2]

An example of his shield as Earl of Chester has survived to a charter of the Cordwainers of that city, dated 20 January 1482. This shows on the obverse, the arms of France and England quarterly, a label of three points, impaling three garbs; on either side of the shield a single ostrich feather; the shield being surmounted by a prince's coronet and cap. The reverse shows the Prince in armour, mounted, carrying a shield charged with France and England quarterly, a label of three points: the crest a lion statant guardant crowned. The legend reads, SIGIL' EDWARDI PRIMOGENITI EDWARDI QVARTI.[3]

---

[1] *B.M. Catalogue*, ii. 224, no. 5563: *Archaeologia*, xx (1824), pp. 379–82, engr.: *Arch. Cam.* Ser. 3, vol. ii (1856), engr., p. 216.

[2] For engravings of these swords and a description by George Ormerod, see 'Observations on Several Ancient Swords of State Belonging to the Earldom of Chester' in *Vetusta Monumenta*, vol. v, pl. L (1835).

[3] *Journal of the Architectural, Archaeological and Historical Society for . . . Chester*, i. 161–81, sketch.

7. EDWARD OF MIDDLEHAM

(Son of King Richard III. Prince of Wales 24 August 1483–9 April 1484.)

A description of the heraldry on the Prince's tomb in the north chapel of Sheriff Hutton church, Yorkshire, by Dugdale in 1619, reads as follows: quarterly France modern and England, a label of three points, each point charged with two ermine spots. All that now remains are two large shields, one plain and the other charged with a red cross.[1] It is said that among the arms formerly shown on the tomb were those of the House of Nevill,[2] the Prince's mother being Anne, daughter of the Kingmaker.

8. ARTHUR OF WINCHESTER

(Son of King Henry VII. Prince of Wales 29 November 1489–2 April 1502.)

Seal to a grant by Prince Arthur, dated at Caernarvon, 20 September 1495, shows the same arms as those of Prince Edward (No. 6 above) son of Edward IV, with dragons as supporters in place of the lions: legend, ARTHVRVS ILLVSTRISSIMI HENRICI SEPTIMI REGIS ANGLIE & FRANC̄ & DV̄S HIB̄N PRIMOGENTVS PRINCEPS WALL DVX CORNVB & COMES CESTR.[3]

In a manuscript, marked D2 in the College of Arms, the arms of the Prince and his Princess (Catherine of Aragon) are shown on a banner supported by a black eagle; the arms are France and England quarterly, a label of three points *argent*, impaling, quarterly 1st and 2nd Castile and Leon quarterly, 2nd and 3rd per pale Aragon and Sicily: at the base point, a pomegranate of Granada.[4]

On Arthur's tomb at Worcester Cathedral, the following arms appeared: France and England quarterly, a label of three points, supported by two antelopes; surmounted by the Prince's coronet above which is a single ostrich feather, while underneath the shield are three such feathers.[5]

---

[1] *V.C.H. Yorkshire, North Riding*, ii. 185.

[2] Dodsworth, *Church Notes* (Yorks. Arch. Soc.), p. 176.

[3] *Archaeologia*, xx (1824), pp. 379–82: *Arch. Cam.* 1856, engr. opp. p. 217: *Cambrian Journal*, iii (1856), pp. 199–200.

[4] Sandford, op. cit., p. 475.   [5] Ibid.

9. HENRY OF GREENWICH

(Son of King Henry VII. Prince of Wales 18 February 1503–4 April 1509.)

Page 90 of 'Prince Arthur's Book' (College of Arms, Vincent MS. 152) contains an elaborate pen-drawing of Henry VIII, which includes his arms as King and also as Prince of Wales,[1] namely, (i) France and England quarterly; (ii) a harp (Ireland); (iii) quarterly, four lions statant guardant (Wales); (iv) three lions passant coward; (v) bezanty 5, 4, 3, 2, 1; (vi) quarterly, France and England a label of three points. The shields iii–vi are surmounted by coronets.

A painting made about 1505 of the arms of Prince Henry shows them as France and England, quarterly, a label, with a red dragon as a dexter supporter and a white greyhound as sinister supporter.[2]

10. HENRY OF STIRLING

(Son of King James I. Prince of Wales 4 June 1610–5 November 1612.)

The singularly beautiful charter of King James creating his son Prince of Wales and Earl of Chester, dated 4 June 1610, contains elaborate heraldic decorations in the margins,[3] namely, 1. Shield, quarterly *gules* and *or*, four lions passant guardant counterchanged (Wales); above the shield the Prince's coronet, and above that a helmet affronteé with seven ostrich feathers issuing from it. 2. Two shields each bearing quarterly 1st and 4th England and France quarterly, 2nd Scotland, and 3rd Ireland. 3. On a sun in splendour, three ostrich feathers enfiled with a crown, and a label inscribed with the words *Ich dien*, and above the whole the Prince's coronet. 4. On a shield, fifteen bezants, 5, 4, 3, 2, 1, surmounted by a duke's coronet (Cornwall). 5. On a shield, three garbs 2 and 1, surmounted by an earl's coronet (Chester).

Prince Henry possessed a very fine library, and the covers of the books bore his various heraldic book-stamps, namely: 1. Quarterly, (i) and (iv) France and England quarterly, (ii) Scotland, (iii) Ireland, over all a label *argent* of three points; 2. Arms as before, within the Garter, the whole ensigned with the Prince of Wales's coronet; 3. Three ostrich

---

[1] *Heralds' Commemorative Exhibition*, London, 1936, No. 108.
[2] *Archaeologia*, xx. 195.   [3] B.M. Add. MS. 36932.

feathers enfiled with a coronet; 4. A lion rampant guardant wearing the Prince's coronet; 5. A Tudor rose with the Prince's coronet above it; 6. A fleur-de-lis; 7. A thistle; and 8. A unicorn rampant.[1]

The following heraldic banners were borne at the Prince's funeral on 7 December 1612,[2]—1. The Standard, *gules* a lion passant guardant crowned *or*, and a (? greyhound) *or*, carried by Sir John Wynn of Gwydir, Knight and Baronet; 2. 'Ye Cornett', on a sun in splendour a plume of three ostrich feathers *argent* enfiled with a coronet *or*, carried by Sir Roger Dalison of Laughton, Lincolnshire, Baronet; 3. Banner, *or* a saltire *gules*, on a chief [   ] a lion passant guardant *or* (Earldom of Carrick), carried by Sir David Foulis of Ingleby House, Yorkshire; 4. Banner of Chester, carried by Lord Effingham; 5. Banner of Rothesay, carried by the Baron Kinloss; 6. Banner of Cornwall, carried by Lord Clifford; 7. Banner of the Principality of Scotland (i.e. Prince of Scotland, one of Henry's titles), carried by Viscount Fenton son of the Earl of Mar; 8. 'A baner of ye Principality of Wales' carried by the Viscount Lisle,[3] which showed quarterly, (i) France and England quarterly, (ii) Scotland, (iii) Ireland, and (iv) *gules* and *or* four lions passant guardant counterchanged, Wales; and 9. 'The great Embrodered Baner of ye Prince's Armes', which were the Royal Arms (as borne by James I) with a label, carried by the Earls of Montgomery[4] and Argyll.

11. CHARLES OF DUNFERMLINE

(Son of King James I. Prince of Wales 4 November 1616–27 March 1625.)

Seal as Prince of Wales[5]—*obverse*: the prince in armour, mounted, wearing his coronet, and on his shield quarterly four lions passant guardant counterchanged; on the horse's trappings, a shield charged with three garbs, and over it a cordelière knot: a shield charged with 15 bezants, 5, 4, 3, 2, 1. In the field on the left, above the horse, a shield of

---

[1] C. Davenport, *English Heraldic Book-Stamps*, London, 1909, pp. 223–8, illustr.

[2] Hon. Mrs. Bulkeley Owen, 'Banners Borne at the funeral of Henry, Prince of Wales', *The Home Counties Magazine*, i (1899), London, pp. 136–8.

[3] Robert son and heir of Sir Henry Sidney, President of the Council of Wales and the Marches. Created Viscount Lisle in 1605. See *The Complete Peerage*.

[4] Philip Herbert, 2nd son of Henry Earl of Pembroke. Created Earl of Montgomery in Wales in 1605. See *The Complete Peerage*.

[5] *B.M. Catalogue*, ii. 225, no. 5565.

the Royal Arms as borne by James I, with a label of three points, en-signed with the Prince's coronet: no legend.

Reverse: On a mount on which grows herbage and flowers, a shield of the royal arms with the label: the dexter supporter a lion rampant guardant crowned; the sinister supporter a wyvern or dragon, tail nowy, each animal charged with a label of three points. In base on the mount, a plume of three ostrich feathers within the Prince's coronet. Legend: MAGNVM SIGILLVM CAROLI PRINCIPIS WALL . . . EBORVM ET COMITIS CESTRIE ET C.

A portrait of Prince Charles, probably painted when he was eighteen years of age, is decorated with the following heraldic embellishments: 1. The royal arms with a label of three points, surmounted with the Prince's coronet; and 2. On a sun in splendour, a plume of ostrich feathers enfiled by a Prince's coronet; the label inscribed *Ich Dien*.[1] On another portrait made when he was twenty-three, the same arms and badge are displayed.[2]

12. CHARLES OF ST. JAMES'S

(Son of King Charles I. Prince of Wales, *circa* 1641–29 January 1649.)

No examples are known to me of a seal or other heraldic forms used by Charles during the period of his principate. By the laws of heraldry he would have borne the royal arms as used by his father, differenced with a label.

13. JAMES FRANCIS EDWARD

(Son of King James II. Prince of Wales June 1688–11 December 1688. 'The Old Pretender.' Died 1766.)

No examples are known to me of a seal or other heraldic forms used in the period when James was both *de iure* and *de facto* Prince of Wales. The following book-stamp appears on the cover of one of his books (printed in 1699): Quarterly, 1 and 4 France and England quarterly; 2. Scotland. 3. Ireland, the whole ensigned with the Prince's coronet.[3] The composition is intriguing, for his father, the dethroned James II, from 1689 until his death in 1701, omitted the lilies of France, probably

---

[1] E. Beresford Chancellor, *Life of Charles I, 1600–1625*, frontispiece.
[2] Ibid., p. 64, illustr.   [3] Davenport, op. cit., p. 256, illustr.

because he was receiving hospitality from the French monarch. It is interesting to note that James's revised coat—1 and 4 the leopards of England, 2 Scotland, 3 Ireland—subsequently became the royal arms of Great Britain.

14. GEORGE AUGUSTUS

(Son of King George I. Prince of Wales 22/27 September 1714–10 June 1727.)

The arms of this Prince, impaling those of his wife, were as follows:[1] Quarterly, 1. Three leopards passant impaling Scotland; 2. France; 3. Ireland; 4. Per tierce, (i) two leopards passant, (ii) a lion rampant, between hearts, (iii) a horse courant, on a shield of pretence the Crown of the Dominions in Germany; over the quarters 1 and 2 above, a label of three points: impaling the arms of Caroline of Brandenburg-Anspach, Princess of Wales (a marshalled coat of fifteen shields). Crest—On a Prince's coronet, a lion statant guardant wearing a coronet. The supporters were the Lion and Unicorn, each charged with a label, the former wearing the Prince's coronet. On a scroll below the shield is the motto *Ich Dien*.

15. FREDERICK LEWIS

(Son of King George II. Prince of Wales 8 January 1728–9–20 March 1750–1.)

The Prince's seal for the Council was as follows:[2] the three feathers badge within an open jewelled coronet, and a scroll inscribed *Ich Dien*: all placed on a sun of thirty-two rays, alternately wavy and plain: legend, PRO CONSILIO FREDERICI PRINCIPIS WALLÆ ETᶜ.

Tindal dedicated his edition of Rapin's *History of England* to Frederick Prince of Wales, and an engraving of his arms shows as follows: Quarterly, 1. *gules* three leopards in pale *or*, impaling the tressured lion of Scotland; 2. *Azure* three fleur-de-lis, 2 and 1, *or*; 3. *Azure* a harp [   ]; 4. Per tierce, (i) *gules* two lions passant guardant in pale, (ii) *argent*, semee of hearts a lion rampant [   ]; (iii) *gules* a horse courant *argent*, and in the centre of the tierce a small escutcheon *argent*; over all, a label

---

[1] Davenport, op. cit., p. 176, illustr.

[2] *B.M. Catalogue*, ii. 226, no. 5567. For his book-stamps, see Davenport, op. cit., p. 168. illustr.

of three points. The whole is ensigned by the Garter, surmounted by a crown. The supporters are, dexter a lion guardant crowned; sinister a unicorn, a crown around its neck, both charged on the breast with a label of three points.

16. GEORGE WILLIAM FREDERICK

(Son of Frederick Lewis, Prince of Wales. Prince of Wales 20 April 1751–24 October 1760.)

No example of his heraldry as Prince of Wales is known to me. He would have been entitled to bear the royal arms suitably differenced.

17. GEORGE AUGUSTUS FREDERICK

(Son of King George III. Prince of Wales 17 August 1762–29 January 1820.)

Seal (A.D. 1790)[1]—the arms of Great Britain as used by George III, i.e. quarterly 1 and 4 England; 2 Scotland; 3 Ireland; on an escutcheon of pretence the arms of the dominions of the Crown in Germany, ensigned with the crown of Hanover, with a label of three points, the whole encircled with the Garter, and ensigned with the Prince's coronet: supporters, a lion and a unicorn, both charged with a label.

On 16 April 1816 Exemplification was made of the arms of Charlotte Augusta, Princess of Wales, namely, the royal arms within a lozenge, differenced with a label of three points *argent*, the centre point charged with a rose *gules*; ensigned with a coronet composed of crosses pattee, fleur-de-lis and ducal leaves; together with the royal supporters differenced with a like label, the lion wearing a coronet, and the unicorn wearing a coronet around its neck.[2]

18. ALBERT EDWARD

(Son of Queen Victoria. Prince of Wales 4 December 1841–22 January 1901.)

Shortly after his birth the Queen commanded that a coat of arms be designed for the Prince quartering those of Britain with those of Saxe-Coburg.[3]

[1] *B.M. Catalogue*, ii. 227.
[2] *The Herald and Genealogist*, ed. J. G. Nichols, i (1863), p. 118.
[3] Burke, *Peerage*, 1869.

Arms—Quarterly, 1st and 4th *gules* three lions passant guardant in pale *or* (England); 2nd *Or* a lion rampant in a double tressure flory and counterflory *gules* (Scotland); 3rd *Azure* a harp *or* stringed *argent* (Ireland); and a label of three points *argent*: an escutcheon, barry of ten *or* and *sable*, a crown rue in bend *vert* (Saxe-Coburg). Crest, on a Prince's coronet, a lion statant guardant *or*, crowned with a like coronet, and differenced with a label of three points *argent*.

19. GEORGE FREDERICK ERNEST ALBERT

(Son of King Edward VII. Prince of Wales 9 November 1901–6 May 1910).

Arms and crest as for No. 18.[1]

20. EDWARD ALBERT CHRISTIAN GEORGE ANDREW PATRICK DAVID

(Son of King George V. Prince of Wales 23 June 1910–20 January 1936.)

In 1910 Welsh local authorities petitioned King George V for the introduction of the red dragon into the Royal Standard and into the coinage of the realm. The prayers of the petitioners were not granted, but whatever feelings of disappointment this may have occasioned gave way before the King's further action in recognizing and placing in a position of honour in Britain's royal heraldry the coat of arms of the ancient Welsh princes. The decision was announced in the following terms:

At the Court of Buckingham Palace,
The 4th Day of February, 1911.
Present,
The King's Most Excellent Majesty in Council.

Whereas there was this day read at the Board a Report from a Committee of the Privy Council, dated the 12th day of December 1910, in the words following, viz.:

'Your Majesty having been pleased, by Your Order in Council of the 19th day of July 1910, to refer unto a Committee humble Petitions from the Council of the Municipal Borough of Aberavon, in the County of

---

[1] For bookplates of this Prince see *Journal of Ex Libris Soc.* July–Oct. 1905, Aug.–Oct. 1907.

Glamorgan, and other local bodies in Wales, praying that Your Majesty in Council would be pleased to order that the Red Dragon of Wales be introduced into the Royal Standard and the coinage of the United Kingdom: The Lords of the Committee have taken the said Petitions into consideration, and do this day agree humbly to report, as their opinion, to Your Majesty, that it would not be expedient for Your Majesty to comply therewith, but Their Lordships are at the same time of opinion that if it appears fitting to Your Majesty that the Arms of Wales, *videlicet*, 'Quarterly Or and Gules, four Lions passant guardant counterchanged', should again be brought into use, Your Majesty might very properly be advised to include them in some form in the Arms of the Prince of Wales.'

'His Majesty having taken the said Report into consideration was pleased, by and with the advice of his Privy Council, to approve thereof. (signed) Almeric Fitzroy.'

The form in which these arms were again 'brought into use' will be seen from the following description of the arms of the twentieth Prince of Wales who bore from 1911 onwards: Quarterly. 1st and 4th, *gules* three lions passant guardant in pale *or* (England). 2nd *or* within a double tressure flory counterflory a lion rampant *gules* (Scotland). 3rd *azure* a harp *or*, stringed *argent* (Ireland); a label of three points *argent*; in pretence, the arms of Wales (described above) ensigned with the Prince's coronet: the whole encircled with the Garter inscribed 'Honi Soit qui mal y pense', and surmounted with the Prince's coronet. Crest, on the Prince's coronet a lion statant crowned guardant, a label of three points *argent* around its neck.

21. H.R.H. PRINCE CHARLES, PRINCE OF WALES

The achievement of His Royal Highness was published for the first time in the 1963 edition of Debrett's *Peerage*. It consists of the royal arms with a silver label of three points and the Arms of the Principality on an inescutcheon, the whole encircled with the Garter. The supporters, the lion rampant guardant and the unicorn, are both charged on the shoulder with a similar label. The crest is the well-known lion statant guardant on a crown. Below the shield, in the compartment, is the shield of the Duchy of Cornwall, *azure* 15 bezants, the shield surmounted by a

Prince's coronet, and on the dexter side is the Plume of Ostrich feathers, and on the sinister a Red Dragon passant. The motto *Ich Dien* is borne on a label which forms the base of the achievement.

IV. HERALDS CONNECTED WITH WALES AND THE PRINCES

No officers of arms were appointed by the native Welsh princes. Although from the fourteenth century onwards the bards acquired a thorough knowledge of heraldry, such knowledge never became necessary for the performance of their duties or profession. It is true that during the Tudor period, a knowledge of the subject was listed as one of the skills that a bard should possess; nevertheless it remained subordinate to the primary function of composing and reciting poetry. The bards never acquired the indicia of their English counterparts, and all officers of arms who have been in any way connected with Wales and the Princes of Wales owe their appointment either to English monarchs or to senior officers of the Heralds' College.

Heraldry is first met with in Britain in the decade 1120–30, and officers of arms about 1170. Heralds were appointed by kings, princes, and other august personages, and carried out a variety of duties. They were employed on ceremonial and public occasions, at tournaments where they combined the duties of masters of ceremonies and recorders, in military campaigns and on diplomatic embassies, they were the experts on heraldic and genealogical matters and questions of precedence, they were the personal and trusted servants of their masters.[1]

An idea of the range of their activities may be derived from the following examples. In 1473 Chester Herald travelled to Arlon to inform the Duke of Burgundy of the birth of Prince Richard; in 1487 Henry VII sent Falcon Pursuivant to South Wales and Ireland on royal affairs, and in 1630 Portcullis Pursuivant was sent to Ireland to announce the birth of the Prince of Wales (later Charles II) with orders to report back to the King how the news had been received. Garter King of Arms helped to arrange the Treaty of Picquigny between England and France in 1475. Heralds carried messages of defiance from the monarch and accompanied his armed forces to the wars. Henry Grene, Leicester King of Arms, accompanied Henry of Monmouth in the war against Owen Glyndwr in

[1] For lists of heralds and their activities see Walter H. Godfrey, *The College of Arms . . .*, London Survey Committee, 1963.

PLATE III

ARMORIAL BEARINGS OF H.R.H. PRINCE CHARLES
PRINCE OF WALES

1404–5, and petitioned for payment of the arrears of his yearly salary (10 marks) which had been granted him by the Prince for making two journeys to Coity Castle, Glamorgan, 'in the time of rebellion'. Ten years later he was with his master, then King Henry V, at the Battle of Agincourt. Pembroke Herald took challenges to Burgundy in 1424 and 1436, and Rouge Croix Pursuivant carried the English challenge to Flodden Field to James IV of Scotland, and later took the news of the victory to Henry VIII who promoted him to be Carlisle Herald. In 1465 Chester Herald carried Lord Scales's challenge to the Bastard of Burgundy to meet him in tournament.

Such work was often arduous and dangerous. During Jack Cade's rising in 1451, Lancaster Herald rode post-haste with messages up and down the country, foundering two horses and having to hire a third. When so employed the person of the herald was inviolate, but this was not always a sure shield, and Froissart mentions the violent death of some of them in the French wars of Edward III. For instance, when Somerset Pursuivant took messages to Scotland in 1542 he was attacked by horsemen in Dunbar, and slain. Clarenceux King of Arms was drowned in Spanish seas while on embassy in 1476. Some tasks required stout hearts as Rouge Croix Pursuivant discovered in April 1462 when sent to arrest a pirate in the Thames estuary.

On the other hand, journeys could be profitable sometimes. Windsor Herald received a yearly pension of 20 marks for bringing 'the good news' to the Prince of Wales in 1367, presumably a report of the victory at Najara.

Sometimes a man received heraldic office as a reward for personal services rendered to the monarch, such as Richard Greenwood, Henry VII's trusted servant in pre-Bosworth days, who was rewarded on the occasion of that king's coronation by being made Rouge Croix Pursuivant. Heralds were occasionally rewarded with extra appointments; for instance, Henry Hastings appointed Surveyor of the Stables to the Prince of Wales in 1757, retaining his office of Rouge Croix Pursuivant which he had held since 1752.

More agreeable were attendances at banquets, receptions, weddings, coronations, investitures, progresses, proclamations, and visits to foreign princes to invest them with the insignia of chivalric honours that British monarchs conferred on them. Among the heralds at the coronation of

Henry VII were Garter and Normandy King of Arms. Northumberland Herald, Berwick and Fitzwalter Pursuivants, attended the creation of Jasper Tudor as Duke of Bedford in 1485. Scales Pursuivant was present in 1477 when Lord Rivers did homage to the Prince of Wales for lands held of him. Gloucester King of Arms attended the St. George Feast in 1416 when the Emperor Sigismund was elected Knight of the Garter. Wallingford Pursuivant attended the funeral of Arthur, Prince of Wales, in 1502; Chester Herald compiled an account of the funeral of Richard, Duke of York in 1476, and also wrote a poem about him; Ireland King of Arms wrote a metrical life of the second Prince of Wales (the Black Prince). Lancaster Herald proclaimed King Charles II at Westminster in 1660, borrowing for the occasion a tabard from James I's achievements in the abbey. As I have shown in an earlier chapter, royal officers of arms took a prominent part in the Investiture of the Princes of Wales.

I have found a few examples of Welshmen attended by personal heralds. Thus Richard Gethin, when on service in France, employed Corbin Pursuivant (1431) who derived his title from the raven (corbie) in his master's coat of arms. Attached to the famous soldier Matthew Goch, Captain of Bayeaux Castle, was Beul Pursuivant who was present at the duel between Chalons and Du Breuil in 1446. Lord Herbert of Gower, later created Earl of Worcester, who died in 1526, had several officers of arms, all pursuivants, namely Herbert, Esperance Herbert, and Fraunceys.

Titles born by officers of arms derived from territorial connexions, the heraldic emblems, badges, mottoes, names, and titles of their employers. Some seem to have derived from a playful whim or fancy. These titles formed an essential part of the herald's description, as a young lady discovered in 1730 when she sued Clarenceux King of Arms for breach of promise. The defendant pleaded that he had been improperly described in the legal papers as 'Knot Ward, Esquire', whereas by his royal Patent the title Clarenceux formed part of his name, with the result that the case was dismissed. However, in the following year she sued him again, this time as 'Ward Clarenceux', and was awarded damages of £2,000.

During the latter half of the fifteenth century heralds added the tracing and recording of genealogies to their activities, and this, together with the granting of arms, has been their main work ever since. They continued to carry out ceremonial duties, and by today these are all associated with royal and state occasions, namely, the Coronation, the Investiture of the Prince of Wales, Proclamation of a new Monarch, Proclamation of Peace, Opening of Parliament, and State Funerals. In addition, Garter Principal King of Arms takes part in the introduction of new peers into the House of Lords.[1]

The heralds of the Princes of Wales took their titles mainly from territories held by their masters. Some of the Princes also employed the King's heralds. When occasion demanded, the Prince might employ more than one, such as the Black Prince, who retained Muschamp Herald (1353–8), Sir Roger de Mortimer, King of Arms (1357), Lancaster Herald (1358–66), Chester Herald (1373), and Guyenne and Aquitaine King of Arms was also a member of his retinue. It is interesting to note here that our present Royal Family has a herald ancestor. He was Sir Payne Roet, a knight of Hainault, Guyenne King of Arms about 1333, father of Catherine, third wife of John of Gaunt. From this marriage descended the Lady Catherine Beaufort, mother of Henry VII. Sir Payne Roet's other daughter, Philippa, married Geoffrey Chaucer.

Edward III is said to have instituted the office of Chester Herald, whose first holder was attached to the Household of the Prince of Wales. However, its earliest appearance in public records is in 1393, and five years later William Bruges was appointed herald to the newly formed Principality of Chester. Bruges continued as Chester Herald under the new dynasty and was a member of the Household of Henry of Monmouth, Prince of Wales. Incidentally, he was the first holder of the office and title of Garter King of Arms, instituted in 1415. Chester Herald walked in the retinue of the Prince of Wales at his Investiture at Caernarvon in 1911. Only two Welshmen have ever held this appointment—James Thomas of Llanfihangel (1592), and T. M. Joseph-Watkin who held it from 1913 to 1915.

The office of Wales Herald occurs in 1393, and probably existed some years before. It is believed that Richard II, who had been Prince of Wales and was descended from Llywelyn the Great, intended that this herald should be attached to the household of the future Princes of Wales. The first incumbent subsequently became Percy Herald to the Earl of Northumberland around 1401, and Shrewsbury Herald to the Earl of

[1] See Sir Anthony Wagner's books, *Heralds and Heraldry in the Middle Ages* (2nd edn., 1956) and *English Genealogy* (1960), both published by the Oxford University Press.

March in 1403. The title was revived in 1963 when Major Francis Jones of Carmarthen was appointed Wales Herald Extraordinary.

The office of Cornwall Herald was certainly instituted by Richard II, in 1398, and although no Duke of Cornwall existed at that date, it seems that he intended the herald should be attached to the holder of the dignity. Cornwall Herald may thus have been an officer of arms to Henry, Prince of Wales, whose coronation, as King Henry V, he attended in 1413. The earliest holder of the title was John Hilton, harper, to whom Richard II granted an annuity of 10 marks in 1398.

An officer of arms, Ich Dien Pursuivant, described in 1476 as 'Hic Dien pour le Prince de Gales', served Edward, Prince of Wales (later Edward V), and in that year attended the translation of the body of Richard, Duke of York, on behalf of his master who was then but six years of age. This title is derived from the motto contained on the scroll in the Plume of Feathers badge of the Prince. The office and its attractive title was short-lived and I have found no further reference to it.

Among the new heralds created by Henry VII was Rouge Dragon Pursuivant, instituted on 29 October 1485, as a compliment to the Welsh antecedents of the Tudors. The red dragon standard had flown over his troops at Bosworth, and he introduced the animal as a supporter of the royal arms after he ascended the Throne. The office of Rouge Dragon Pursuivant has continued unbroken to the present day.

Wallingford Pursuivant derived his title from the manor of Wallingford, formerly part of the Duchy of Cornwall and property of the Heir Apparent. The first holder of the pursuivancy was Thomas Wrythe (later Wriothesley), appointed in 1489 as officer of arms to Arthur, Prince of Wales. He attended the funeral of the young prince in 1502, when 'sore weeping he toke off his cote of armes and cast it alonge over the chest right lamentably'. Wrythe continued as Wallingford Pursuivant to the succeeding Prince of Wales, Henry, created in 1504, whom he accompanied (as King) to the Field of Cloth of Gold in 1520. He was advanced to Garter King of Arms in 1505, and the pursuivancy lapsed, never to be revived.

Two Kings of Arms, March and Gloucester, exercised a general heraldic jurisdiction over Wales in the fifteenth century. March King of Arms, originally herald of Edmund Mortimer, third Earl of March, was placed on the Royal establishment before 1384, and under Edward

IV and Henry VI his successors included Wales, Cornwall, and England in their territory. In 1483 he was superseded by Gloucester as King of Arms for Wales. The last March King of Arms, William Ballard, made a visitation into South Wales, about 1470–80, when he recorded valuable genealogical and heraldic data now preserved in the College of Arms.

Gloucester Herald was originally an officer of arms of the dukes of Gloucester and reference is found to the title in 1406. Subsequently he entered the royal service as Gloucester King of Arms. The last holder of the office, Richard Champneys, attended the coronation of Richard III in July 1483. His patent, dated 14 September 1483, describes him as Gloucester King of Arms, and Principal Herald of the parts of Wales. The last reference to him is in 1484 when the office lapsed. Early in the eighteenth century an effort was made to revive the title. Bath King of Arms of the Order of the Bath was instituted at the creation of that Order, by patent dated 18 May 1725. By an additional statute dated 14 January 1726, Bath was constituted Hanover Herald and Gloucester King of Arms and Principal Herald of the parts of Wales. To this, Clarenceux and Norroy, Kings of Arms, strongly objected, and after consideration the statute was adjudged to infringe their rights, whereupon the additional titles were discontinued.

Several Welshmen have been appointed regular officers of arms— David Griffith (Warwick Herald *c.* 1461), Richard Johns (Calais Pursuivant 1528), Fulk ap Howel (Guisnes Pursuivant 1532, Rouge Dragon 1536, Lancaster Herald 1538), James Thomas of Llanfihangel, Glamorgan (Bluemantle Pursuivant 1587, Chester Herald 1592), John Guillim (Rouge Croix Pursuivant 1613), author of *A Display of Heraldry*, George Owen of Henllys, Pembrokeshire (Rouge Croix Pursuivant 1626, York Herald 1633), Robert Chaloner of Lloran, Denbighshire (Bluemantle Pursuivant 1660, Lancaster Herald 1667), Philip Jones (York Herald 1722) ,John Monson Phillips, grandson of Thomas Phillips, coroner of Breconshire (Rouge Dragon 1786), Ralph Owen, born in Lancashire, who changed his name to Bigland and was Garter King of Arms from 1831 to 1838, and Thomas Morgan Joseph-Watkin, born at Aberdare, Glamorgan (Portcullis Pursuivant 1894, Chester Herald 1913).

Several Garter Kings of Arms in modern times can claim descent from ancient Welsh stocks through the distaff side. Among them we find Sir Alfred Scott-Gatty, descendant and heir at law of the Vaughans of

Golden Grove, Carmarthenshire, who traced to the Princes of Powys; and Sir Algar Howard, who attended the Investiture of 1911 as Fitzalan Pursuivant Extraordinary. The Hon. Sir George Bellew descends from the illustrious house of Herbert; and the present incumbent, Sir Anthony Wagner, in addition to having a Welsh grandmother, has a proven descent, generation by generation, from no less a personage than the renowned Owen Glyndwr.

Kings of Arms occasionally appointed Welshmen to be deputy officers within the land of Wales, such as Griffith Hiraethog of Denbighshire (died 1564), deputy herald over the whole of Wales under Garter, Norroy, and Clarenceux; Lewys Dwnn of Montgomeryshire (died about 1616), appointed in February 1585 deputy of Clarenceux and Norroy for 'the three provinces of the Kymry' (i.e. Gwynedd, Powys, and Deheubarth); Griffith Hughes, 'deputy to the office of Arms for North Wales' in 1639; David Edwardes of Rhydgorse, Carmarthenshire, appointed on 1 August 1684 to be Clarenceux's deputy for the shires of Brecon, Cardigan, Carmarthen, Pembroke, and Glamorgan; and Hugh Thomas, member of an ancient but impoverished Breconshire family, appointed before 1703 deputy by Garter for heraldic and genealogical duties in Wales. To these we can add the name of another Welshman, Robert Owen of Shrewsbury (died 1632) who acted as deputy for Shropshire and the borders.

From this we see that Wales was by no means ignored by the 'heraldic establishment', although the number of Welsh officers of arms has never been considerable. The appointment of officers of arms to the households of the Princes of Wales seems to have been sporadic, and the main reason for this lies in the fact that the heraldic officers in ordinary, specified and limited in number by their Charter of Incorporation, were regarded as sufficient for normal requirements.

NOTE

Since this chapter was written, Her Majesty The Queen has granted The Prince of Wales a 'Personal Flag for use in Wales', namely, the Arms of the Principality (quarterly, *or* and *gules*, four lions passant guardant counterchanged) with an inescutcheon *vert* charged with the Prince's Coronet.

PRINTED IN GREAT BRITAIN
AT THE UNIVERSITY PRESS, OXFORD
BY VIVIAN RIDLER
PRINTER TO THE UNIVERSITY